W9-DJG-500

Edgar H. Lehrman

A GUIDE TO THE RUSSIAN TEXTS OF TOLSTOY'S *WAR & PEACE*

ardis / ann arbor

Published by Ardis Publishers,
2901 Heatherway,
Ann Arbor, MI 48104

Printed in the United States of America

ISBN 0-88233-441-7

I dedicate this book with love
to my parents
Jacob and Frances Wittenberg Lehrman

Acknowledgments

I am grateful to those who helped answer my *War and Peace* questions for this book, or who helped me in other ways connected with it.

Robert V. Allen
Aleksandr Anikst
Michael Astour
Miriam Astour
David Caplan
Patricia Carden
Marianna Tax Choldin
Liselotte Dieckmann
Terence Emmons
Kathryn Feuer
Maurice Friedberg
Ernest P. Gray
Alfred M. Holtzer
Paul L. Horecky
Olga Raevsky Hughes
Assya Humesky
Simon Karlinsky (see below)
Alla Ktorova
Emily R. Lehrman
Ruth M. Lehrman
Hugh McLean
Forrestt A. Miller
Lawrence Miller
Catharine O'Donnell
Rose Raskin
Mary (Mrs. Norris) Smith
George Spater
Kiril Taranovsky
Christopher Wertz
Lynn Wishart
Evelina Zaidenshnur
Piotr Zaionchkovskii

I also would like to thank those who have tried to help solve the mystery of the song Natasha sings (see p. 62 below).

Anna di Palma Amelung
Harold Barlow
Carlo Bianconi
James Fuld
Boris Goldovsky
Philip Gossett
Rembert Herbert
Leonard J. Lehrman
Mark Lindley
O.W. Neighbour
Pierluigi Petrobelli
Boris Schwarz
Wayne D. Shirley
Nicholas Slonimsky
Reinhard Strohm
Nicholas Temperley
Carlo Vitali
Emilia Zanetti

The staff of the Olin Library at Washington University (especially the Reference and Inter-Library Loan people) deserve my special gratitude. The people at the Gaylord Music Library of Washington University were also very helpful.

Special thanks go to the Tolstoy Museum of Moscow, which answered some very difficult questions.

Above and beyond the help with individual problems, Simon Karlinsky consented to read the manuscript through before the final version was sent to the publisher. I would like to thank him, publicly and humbly, for taking time from a busy schedule of outstanding teaching and scholarship to help a *zemliak* from Riemeister Street; his detailed, lucid, well-informed, and highly relevant comments filled eight typewritten pages.

Washington University in St. Louis has been more than generous in supporting so slow-moving a piece of work as this book. After many years, including a term on leave at full pay, I have finally finished it.

I would also like to thank the *Times Literary Supplement* of London for publishing, on September 8, 1978, my letter requesting aid for three particularly thorny problems connected with this work.

Ideally, to write such a work as this, the author should have native fluency in both Russian and English. My English is native, but my Russian (which I have been using for over a third of a century) is not. Therefore, I am particularly grateful to those native speakers of Russian in the St. Louis area who have been more than kind with their help to me.

Not just any native Russian will do. All too frequently, native-speakers of a language have no idea what rules they are following when they speak, and they tend to give foreigners an idealized version of what they do. For the sort of project undertaken here, native sources must be intelligent, responsive, available, educated, well read—and plural in number. Professor and Mrs. Michael Astour of Southern Illinois University (Edwardsville) are all this and more; they have been wonderful. But I would never have dared to embark upon this endless project without the continual aid of my favorite Muscovite—my wife.

It goes without saying that any mistakes in this book are all my own.

A NOTE ON THE TEXTS

As early as 1931, Boris Eikhenbaum lamented, "Перед нами разительный и непоправимый факт: окончательного, несомненного, 'канонического' текста *Войны и мира* нет и никакими средствами создать его невозможно".[1]

An enlightening essay on the various early editions of the work has been written by L. D. Opul'skaia, from which much of the following information has been taken.[2] What would become the start of the work (through the Schöngraben battle)—"1805-ый год"—was first published in Katkov's *Русский вестник,* Nos. 1 and 2 for 1865, and 2, 3, and 4 for 1866. F. F. Ris in Moscow published the first complete edition of *Война и мир* in 1868 and 1869; almost at the same time, and during the same years, the second edition was published, and Tolstoy himself read the proofs for it. Tolstoy divided each of these two editions into six volumes; volumes five and six of both were printed from the same plates.

The third edition of *Война и мир* came out in 1873, in volumes V through VIII of Tolstoy's *Собрание сочинений,* published in Moscow. Tolstoy now divided the previous six volumes of the text into four new volumes. The epilogue retained only those parts connected with the fate of the characters. Reflections on the 1812 campaign, the first four chapters of the first part of the Epilogue, and the entire second part of the Epilogue were relegated to an appendix entitled, "Статьи о кампании 1812-го года". The fourth edition of 1880 followed the text of the third edition. *Война и мир* was published again—in both the fifth and the sixth editions—in 1886. Both editions of that year were based on the 1868-1869 second edition, but retained the 1873 division into four volumes. The fifth edition retained the French passages, but the sixth edition translated them into Russian. Incidentally, one of the leading Soviet Tolstoy scholars has written that these translations were not made either systematically or by the author himself.[3] Opul'skaia states, "Таким образом, при жизни Толстого существовало четыре отличающихся один от другого текста *Войны и мира* ."[4] From now on until after Tolstoy's death, the 1886 edition with the French in it was considered basic.

The *Полное собрание сочинений (Юбилейное издание)* in ninety volumes published *Война и мир* twice. The first printing was edited by Gruzinskii and Tsiavlovskii from 1930 through 1933.[5] The so-called second printing came out in 1937 and was edited by G.A. Volkov and M.A. Tsiavlovskii. The earlier Jubilee version took the 1886 text as basic, but inserted certain stylistic changes from the 1873 edition. The 1937 variant took the 1868-1869 text of the second edition as basic and inserted corrections from the 1873 edition in the belief that Tolstoy had made them all. However, time proved this presumption false.

This is an important theoretical reason for avoiding the "second printing" of the Jubilee Edition. There was also a very practical consideration: the very diligent and efficient people at the Inter-Library Loan service at Washington University in St. Louis were unable, despite well over a year of effort, to locate a copy of this printing in the United States; when a borrowed copy of it finally did arrive, the lending organization was the Lenin Library in Moscow.

It would have been more accurate to refer to these two different variants in the Jubilee Edition as different editions, but Soviet sources such as Opul'skaia use the expression "второй тираж".

In any case, after 1937, a copy of Volumes 5 and 6 of the second edition (1868-1869) turned up with corrections in the handwriting both of Tolstoy and of Nikolai Nikolaevich Strakhov (1828-1896)—and most of the changes are in Strakhov's hand. So the 1937 version was on the wrong track.

To make matters worse, the editors of both versions given in the *Полное собрание сочинений* had relied exclusively on published sources. A group of highly professional Soviet scholars later complained, "Вопрос же о выверке текста по рукописным источникам даже не ставился, и все обилие ошибок переписчиков и наборщиков, частичные исправления Бартенева, сделанные в 1869 г., в третьей части первого тома, а также правка по всему тексту, сделанная Страховым в 1873 г., полностью сохранились в романе."[6]

What did Strakhov actually do in preparing the 1873 edition for publication? Some tend to see him as an intruding villain; his "reactionary" politics do not help his reputation in Soviet Russia today either. The first contact between Strakhov and Tolstoy came in November 1870, when Strakhov wrote Tolstoy for a contribution to the magazine *Заря.* Tolstoy answered on November 25, 1870, inviting Strakhov to come visit him at Iasnaia Poliana. Strakhov did so in June of the following year, and almost annually thereafter.

The initiative for Strakhov's role in the proofreading came not from him but from the novelist. On May 11, 1873, Tolstoy wrote Strakhov that he was revising *Война и мир* and "ужасно желал бы вашего совета."[7] Strakhov agreed. On May 31, Tolstoy wrote him, "Очень, очень вам благодарен за предложение просмотреть *Войну и мир.* Вы не поверите, как это для меня дорого." On June 22, Tolstoy again requested Strakhov's opinion about the changes Tolstoy had already made, writing, ". . .если вы найдете, что дурно, даю вам право уничтожить поправку и поправить то, что вам известно и заметно за дурное . . . . Если вы захотите и успеете сделать поправки и просмотреть, то сделайте и пошлите в Москву."

Thus, Tolstoy gave Strakhov a free hand to the point that Tolstoy did not even wish to see what Strakhov had done. This carte blanche was again offered Strakhov in Tolstoy's letter to him of September 3 or 4; Tolstoy then wrote, "Даю вам это полномочие и благодарю за предпринимаемый труд." In between, on August 24, Tolstoy had written Strakhov, "Не знаю как благодарить вас за ваши тяжелые, скучные труды над *Войной и миром.*" Tolstoy largely repeated these words in his letter to Strakhov of September 3 or 4.

The reference to "скучные труды" gives us part of Tolstoy's motivation in making the request. In the June 22 letter, Tolstoy told Strakhov that the novel "мне очень редко нравилась, когда я перечитывал ее, а большей частью возбуждала досаду и стыд."

Tolstoy in general seems to have had singularly little patience with the filigree-type work of scholarship. Nabokov has remarked somewhere that pedantry is not one of the Russian vices. R.F. Christian has shown that, in *Anna Karenina,* there is a good deal of arithmetical inconsistency about how long Anna has been married, the age of her son, etc.[8] This same disregard for what must have impressed Tolstoy as trivial details can also be seen in *Война и мир* in which the ranks, titles, and even names of certain historical characters are occasionally given incorrectly, and were never changed. The fact that Tolstoy was a literary genius does not mean that he was always right about everything. Abraham Lincoln, we are told, once instructed a portrait painter not to forget the warts; the fact that Tolstoy also had some warts does not negate his literary genius. What Strakhov did, he did at Tolstoy's repeated request. On September 23 or 24, 1873, Tolstoy again wrote Strakhov, "Очень благодарю вас . . . за все, что вы сделали с *Войной и миром.*" The proofreading had to be done, after all, and Tolstoy was unwilling to do it himself. Strakhov thus saved the novelist from some depressing and painstaking work.

The most recent scholarly edition of the novel published in the Soviet Union is the 1961-1963 edition; *Война и мир* comprises Volumes IV through VII of his *Собрание сочинений в двадцати томах.* In the Opul'skaia article which has already been referred to, she cites many misprints and other inaccuracies which had crept into earlier editions.[9] The 1961-1963 edition goes back to the 1868-1869 second edition, and was collated with the first edition. However, the 1961-1963 edition retains the four-volume division of the 1873 edition on the thoroughly legitimate grounds that Tolstoy himself introduced the four-volume division. This time, the manuscripts also were consulted.

But that did not lay the problem to rest. In April 1963, N.K. Gudzii, who had been on the editorial boards for both the 1937 and the 1961-1963 versions, published an article about which text should be considered canonical. He wrote, "Таким текстом . . . необходимо считать текст романа в издании 1873 года, представляющий собою результат последней активной работы Толстого над романом."[10]

Some problems of scholarship, it would seem, simply cannot be solved once and for all.

Because of this textual mess, the question arises as to which text should be used in preparing this "handbook." My answer is to utilize two different texts from start to finish. They come from the first version of the Jubilee Edition (1930-1933) and the 1961-1963 edition. Except in Volume One, Part I, the chapter divisions of these two texts coincide completely. For Volume One, Part I, chapter divisions of both editions are indicated in the "handbook." When a chapter of Volume One, Part I is referred to later, it is referred to in the divisions of the Jubilee Edition because there are more of them.

It would, of course, have been simpler to use the 1961-1963 edition exclusively. However, judging from the printed texts (and I have not been able to consult the manuscripts), I suspect strongly that this edition has modernized some of Tolstoy's spellings. Furthermore, the earlier text (or versions very much like it) must still be available in many, many thousands of copies. In addition, by using two editions, I have been able to reduce the number of misprints in the texts.

When one considers the number of outsiders who had a hand in the text of *Война и мир*—the author's wife, P.I. Bartenev, S.S. Urusov, S.V. Golitsyn, Strakhov, and various copyists—one is amazed that the texts we have are so good. The fact that none of them is perfect does not mean that any of the principal ones is not excellent. My hope is that the reader will be able to use my "handbook" with whatever edition of *Война и мир* he is reading. But Eikhenbaum was probably right.

NOTES

1. Б. М. Эйхенбаум, *Лев Толстой: Книга вторая, 60-ые годы,* Ленинград-Москва, ГИХЛ, 1931, стр. 401.

2. Л.Д. Опульская, "История писаниия и печатания",in Л. Н. Толстой, *Собрание сочинений в двадцати томах,* том VII, Москва, ГИХЛ, 1963, pp. 395-438, especially pp. 420-436.

3. Н. Гудзий, "Что считать 'каноническим' текстом 'Войны и

мира'?", *Новый мир, № 4, 1963, стр.* 234.

4. Опульская, *op. cit.,* p. 421.

5. Vol. IX (Vol. I of novel), М-Л, 1930, редактор: А.Е. Грузинский; Vol. X (Vol. II of novel), М-Л, 1930, редактор: А.Е. Грузинский; Vol. XI (Vol. III of novel), М-Л, 1932, редакторы: А.Е. Грузинский и М.А. Цявловский; Volume XII (Vol. IV and Epilogue of novel), М-Л, 1933,редакторы А.Е. Грузинский и М.А. Цявловский. We are told on an unnumbered page at the start of Vol. IX that Gruzinskii died on January 22, 1930, and "Окончательная сверка текста выполнена Г.А. Волковым при участии М.А. Цявловского." However, Volkov's name is not given as one of the editors of the so-called "first printing."

6. Н.К. Гудзий, Н.Н. Гусев, В.А. Жданов, Э.Е. Зайденшнур, В.С. Мишин, А.И. Опульский, Л.Д. Опульская, Н.С. Родионов, С.А. Розанова и А.И. Шифман, "О Полном собрании сочинений Толстого ('Юбилейном')," in *Литературное наследство,* том 69, книга вторая, стр. 448. The article, a detailed study, is on pp. 429-541. On p. 455, various articles are mentioned which cite numerous mistakes made in the Jubilee Edition printings of *Война и мир* and *Анна Каренина.* In one such article, Zaidenshnur complains that only *Война и мир* was printed in the Jubilee Edition without checking the manuscripts. (Э. Зайденшнур, "По поводу текста 'Война и мира'," *Новый мир,* № 6, 1959, стр. 279.)

7 The information about Strakhov comes from "Неизданные письма Л.Н. Толстого к Н.Н. Страхову. Публикация и комментария А.И. Опульского." *Лев Николаевич Толстой: Сборник статей и материалов,* pp. 511-576. Tolstoy's letters can also be found in the Jubilee Edition, Vol. LXII.

8. R.F. Christian, "The Passage of Time in *Anna Karenina*," *Slavonic and East European Review,* Vol. 45, pp. 207-210.

9. Опульская, *op. cit.,* pp. 427-436.

10. Гудзий, *op. cit.,* p. 245.

11. Note: The two editions of the Russian text used here are the First Printing of the Jubilee Edition (mentioned in Note 5 above) and the most recent scholarly edition as this is written (Volumes IV, V, VI, and VII of the 1961-1963 edition of Tolstoy's collected works in twenty volumes, mentioned in Note 2 above). Parentheses ( ) indicate an entry occurring only in the 1930-1933 edition; square brackets [ ] indicate an entry occurring only in the 1961-1963 edition.

Abbreviations used

acc	accusative; according	lit	literally
adj	adjective	LNT	Lev Tolstoy
adv	adverb	l-x; lx	one-time
aff	affectionate	M	Moscow
aug	augmentative	m	masculine
betw	between	many-x	many-time
book	bookish	mil	military
cent	century	N	Napoleon; North
cf	compare	n	noun; note
coll	colloquial	nom	nominative
collec	collective	nr	near
comp	comparative	nt	neuter
cont	contemptuous	obs	obsolete
cuss	cussing	obseq	obsequious
dat	dative	OCS	Old Church Slavic
deep	*deeprichastie*	orig	originally
dial	dialect	P	Polish, Poland
dim	diminutive	pass	passive
E	English, East	pej	pejorative
emph	emphatic	pf	perfective
encl	enclitic	pl	plural
esp	especially	pop	popular
euph	euphemism	posit	positive
f	feminine	poss	possessive
F	French, France	pr	present
fam	familiar	pref	prefix
fig	figurative	prep	preposition
fr	from	prich	*prichastie*
ft	future	pron	pronoun
G	German, Germany	R	Russia; Russian; Russians
g	grams		
Gall	Gallicism	r	ruble
gen	general; genitive	rel	religion
Gk	Greek	rhet	rhetorical
impf	imperfective	RL	Russian literature
impv	imperative	Rv	river
indecl	indeclinable	S	South
inf	infinitive	sing	singular
inst	instrumental	smb	somebody
interj	interjection	sq	square
kop	kopek, kopeks	st	street
L	Latin, Leningrad	sth	something

St P	Saint Petersburg	Ukr	Ukrainian
subst	substandard	vb	verb
suff	suffix	vulg	vulgar
superl	superlative	W	West
swh	somewhere	w	with
tr	transitive, translator, translated, translation	W&P	*War and Peace*

CONTENTS

A GUIDE TO THE RUSSIAN TEXT OF TOLSTOY'S *WAR AND PEACE*

PREFACE

I. Some Explanatory Notes About This "Handbook"

This "handbook" is the second in a series. The first was a *"Handbook" to the Russian Text of "Crime and Punishment"* (Mouton/Walter de Gruyter, The Hague-Paris-Elmsford, N.Y., 1977, 124 pages).

The object of this "handbook" is to help enable the advanced student of Russian, who has had no contact with that language before high school or college, to read the original text of *War and Peace* with both pleasure and understanding. Although students differ in capabilities, this "handbook" has been designed for those who have had at least three years of college Russian or the equivalent. It would also be helpful if the student has read some nineteenth-century Russian literature (especially Tolstoy) before this, even if only in translation.

The "handbook" could fit into a survey of nineteenth-century Russian literature (or of Tolstoy) in which at least part of the reading is done in the original. It could also be used in graduate seminars on Tolstoy. My hope is that this "handbook" will help free the teacher from the need to provide a detailed commentary to the geography, language, history, and culture involved in reading *War and Peace* in the original. The time thus gained can be used as the teacher sees fit.

This "handbook" does *not* aspire to be a rigorously scholarly linguistic treatment of the novel. It is *not* intended to serve as a teaching aid in a course dealing with the history of the Russian language.

Although the "handbook" has been devised largely with the classroom in mind, it can be used by a student working alone. In either situation, he should have ready access to an ordinary Russian edition of the novel, and to any edition of Smirnitsky's *Russian-English Dictionary,* as published by the Soviet Encyclopedia Publishing House in Moscow.

My hope is that professors of Russian literature will also find this "handbook" helpful. Thus, in one recent volume dealing with *Crime and Punishment,* one of the best Dostoevsky scholars in the United States allowed *promyshlennik* to appear in its contemporary meaning of "industrialist" rather than in the obsolete meaning Dostoevsky uses of "dealer; artisan; peddler (possibly shady)." In another work of American criticism also dealing with *Crime and Punishment,* the author mistakenly believed that *liniia* refers to "line" (on a printed page) rather than to the numbering of streets on Vasilevskii Island. (At the time the books indicated were published, my

"Handbook" to the Russian Text of Crime and Punishment did not yet exist.) My hope is that future critics of that novel—and of *War and Peace*—will not always repeat this type of mistake. While it is true that the errors mentioned are quite minor, it is also true that no outstanding scholar wishes to be inaccurate.

A review of my *"Handbook" to the Russian Text of Crime and Punishment* stated that the work contained a good deal of "trivia." My standard has been and is that if the novelist considered the "trivia" worth including, then I consider it worth identifying. Besides, one can never tell when someone else will make meaningful connections of the "trivia." Thus, James Curtis at the University of Missouri, in his fine article "Spatial Form as the Intrinsic Genre of Dostoevsky's Novels," (*Modern Fiction Studies,* Vol. XVIII [Summer, 1972], p. 153) writes, about Raskolnikov's standing on the Ascension Bridge in *Crime and Punishment,* ". . . we can be certain that it is Sonya's window that Raskolnikov is looking at." Curtis also states that he relies on my *Crime and Punishment* "Handbook" for understanding the geography of St. Petersburg. One man's trivia is another man's catalyst.

My hope is that my work on *War and Peace* too will serve as some critics' catalyst. The large number of Biblical references given here, for example, should disprove once and for all the legend that Tolstoy became interested in Christianity only around 1880 with his so-called "conversion."

This book should also be of use to professors (not just of literature but also in other branches of Russian studies) who have always wanted to read *War and Peace* in the original, but have never felt up to it. A historian may well look at Tolstoy's peasants (or Church Slavic) and think to himself, "Why couldn't he say something simple, such as 'After prolonged negotiations, the treaty was finally agreed on' "? All too frequently in our profession, we have tended to sweep problems of meaning under the rug by pretending that they are "minor" and "unimportant." But how can we always tell that until we know the answers? Problems should be solved, and not dodged!

My hope too is that this work will be of value to future translators of *War and Peace,* despite the fact that there are seven versions of the work now extant in English. Each has its own errors, at least some of which, I hope, can now be corrected.

This work is also designed for the English-speaking foreigner in the Soviet Union, be he journalist, diplomat, businessman, or anyone else. He may have always wanted to read *War and Peace* but lost his courage when he ran into the "trouble points" explained in this "handbook." Much of the material given below is not known to ordinary native speakers who, when dealing with foreigners (in any country), all too often assume a mantle of infallibility which no one possesses.

The theory behind my approach was set forth in my article, "Needed: American 'Handbooks' for Masterpieces in Russian" (*Slavic and East European Journal,* Volume XIII, No. 3 [1969], pp. 363-375). What follows here is the second published attempt to put the theory into practice.

The aim of the whole effort is to make *War and Peace* available to non-Russian readers on Tolstoy's terms. The problem is not to bring Tolstoy down to us, but to bring ourselves up to him. That is the law and the prophets; the rest is commentary.

II. How To Use The Glosses Below

A complete list of abbreviations is given on pp. xiii-xiv. It should be consulted as needed.

Tolstoy divided *War and Peace* into Volumes, Parts, and Chapters. They are all numbered. To keep them apart, the numbers of the Volumes have been written out in letters (e.g. Volume One), the number of the Parts has been written in Roman numerals (e.g. Part I) and the number of the Chapters has been given in Arabic numerals (e.g. Chapter 1). It should be realized that the chapter numbers for most of Volume One, Part I differ in the two editions of *War and Peace* used in preparing this "handbook." The varying chapter numbers have been indicated in Volume One, Part I. The chapter breaks for the rest of *War and Peace*—all of it—are identical in the two editions.

The "handbook" attempts to define—always within the context of the novel--phenomena which Smirnitsky's dictionary either omits or has in hard-to-find places. By "hard to find," I mean, "not in the first ten lines of the first definition in Smirnitsky and, if Roman numerals divide the definition (as under как which has II, or что which has III), not in the first ten lines under I, and not in the first two lines of each subsequent Roman numeral." Also given are words common in Tolstoy's Russia (but untranslatable), and substandard language.

The student is strongly urged to familiarize himself with the prefaces (at least in English) and the abbreviations (in both languages) given in Smirnitsky. He should be able to recognize a compound word if its component parts are in Smirnitsky.

The "handbook" is organized for use from the beginning of the novel onwards, cumulatively. Its effectiveness will be impaired by a decision to start by sampling a chapter in the middle because the notes themselves are not repeated. However, the point of the index given in Appendix Two is to help the student locate definitions or explanations of items already included. Perhaps the best way to use this "handbook" is to read the notes to a given chapter a few times just before reading that chapter in Russian. In this way, the mind should retain (at least passively) some idea of the material being glossed.

The perceptive student may well ask why this "handbook" is keyed to the Smirnitsky dictionary rather than to the *Oxford Russian-English Dictionary* by Marcus Wheeler (Oxford at the Clarendon Press, 1972). There are two reasons for this. The first is the substantial difference between the American price of the two books; students would probably find the Smirnitsky cheaper to buy than the Oxford. The second is that the Smirnitsky dictionary, in one edition or another, has been readily available in the West for about a quarter of a century. Based on this background, it seems less likely to go out of print than does the Oxford dictionary. However, the Oxford dictionary is a fine one and, in my opinion, the best Russian-English dictionary now available, at least for native speakers of English.

III. Further Observations

Tolstoy's syntax is generally not very difficult, at least when peasants are not talking. Dostoevsky is much harder and some of Gogol' and Leskov harder yet. Therefore, the student may be wise in reading *War and Peace* before reading some of the masterpieces of the other authors just mentioned.

Students must be extremely cautious, however, about imitating the Russian used in this novel. As is natural in a work written over a century ago, many of the words and phrases used in it are now obsolete. Although attempts have been made here to indicate what is obsolete, dialect, popular, with a German accent, or substandard Russian, the flavor of a word cannot always be defined with scientific precision. Indeed, the most authoritative dictionaries may disagree. I have tended to rely most on the seventeen-volume Academy of Sciences dictionary published between 1950 and 1965 and on the four-volume Academy of Sciences dictionary published between 1957 and 1961. Even among educated, intelligent, native Russians who love Tolstoy, there are reasons for honest disagreement about the meanings and implications of various words and expressions in *War and Peace.* We must not forget this. Like other living entities, the Russian language is constantly changing.

The student is asked to note the following "ground rules" in using this "handbook."

1. Each word is glossed the first time it appears and in the meaning that makes sense within the given context. The other meanings that may be added to it may make sense in later contexts. To facilitate the retrieval of information, users of this "handbook" should consult Appendixes One

and Three (for the historical characters mentioned by name) and Two (for Russian idioms).

2. Egregious misprints will be noted if they convey an incorrect meaning, e.g. молнии for молчании in Three, III, 23.

3. In Tolstoy's day the instrumental singular of feminine soft sign nouns was sometimes written in ordinary prose with an и rather than with a soft sign, e.g. мыслию rather than мыслью in One, I, 13. Nowadays the мыслию form is considered bookish.

4. A word which starts with a vowel stresses that vowel if no other stress mark on that word indicates the contrary. It is impractical to put stress marks over capital letters in this kind of work.

5. When a Western character is referred to for the first time, his name will be given in Latin letters. Within the note which explains who he is, the Latin initial of his name will replace his surname, e.g. (from One, I, 1):

Гаугвиц — Haugwitz [Count Christian-August H. etc. . . .]

6. A word with two accent marks can be stressed on either one, e.g. о́бли́тый in Two, III, 12.

7. The Library of Congress transliteration system without ligatures is used in this "handbook." However, efforts have been made to restore the original Western spelling to Western names, e.g. Wintzingerode rather than Tolstoy's Vintsengerode.

8. In view of the fact that Tolstoy spelled his name when writing English with a "y" at the end, and that most of the good translations of his works into English (such as the Maudes') spell it with a "y," his name has been spelled with a "y" here except when a Russian title containing his name is being transliterated.

9. When *obs* (for "obsolete") is placed after a Russian word, then the word itself is obsolete, e.g. середа or пиеса in the first chapter. When *obs* is placed after the English translation, however, then the English meaning given (for the Russian word concerned) is obsolete. Thus фамилия in One, I, 1 is obsolete in the meaning of "family" as indicated, but the Russian word itself is not obsolete in at least one other meaning, e.g. "family name." [N.B. French expressions are not usually glossed in this "handbook," but the Russian translations of them are. This is why the first entry under Volume One, Part I, Chapter 1 below is not to the French "Gênes et Lucques," but to the Russian "Генуа и Лукка." But French is glossed (e.g. Three, I, 22) if there is no Russian translation.]

IV. Language

Russian has changed a good deal in the century and more since *War and Peace* first appeared. Words that are either completely obsolete or obsolete in the way Tolstoy uses them in *War and Peace* are indicated in the "handbook."

The spelling of many words has changed slightly since Tolstoy's day. Many infinitives which he ended with -оивать (ся) are now spelled in -аивать (ся) , e.g. his успокоиваться, усвоиваться, удостоивать, and пристроиваться. One "o" has turned to "a" in such words as затрогивать, потрогивать, росписной, and сплочивать; on the other hand, Tolstoy's тароватый is nowadays spelled тороватый. The -овать ending of his танцовать is now spelled -евать.

Sometimes с has changed to ш as in his статский and стора. Sometimes, the reverse change as taken place, as in his штиль and гошпиталь.

The у ней contraction, so common in nineteenth-century prose, is not nearly so common nowadays as у нее. Our contemporaries are less given to coining possessive adjectives than Tolstoy and his contemporaries were; such a form as Херубиниевский (Cherubini's) would be considered highly unusual nowadays.

As the Russian way of life has changed, so has the Russian language. The Soviet regime does not use the "Table of Ranks" (see Appendix Four below), which is now obsolete both for civilians and for the military. Similarly, wolf-hunting, and many terms dealing with horses, horse-drawn vehicles, and the early nineteenth-century military have also become rare at best.

Tolstoy, like any other great writer, has his own linguistic individuality. R.F. Christian has devoted Chapter Five ("Language") to this question in *Tolstoy's War and Peace: A Study* (Oxford, 1962, pp. 148-167). The Soviet scholar Viktor Vladimirovich Vinogradov has written more fully on the same theme in "О языке Толстого (50-60-е годы) ," *Литературное наследство,* Vols. 35-36, Москва, АН-СССР, 1939, pp. 117-221; reprinted in Vaduz, Lichtenstein, 1963). My observations here are indebted to these works.

The reader of *War and Peace* should be prepared for paragraphs that may start and end with simple statements, but which may grow quite lengthy in between. Yet, they are not too difficult to follow because, as Christian remarks, "the hallmark of Tolstoy's style is lucidity" (p. 162). Repetition is one of the most characteristic features of *War and Peace.* Another is the way что and который spring up out of the text like mushrooms from the Russian earth after a sunshower. The uses of metaphor, metonymy and similes are rather rare.

Vinogradov points out that, particularly in the early editions of *War and Peace,* there were many linguistic usages which were out of date when Tolstoy wrote them in the 1860s. The Soviet critic even declares that Tolstoy's own narrative in *War and Peace* shows the Russo-French verbal styles of the Russian gentry characteristic of the first third of the nineteenth century (p. 124), complete, of course, with many Gallicisms, some of which Vinogradov identifies.

Tolstoy did not always use деепричастия in accordance with the grammatical rules of the twentieth century. As a result, they sometimes seem to dangle.

He also uses dialect words, the talk of common people (просторечие) and verbs which show many-time action, which he derives from standard imperfective verbs, e.g. делывать from делать, танцовывать from танцовать, and угащивать from угащать.

Like many another literary genius, the author of *War and Peace* employs highly specific and technical terms when dealing with various subjects. In his case, this observation applies to wolf-hunting, beekeeping, soldiering, horses, officialese (канцелярский язык), mathematics, and Church Slavic (as connected with religion). This is not the place to discuss Tolstoy's use of interior monologues or the way, in *War and Peace;* "диалог движется скачками" as Vinogradov puts it (p. 197). Again the reader is referred to the essays by Vinogradov and Christian for further comments about Tolstoy's use of language in *War and Peace.*

V. The Appendixes

Each of the six appendixes has its own purpose. Appendix One gives proper nouns in Russian occurring in *War and Peace.* The names on this list include those of people, places, medals, and even works of art. The names of Western Europeans in the Russian service can be found in this list.

The purpose of Appendix Two is to help the student locate the definitions of pesky, Russian words and phrases which recur in the novel by pointing out where they are defined. *War and Peace* is simply too long for the student to remember everything.

Appendix Three gives proper nouns in the Latin alphabet. These include the names of places, people, books and institutions. Naturally, there is some overlapping between Appendix One and Appendix Three.

Appendix Four gives the Table of Ranks so prominent in so many Russian novels in the nineteenth century. A civil service rank is mentioned along with its military equivalent, if any, in the hope that the student will be able to see the various inter-relationships among them.

Appendix Five is a short bibliography of Tolstoy materials. This has sections on bibliographical, biographical, memoir, critical and general material, and then criticism of *War and Peace*. Each section of Appendix Five contains material both in Russian and in English.

The sixth Appendix lists the reference works which have been repeatedly consulted in the preparation of this "handbook." Webster's Second International has been preferred to Webster's Third International because it contains more words and is more normative.

The seventh and final Appendix lists those problems which, as of this writing, still elude solution.

VI. Napoleon Bonaparte

The most important historical figure of *War and Peace* is Napoleon Bonaparte (1769-1821). A military school graduate, this Corsican was made a brigadier-general in the French army after Toulon (q.v.) in 1793. He made himself dictator in Brumaire (q.v.) of 1799, and had himself proclaimed Emperor of the French in 1804. The following year, he defeated the Russian and Austrian armies together at Austerlitz (q.v.). He invaded Russia in 1812 without a declaration of war, forced the Russians off the field at Borodino (q.v.), captured Moscow, and then saw his army irretrievably melt away almost completely. He was forced to abdicate in 1814, returned to France thereafter for the Hundred Days (which ended in his defeat at Waterloo), and was then exiled for life to St. Helena (q.v.). Readers should remember, however, that Tolstoy's historical figures (especially Napoleon) are the creations of a novelist, and not of a historian. (Shklovskii's book, *Матерьял и стиль,* is very informative on this point.)

VII. Final Observations

1. During the nineteenth century, the Gregorian, New Style (N.S.), calendar in use in Western Europe was twelve days ahead of the Julian, Old Style (O.S.), calendar then in use in the Russian Empire.

2. Moscow street names have been given here as in *War and Peace*. Many of them have been changed since, and there will no doubt be other changes in the future. The best way I know to identify the modern equivalents for Tolstoy's names of Moscow streets is to place Baedeker side by side with more modern maps of Moscow. Some new names can be found in *Guide to the City of Moscow* (Moscow, Cooperative Publishing Society of Foreign Workers in the U.S.S.R., 1937). The United States Embassy in Moscow used

to (and perhaps still does) have a large map of that city hanging on one of the office walls; no doubt the State Department in Washington also has this map. It would be very helpful if the Soviet government would again authorize the publication of this type of map, as it did in 1937.

3. A comparison of pre-1917 and contemporary maps of the towns and villages mentioned in *War and Peace* can also enable the reader to learn their present names.

4. For questions whose answers were particularly hard to find (e.g. Talleyrand's chair in Epilogue, II, 1 or the Austrian officer named Schmidt in One, II, 9), I have noted the source of my information.

St. Louis, Missouri
October, 1978

ONE, I, 1

ТОМ ПЕРВЫЙ, ЧАСТЬ ПЕРВАЯ, ГЛАВА ПЕРВАЯ

1. Ге́нуа и Лу́кка — Genoa and Lucca. [On June 4, 1805, N.S., N received a delegation fr Genoa, in which an open, F-dominated plebiscite had called for annexation of Genoa to the F Empire. N "granted" the request, thus violating a promise he had made to annex no further Italian territory. The small Republic of Lucca was pressured into following suit. N thereupon handed Lucca over to his older sister, Elisa, and to her husband Prince Bacciochi, to be added to Piombino, which the Bacciochis already ruled. R today is Ге́нуя.]
2. фами́лия — family *(obs)*
3. императри́ца Мари́я Фёдоровна — [(1759-1828). Widow of Tsar Paul I and mother of Tsar Alexander I. She had been born Sophie Dorothea, Princess of Württemberg and was Empress-Mother during time of *W & P.*]
4. кра́сный — in red [court footmen wore red]
5. звезда́ — star [decoration]
6. состаре́ться *(pf, obs)* = соста́риться *(pf)*
7. уча́стие — interest
8. середа́ *(obs)* = среда́
9. заводи́ть/ завести́ — to wind up
10. Новоси́льцов or Новоси́льцев — [Никола́й Никола́евич Н. (1761-1836) Diplomat sent by Alexander I to negotiate with N in Paris about peace between F and E. N agreed on June 4 to receive him in July. Meantime, N annexed Genoa and Lucca. Nov. learned of the annexations when still in Berlin. His trip to Paris was cancelled and war followed with F and some S G states on one side, and Austria and R on the other. N marched at the end of August E into the Danube valley. *W & P* starts in July.]
11. пие́са *(obs)* = пье́са — a literary work *(obs)*
12. наш благоде́тель = царь Алекса́ндр
13. э́тот уби́йца = Наполео́н
14. кровь пра́ведника — [Louis-Antoine-Henri, duc d' Enghien (1772-1804), was a Prince of the F former royal house. He

lived in exile in Ettenheim, Baden, G. After a royalist conspiracy against the F government was discovered in Paris, F police invaded Baden and took the Duke back to F (March 14, 1805, N.S.). He was tried by a military court and shot one week later, although he had not been involved in the conspiracy. This high-handed action by N scandalized much of Europe.]

15. Ма́льта — Malta [In 1802, the treaty of Amiens called for the E to evacuate Malta, but they had not done so. War broke out between F and E in May, 1803. Tsar Alexander put forth a plan for a settlement that year under which R troops would occupy Malta. Thus the antagonism to British forces there, expressed here.]
16. за́дняя мысль — ulterior motive
17. Гарденберг — Hardenberg [Prince Karl August von H. (1750-1822). Prussian Minister of Foreign Affairs (1804-1806), and later Chancellor (1810-1822).]
18. Гаугвиц — Haugwitz [Count Christian-August H. (1752-1831) Prussian Minister of Foreign Affairs in 1802. In 1805, he was bearer of Prussian ultimatum to N, which was never delivered because N won at Austerlitz.]
19. Винценгероде — Wintzingerode [Фердинанд Фёдорович В. Also known as Ferdinand, Freiherr von W. A Württemberger in R service, he was a gen during both 1805 and 1812 campaigns. Captured by F nr M in 1812, he was threatened by N personally for alleged treason inasmuch as F controlled Württemberg, but R forces freed him during F retreat fr M.]
20. успоко́иваться *(impf, obs)* = успока́иваться *(impf)*
21. Montmorency — [Famous old, aristocratic F family]
22. Rohan — [Another famous, old aristocratic F family]
23. щелкону́ть or щелкану́ть *(pf, lx, pop)* = щёлкать/ щёлкнуть — *lit:* to crack nuts or sunflower seeds; *fig:* to give smb a fillip; *(here)* to put smb down
24. Лафатер — Lafater or Lavater [Johann Caspar L. (1741-1801). Swiss pastor and writer. Author of *Physiognomische Fragmente zur Beförderung der Menschenkenntnis und Menschenliebe* (1775-1778) tr. into E and published repeatedly in 1790's, in which he sought to correlate a person's character w structure of his head. He also wrote several letters to Empress Mariia Fёdorovna.]
25. при поко́йном импера́торе — [Paul I had been assassinated

in a palace coup four years earlier.]

26. тяжёлый — difficult (person)
27. Куту́зов — Kutuzov [Михаи́л Илларио́нович Голени́щев-К. (1745-1813). Later Светле́йший князь Смоле́нский. R gen. Distinguished veteran of Turkish wars. Commanded R army in Austria in 1805 and R army against F invasion from August 20, 1812, N.S., on.]
28. поко́й — Slavic name of letter п.

One, I, 2

1. шифр — [Jewelled monogram of Tsar or Tsarina given as badge of honor to ladies in waiting]
2. большо́й свет — high society (F *grand monde*)
3. разводи́ть/ развести́ рука́ми — to throw one's hands up in helplessness
4. Екатери́нинский вельмо́жа — [Catherine II had died in 1796]

(5.) Безу́хий — [Later, this name appears as Безу́хов because of numbers involved in Pierre's plan to kill N in M in 1812]

6. пробурли́ть *(pf, pop)* = бурча́ть/ пробурча́ть
7. пригля́дываться/ пригляде́ться — to look at attentively

One, I, 3

1. пу́щен fr пуска́ть/ пусти́ть — to set in motion
2. испла́каться *(pf)* — to shed many tears
3. ме́тр д'отель or метрдоте́ль *(m)* — *maître d'hôtel*
4. убие́ние *(obs)* — murder
5. Louis XV — [(1710-1774). King of F (1715-1774)]
6. ро́ба — gown *(obs)*
7. убира́ть/ убра́ть — to decorate; to adorn
8. хоро́ш — good-looking *(always short form in this meaning!)*
9. облока́чивать/ облокоти́ть — to lean one's elbow on sth
10. ду́рен [собо́й] — bad looking; ugly *(always short form in this meaning)*
11. анти́чный — fr antiquity; classical
12. Mlle. George — [Stage name of F actress Mar-

guerite Josephine Weimer (1787-1867), mistress of N. Famous in tragic and dramatic roles. Visited St. P. in 1808.]

13. на́чал было — [было is often used thus after past tense vbs to indicate that the action was just begun or about to begin when sth happened to stop it. Note this use!]

One, I, 4

[No new chapter in 1961-1963 ed.]

1. притя́гивать/ притяну́ть — to pull
2. образо́вывать/ образова́ть — to educate
3. медве́дь *(m)* — *lit:* bear; *fig:* awkward, clumsy, strong, bear-like man

One, I, 5

[One, I, 4 in 1961-1963 ed.]

1. приходи́ться родня́ (роднёй) — to be related to *(impf only)*
2. по отцу́ — on father's side of the family
3. Румя́нцев — Rumiantsev — [Famous, R aristocratic family. Никола́й Петро́вич Р. (1754-1826) was Minister of Commerce from from 1802-1811, Minister of Foreign Affairs from 1807 and Chancellor from 1809. He is mentioned repeatedly later in *W & P.*]
4. Голи́цын — Golitsyn [Famous R aristocratic family. Князь Алекса́ндр Никола́евич Голи́цын (1773-1844) was оберпрокуро́р of the Synod in 1803. From 1816 to 1824 he was Minister of National Enlightenment. He is mentioned repeatedly in Epilogue.]
5. чту fr чтить *(impf)*
6. не шла — was not suitable
7. пуска́ть/ пусти́ть в ход — to set in motion
8. коме́дия корона́ции в Мила́не — [N had himself crowned King of Italy in Milan, May 26, 1805, N.S.]
9. для Людови́ка XVII, для короле́вы, для Елизаве́ты — [Louis XVI of France (1754-1793) reigned fr 1774 until he was removed and executed by the National Convention, which also executed his wife, Queen Marie-Antoinette (1755-1793) and his sister, Philippine-Marie-Elisabeth (1764-1794). Louis XVII (1785-1795) never ruled and died in prison during the F Revolution.]
10. Бурбо́ны — The Bourbons (the F former

ruling house]

11. *bâton de gueules, engrêlé de gueules d'azur* — baton of gules engrailed w azure gules. [Gules are red and azure is blue, so Ippolit is talking nonsense. Maude gives the arms of the House of Condé as *"D'or à la fasce de gueules,"* or fess gules.]
12. Алекса́ндр [Па́влович] — [Alexander I, Tsar. (1777-1825). Reigned fr 1801 to death. On throne throughout period of *W & P.*]
13. *Contrat social* — [*Le Contrat Social* (1762) Famous book by Jean-Jacques Rousseau (1712-1778). Hobbes and Locke in Gt Britain formulated idea that men abandon nature for society. Rousseau developed this idea. The aim of this contract is to make government possible, but the people retain sovereignty. These ideas influenced people as different as Jefferson and Robespierre.]
14. права́ челове́ка — the rights of man. [Subject of famous F Declaration of 1789. Declared that men are all equal, that the people is sovereign, and that individuals have rights to liberty, property and security.]
15. выходи́ть/ вы́йти из себя́ — to grow furious
16. 18 брюме́ра — [N's coup d'état on Nov. 10, 1799, N.S. (the 18th of Brumaire on the F revolutionary calendar), when he overthrew the Directory and proclaimed a consulate which soon led to his absolute power.]
17. пле́нные в Африке, кото́рых он уби́л — [N repeatedly ordered prisoners of war murdered during his 1798-1799 campaign in Egypt and Asia Minor including 2,000 at Jaffa alone]
18. Арко́льский мост — [Arcola is on Alpino Rv in N Italy nr Verona. At the Battle of Arcola on Nov. 15-17, 1796, N.S., N risked his life on the bridge to inspire his troops to victory over the Austrians thus helping to bring about Treaty of Campo-Formio.]

One, I, 6

[One, I, 5 in 1961-1963 ed.]

1. мсьё — monsieur
2. мне́ния мне́ниями — there are opinions and opinions; opinions differ

(3.) шо́пот *(obs)* = шёпот

4. княги́нин *(poss)* fr княги́ня
5. рединго́т *(obs)* — [Long wide coat originally used for riding *(E-riding coat)*]
6. па-зво́льте = позво́льте

7. дома́шний челове́к — a friend of the family; a frequent visitor to a given house
8. Запи́ски Це́заря — [Perhaps *De bello gallico* (the *Gallic Wars*) by Caius Julius Caesar (ca. 102 B.C.–44 B.C.) describing his conquest of Gaul (58 B.C.–49 B.C.)]
9. не так — not right
10. помо́га — help; aid
11. не по мне — not to my taste

One, I, 7

[One, I, 6 in 1961-1963 ed.]

1. Ане́т — Annette [Scherer]
2. понима́ть толк в чём-либо *(impf)* — to be a good judge of sth
3. за живо́е — to the quick
4. Апра́ксин — [R aristocratic family; counts]
5. как бы — as if
6. что мне за де́ло — what do I care; what does it matter to me

One, I, 8

[No chapter in 1961-1963 ed.]

1. а то — or else; as things are; but; surely
2. никуда́ него́дный — good for nothing
3. да что — but why talk about it
4. коло́дник *(obs)* — convict
5. никуда́ не годи́ться *(impf)* — to be good for nothing
6. что вы [бу́дете де́лать]
7. подма́зка — greasing
8. гуса́рство — hussar-like behavior (loving wine and women)
9. исправле́ние —setting right; reforming

One, I, 9

[No chapter in 1961-1963 ed.]

1. ю́ньская — [In Chapter 1, LNT wrote ю́льская.]

2. изво́зчичий *poss* fr изво́зчик
3. недопи́тый — unfinished; incompletely drunk
4. держа́ть [пари́] *impf* — to bet on
5. одни́м ду́хом — in one breath
6. разойми́ *(impv, pf)* fr
   разыма́ть/ разня́ть (*obs* and *pop*) = разнима́ть/ разня́ть [Maude explains that bettors would shake hands on a bet, and some third party would separate their hands.]
7. семёновский [полк] — [Semēnovskii Guards Inf Regt. One of the first two Regiments of Guards formed by Peter I in 1687.]

[8.] где . . . где — in one place, . . . in another place

9. хва́стать *(impf, coll)* = хва́статься
10. слива́вшихся на нём у́тренней и вече́рней зари́ — [StP lies about 60 degrees N latitude. Hence, there are only a few minutes between sundown and sunup at the time of the summer solstice, when darkness never really takes hold.]
11. империа́л — [10 ruble R gold coin]
12. е́сли кто — if smb
13. лейб-гуса́р — member of Life Guard Hussar Regt, [formed by Paul I in 1796]
14. распира́ться/ расопере́ться — to support oneself against sth
15. переве́с — counterbalance
16. загиба́ть/ загну́ть — to bend back

One, I, 10

[One, I, 7 in 1961-1963 ed.]

1. не в приме́р други́м — as an exception
2. пра́порщик *(obs)* — [lowest ranking commissioned officer in R army or guards]
3. стоя́ть *(impf)* — to stay *(obs)*; to live *(obs)*
4. жива́ть *(impf-many-x, coll)*, fr жить *(impf)*
5. Радзивило́в — Radziwillow [Frontier point with Hapsburg Austria in Volynskaia Province, Kremenetskii District. The R army was headed towards Vienna to help the Austrians fight N.]
6. Ната́лия — [Pre-revolutionary R celebrated the day of the saints whose name they bore rather than their own birthdays. St. Natalie's day is August 26, O.S. and was celebrated both by mother and daughter who bore that name.]
7. цуг — [team of several horses, one or

two abreast]

8. Пова́рская — [A street in M. It ran from Кудри́нская пло́щадь to Арба́тская пло́щадь about a half mile W of Kremlin.]
9. цвето́чная [ко́мната] — room for growing flowers; hothouse
10. официа́нтская [ко́мната]
11. куве́рт *(obs)* — place [at dinner table]; place-setting [F-*couvert*]
12. камча́тный — linen with a silk-like pattern
13. то-то — that's it; really
14. Разумо́вский — [Razumovskii; aristocratic family of counts]
15. и так — as it is; even without that
16. ещё за грани́цей! — abroad to boot!
17. был предоста́влен самому́ себе́ — was left to himself
18. Мо́йка — [branch of Neva Rv in downtown StP close to Winter Palace]
19. в чём де́ло — what it is all about
20. ви́дывать *(impf, many-x)* fr ви́деть *(impf)*
21. троюродный дя́дя — distant cousin of one's parent

One, I, 11

[One, I, 8 in 1961-1963 ed.]

1. запа́хивать/ запахну́ть — to cover sth w folds of a garment
2. на всё есть вре́мя — [Perhaps echoing Ecclesiastes 3:1]
3. сочла́ *(pf, past sing)* fr счита́ть/ счесть
4. на его́ па́мяти — [he] could remember; since [he] first got to know [her]
5. у ней *(less usual variant)* = у неё

One, I, 12

[One, I, 9 in 1961-1963 ed.]

1. отеня́ть/ отени́ть = оттеня́ть/ оттени́ть
2. наклёп *(obs)* — slander
3. Павлогра́дский гуса́рский полк — [a regt of Life Guards, formed in 1783]

4. кро́ме как — except for
5. Арха́ров — Arkharov [well known, rich and noble R family]
6. шит бе́лыми ни́тками — all too obvious
7. ва́ша пра́вда — you are right
8. Саломи́ни – Salomini — [R-born opera-singer and actress who toured M w G troupe in winter of 1805-1806. Also spelled "Solomini."]
9. [вот] поди́те *(impv)* — just imagine; try; attempt
10. держи́ я её стро́го [note this use of *impv*] = е́сли бы я держа́ла её строго
11. что греха́ таи́ть *(impf)* — one must admit
12. проводя́ *(pf, past, act, deep)* — having seen out

One, I, 13

[One, I, 10 in 1961-1963 ed.]

1. ша́пка-невиди́мка — [a fairy-tale cap that makes its wearer invisible]
2. дива́нная *(obs)* — sitting room

One, I, 14

[One, I, 11 in 1961-1963 ed.]

1. с гла́зу на глаз — tête-à-tête; privately

(2.) мока́я fr мока́ть *(impf, obs)* = мака́ть/ макну́ть

3. Madame de Genlis — [Stéphanie-Félicité Ducrest de St. Aubin, Countess de G. (1746-1830). F writer. Governess to ft King Louis-Philippe. She was an educational theorist, author of fiction, and a bit prissy.]
4. добива́ться/ доби́ться своего́ — to get what one is after
5. рассы́паться/ рассыпа́ться — to say many ingratiating things
6. родно́й — a relative
7. Орло́в — [Perhaps граф Алексе́й Григо́рьевич О. (1737-1807). R colonel and favorite of Catherine II. He retired in 1775, but returned to M after Alexander became tsar. O. was famous for his hospitality.]

One, I, 15

[One, I, 12 in 1961-1963 ed.]

1. их [сия́тельство] — [Obsequious usage of pl to indicate a person of high standing. It is obs in this usage.]
2. сия́тельство — [title used to address or refer to count or prince]
3. дотро́гиваться *(impf, obs)* = дотра́гиваться
4. сну́ро́к *(obs)* = шнуро́к
5. го́ресть *(f)* — deep pain
6. что наш дорого́й — how is our dear; what about our dear
7. к тому́ же — moreover
8. не в ду́хе — in a bad mood
9. Пётр Кири́ллович = Пьер

One, I, 16

[One, I, 13 in 1961-1963 ed.]

1. так и *(shows action was involuntary and energetic)* — really *(intensifier)*
2. полови́на — apartments or rooms within a large house *(obs)*
3. прогова́ривать/ проговори́ть — to say; to utter
4. M. Pitt — [William Pitt, the younger (1759-1806). Prime Minister of E (1783-1801). Recalled in 1804. Negotiated with Novosil'tsev and proposed alliance against N in April 1805.]
5. Воробьёвы го́ры — Sparrow Hills [Hillocks just W of M fr which Kremlin can be seen across M Rv. Now called Ле́нинские го́ры and site of M University tall building.]
6. Було́нская экспеди́ция — [N was planning at this time to collect a force at Boulogne for the possible invasion of of E.]
7. Вильнёв — Villeneuve [Pierre-Charles Villeneuve (1763-1806). F admiral to be defeated and captured by E under Nelson at Trafalgar on October 21, 1805, N.S.]
8. причтёте *(pf ft)* fr причи́тывать/ приче́сть — to number *(obs),* to reckon *(obs)*
9. чего́ бы мне ни сто́ило — whatever it costs me
10. мо́жет [быть]

One, I, 17

[One, I, 14 in 1961-1963 ed.]

1. что ли — or what; or sth
2. Тара́ска *(dim, pej)* — [Serfs were generally called by this double dim, which, nowadays, is insulting]
3. чтоб чи́стенькие — let them be nice and clean

One, I, 18

[One, I, 15 in 1961-1963 ed.]

1. охо́тницкий — amateur's; fan's
2. манифе́ст — [Alexander I sent an ukase to senate on Sept. 1, 1805, O.S. about levying recruits and sending R army to Austria for help against F, but there was no manifesto as such]
3. отома́нка *(obs)* = оттома́нка — a wide soft couch with pillows replacing a back (*not* a footstool)
4. босто́н (*adj:* босто́нный) — Boston *(obs)* [card game for 4, using 2 decks of 52 cards each]
5. треть [го́да]
6. на виду́ — in the public eye
7. [он] на о́бухе хлеб моло́тит — [he] can hold on to a penny [The saying is "На о́бухе рожь мола́чивал, зерна́ не утра́чивал."]
8. пойти́ в ход *(pf)* — to become popular
9. тре́пля fr трепа́ть *(impf)*
10. засу́чиваться/ засучи́ться *(pop)* — to roll up one's sleeves
11. зе́лье — pest
12. в слу́чае [быть] — [to be] in great favor (of a ruler)
13. анана́с — [considered a rare delicacy in R]
14. дрей-маде́ра — dry Madeira

One, I, 19

[One, I, 16 in 1961-1963 ed.]

1. Ерёма, Ерёма, сиде́л бы ты до́ма, точи́л бы свои́ веретёна — You should have stayed home and minded your own business
2. Суво́ров — Suvorov [Алекса́ндр Васи́льевич С. (1729-1800), князь Италья́нский, граф Румы́нский, гене-

рали́ссимус, etc. Greatest of R gens. Never lost a battle. Defeated Moreau's F army on Adda R in N Italy in 1799 after Moreau's larger army had surrounded S. S complained bitterly about the behavior of the Austrian Council of War *(Hofkriegsrath).* His Swiss campaign of 1799 is classic. Shinshin underestimates S.]

(3.) на го́лову — to his cost

4. на печи́ лежа́ — [stove is traditional place for old folks to sleep on in R peasant hut]

5. я тебя́! — I'll fix you! I'll get you!

6. пиро́жное — F pastry *(nowadays); (here)* dessert *(obs)*

One, I, 20

[One, I, 17 in 1961-1963 ed.]

1. распуска́ть/ распусти́ть — to open wide; to spread out

2. "Ключ" — [Musical piece attributed to Mozart. Verses quoted just after were taken fr "Запи́ски современника с 1805-1819 гг.", by С. Жихарев (1859). They were written by D.A. Kavelin, father of historian K.D. Kavelin. For music, see Игорь Ильинский и С. Толстой, "Квартет 'Ключ' в романе "Война и мир", "Звенья: Сборник материалов и документов по истории литературы, искусства, и общественной мысли", М, выпуск 2, 1933 г., стр. 625-626.]

3. подра́гивать *(impf)* — to shake gently or fr time to time

4. собира́ться/ собра́ться с си́лами — to summon up one's forces; to brace oneself

5. сам митрополи́т — [Under R church law, this official could permit certain cousins to marry each other, who could not do so otherwise]

(6.) танцова́ть *(impf, obs)* = танцева́ть

7. стро́ить *(impf, obs)* — to tune up

8. что вам за охо́та — what makes you do it

9. экосе́з — écossaise [old fashioned Scottish dance in duple measure]

10. дотанцева́ть *(pf)* — to finish dancing

11. англе́з — anglaise [old fashioned E country dance]

12. переводи́ть дух [or дыха́ние] — *(impf)* — to take a breath

13. ли́ше *comp* fr лихо́й

14. па *(F pas)* — step (in dancing)

One, I, 21
[One, I, 18 in 1961-1963 ed.]

Note: Nos. 8-12 are with a G accent

1. глуха́я и́споведь — mute confession [given by the church to those too sick to talk to the priest who confesses them]
2. собо́рование — extreme unction
3. прейдеши *(OCS)* = прейдёшь
fr преходи́ть/ прейти́ *(obs)* — to exceed
4. собо́ровать *(impf)* — to administer extreme unction
5. ма́тушка — dear *(title of respect and affection given to a woman) (obs)*
6. Екатери́на — Catherine II [(1729-1796). Born Princess Sophie of Anhalt-Zerbst in G. she married the future Peter III and became reigning monarch after he was removed in the palace coup of 1762. She reigned until her death, and was succeeded by son, Paul Petrovich.]
7. брегéт — Bréguet [Fine pocket watch first made by Swiss, Abraham-Louis Bréguet (1747-1823). It could chime the time to the quarter hour.]
8. кремота́ртар — cream of tartar [white, crystalline, purified tartar used as in medicine as cathartic or diuretic]
9. нé пило слу́шай = нé было слу́чая
10. что́пи = чтобы
11. шив = жив
12. око́тник = охо́тник
13. курéнье — [i.e. from incense]
(14.) шка́пчик fr шкап *(obs)* = шкаф
15. как всегда́ — as usual
16. ма́ло ли — lots of
17. э́того то́лько недостава́ло! *(ironic)* — that's all [we] needed!
18. ста́ло быть — as a result; hence
19. раска́т — loud sound; pealing
20. втёрлась *(pf, past)* fr втира́ться/ вторе́ться
21. моза́иковый = моза́ичный

One, I, 22

[One, I, 19 in 1961-1963 ed.]

1. по соло́ме настла́нной под окно́м — [to deaden the sound of wheels on cobblestones]
2. не мог(ли́) не [ви́деть] — could not fail [to see]
3. на полови́не ле́стницы — halfway up the stairs
(4.) аго́ния — final agony
5. повлекла́ *(past)* fr повле́чь *(pf)* — to bring along w oneself
6. приче́тник — sexton; junior deacon
7. италья́нское окно́ — [a wide window with 3 or 4 shutters]
8. зи́мний сад — greenhouse; hothouse
9. гра́фова *(acc, sing, short form)* fr гра́фов *(obs, poss, adj)* fr граф
10. не то что — not quite; not exactly
11. как то́лько — as soon as
12. бо́льше обыкнове́нного — bigger than usual
13. держа́ться *(impf)* — to behave
14. на ходу́ — while walking; on the go; in motion
15. лю́ди *(pl)* — serfs *(obs)*

One, I, 23

[One, I, 20 in 1961-1963 ed.]

1. вольте́ровское кре́сло — Voltaire chair [high-backed, deep, and w arms, as in Houdon's famous statue of Voltaire seated]
2. зажжённый *(past, passive prich)* зажига́ть/ заже́чь
3. не в си́лах — unable [to]
4. поровня́ться *(pf. obs)* = поравня́ться
5. посыла́ть/ посла́ть возду́шный поцелу́й — to throw smb a kiss (by kissing one's hand)
6. перекривля́ть/ перекриви́ть — to distort; to bend too much
7. безотхо́дно *(obs)* — without going away
8. переворoти́ться *(pf, obs)* = переверну́ться *(pf)*

One, I, 24

[One, I, 21 in 1961-1963 ed.]

1. вас не хва́тит — your strength won't hold out
2. заступа́ть/ заступи́ть доро́гу — to block one's way
3. увлажа́ть *(impf, obs)* = увлажня́ть *(impf)*
4. тре́тьего дня — day before yesterday

One, I, 25

[One, I, 22 in 1961-1963 ed.]

1. генера́л-анше́ф *(obs)* — full gen [Second highest rank in R army at end of 18th and start of 19th cent. Corresponds to later генерал-от-инфанте́рии etc. or to Soviet генера́л а́рмии. But LNT may have had lt. gen. in mind. (Cf. Jub. Ed. XIII, 77.)]
2. Па́вел [Петро́вич] — [Paul I, who reigned fr his mother's death in 1796 until he was murdered in 1801, was often hostile to Catherine II's favorites. He was succeeded by his son, Alexander I.]
3. насу́пливаться/ насу́питься — to frown
4. Элои́за — Héloïse [Heroine of *La Nouvelle Héloïse* (The New Héloïse, 1761) by Jean Jacques Rousseau (1712-1778)]
5. abc — [geometric figures in R are labeled according to the Latin alphabet]
6. как же не ду́ра! — isn't she a fool!
7. сте́рпится—слю́бится — get used to sth and you'll like it
8. неразре́занная кни́га — a book whose pages are uncut [F books still often come this way]
9. "Ключ та́инства,, = "Ключ к та́инствам нату́ры,, [R tr of *Aufschlusse zur Magie und mystische Nächte* (Keys to the Mystery of Nature, 1788-1791) by G rel mystic Karl von Eckartshausen (1752-1803). R tr dates fr 1804.]
10. ско́лько ни твержу́ — however much I assert
11. рассе́яние — passing time pleasantly *(obs)*
12. корсика́нское чудо́вище — [i.e. N]
13. сверх того́ — moreover
14. так как — inasmuch as
15. он о́чень хоро́ш — he is very good-looking
16. бу́дет — enough
17. ле́гче верблю́ду — "It is easier for a camel [to go

through the eye of a needle than for a rich man to enter into the Kingdom of God." (Matthew 19:24. The same words occur in Mark 10:25 and almost in Luke 18:25.)]

18. пристращáть *(pf, obs)* — to frighten
19. Апóстолы *(Bible)* — Acts of the Apostles and Epistles (connected w R Orthodox Church service)
20. разгýл — unbridled freedom
21. мáтерь *(OCS,f)* = мать
22. картáвить *(impf)* = грассúровать *(impf)* — to pronounce the sound "r" in the back of the throat rather than between the teeth, i.e. as Parisians say the F "r" rather than as R ordinarily say the R "r"

One, I, 26

[One, I, 23 in 1961-1963 ed.]

1. Дю́ссек — Dussek [Jan Ladislav D. (1760-1812). Czech pianist and composer. Visited StP and R, 1785-1786.]
2. рукá в рýку — holding hands
3. то и дéло — continually; repeatedly
(4.) притрóгиваться *(impf, obs)* = притрáгиваться
5. на твой глазá *(obs)* — in your opinion
6. срок — deadline; date sth is due
7. пудромáнт — a dressing gown worn while powdering one's wig
8. Бог тут не при чём — God has nothing to do with this
9. Михельсóн — Mikhel'son [Ивáн Ивáнович M. (1740-1807) gen in R svc, commanding troops collected on W frontier in 1805]
10. Толстóй — Tolstoi [Пётр Алексáндрович T. (1761-1844). R gen. In 1805, he commanded a corps of 20,000 men supposed to act against F in Pomerania on NE G coast under overall command of King Gustavus IV Adolphus of Sweden. N's victory at Austerlitz squelched the idea, and T. returned to R w his army.]
11. Померáния — Pomerania [S shore of Baltic between Oder and Vistula Rvs. Then Prussian and Swedish; now P.]
12. Штрáльзунд — Stralsund [seaport on Baltic Sea, then in Prussia. Now in E G.]
13. *"Marlbroug s'en va t'en guerre. . . Dieu sait quand reviendra."* [Great song hit of 18th cent. Neither composer nor lyricist is known. "Marlbroug" was the great E gen, John Churchill, first Duke of Marlborough

(1650-1722), who defeated F at Blindheim (or Blenheim) in Bavaria in 1704. The music is still pop today, with such words as "For he's a jolly good fellow," and "The bear went over the mountain." For words and music, see René Deloup, *Vieilles Chansons et Rondes Françaises,* Paris, Max Eschig, and London, Schott and Co., no date (copyright 1939), p. 14.]

One, I, 27

[One, I, 24 in 1961-1963 ed.]

1. Рю́рик — Rurik [Legendary 9th cent., first prince of R, fr whom many R gentry claimed descent, including LNT]
2. посме́иваться *(impf, many-x)* — to snicker periodically
3. [ему́] пло́хо прихо́дится — [he] is hard pressed
4. Потёмкин — Potemkin [князь Григо́рий Алекса́ндрович П. (1739-1791). R Field Marshal and favorite of Catherine II.]
5. Моро́ — Moreau [Jean Victor Marie M. (1763-1813). F gen whom Suvorov defeated in Switzerland in 1799. Later banished for suspected sedition. He lived in New Jersey in 1805.]
6. Фри́дрих — Friedrich [Frederick II (1712-1786), King of Prussia (1740-1786). Famous for generalship, called Frederick the Great.]
7. ему́ чорт не рад — [Rhymes w хофс-кригс-вруст-шнапс-рат]
   вурст = *G Wurst* , = sausage
   шнапс = *G Schnapps. G Hofkriegsrath* — War Council
8. надо францу́зов взять — you have to bring in Frenchmen
9. [что́бы] своя́ свои́х не позна́ша — so that each does not recognize his own kind *(paraphrase of John 1:10-11)*
10. [что́бы] своя́ свои́х побива́ша — so that each of them kill his own kind
11. Па́лен — Palen or Pahlen [Perhaps Фёдор Петро́вич П. (1780-1863). R diplomat who served a time in Washington.]
12. чудеса́ *(nom pl)* fr чу́до
13. Орло́вы — Orlovs [Brothers Григо́рий Григо́рьевич О. (1734-1783), R gen and favorite of Catherine II. Алексе́й Григо́рьевич (see), and Влади́мир Григо́рьевич (1743-1831), who helped Catherine II take the throne fr her husband.]

14. как же — of course
15. а мне оно́ вот где [сиди́т] — I've had it up to here; it hurts me up to here [expression of annoyance, usually accompanied by pointing to neck, head, etc.]

One, I, 28
[One, I, 25 in 1961-1963 ed.]

1. погребе́ц — portable bar
2. Оча́ков — Ochákov [town at Dnieper Delta nr Black Sea. Suvorov captured Turkish fortress there by storm in 1788.]
3. и то и друго́е — both this and that
4. свет — [high] society
5. о, нет — [disagrees with Andrei's foregoing statement]
6. Стерн — Sterne [Laurence S. (1713-1768), E clergyman, initiator of "sentimental" novel, author of *Tristram Shandy* (1759-1767) and *A Sentimental Journey through France and Italy* (1768). A note in first printing of LNT Jubilee Ed. (XII, 475) mentions a 1793 R tr of latter work, but I have been unable to find anything resembling quotation in E original (Sterne, *A Sentimental Journey through France and Italy by Mr. Yorick,* ed. by Gardner D. Stout, Jr., Berkeley and Los Angeles, U. of Cal. Press, 1967). However, LNT's diary entries for March 8, 1851, O.S. and especially for May 31, 1855, O.S. (Jub. Ed. XLVI, 49 and XLVII, 43) indicate some knowledge of Benjamin Franklin's *Autobiography,* in which Franklin refers to "an old maxim" (which he italicizes): "He that has once done you kindness will be more ready to do you another than he whom you yourself have obliged." (*The Autobiography of Benjamin Franklin,* ed. by Leonard W. Labaree *et alii,* New Haven, CT., Yale, 1964, p. 172.)] (See Appendix Seven.)
7. круто́й — stern; harsh
8. оття́гивать/ оттяну́ть — to pull down
9. к чему́ — what for
10. э́то в сиде́нье — put this on the seat
11. Зу́бов — [R family made counts in 1793]
12. шестери́к — a team of six horses *(obs)*
13. расчеркну́ть *(pf)* — to sign sth
14. разжени́ться *(pf, pop)* — to get unmarried
15. печата́ние — sealing

16. Михаи́л Илларио́нович [Куту́зов]
17. рема́рка — stage directions in a play *(nowadays); (here)* remarks or observations *(F remarque)*
18. без чувств — unconscious

One, II, 1

1. Браунау — Braunau [City in Upper Austria on Inn Rv, a tributary of Danube]
2. перекла́няться *(pf)* — to bow too low
3. докла́няться *(pf, obs)* — to bow (low enough)
4. чини́ться *(impf)* — to repair one's things
5. ши́льце fr ши́ло
6. мы́льце fr мы́ло
7. ве́домство — supply service *(mil)*
8. поха́живать *(impf)* — to walk up and down; to stroll
9. Цари́цын Луг — [StP parade grounds. Later called Ма́рсово по́ле.]
10. чехо́л — cap-cover
11. Фердина́нд — [Archduke Ferdinand Karl-Joseph of Austria (b. 1782) commanded left of Austrian army which lost at Ulm]
12. Мак — Mack [Karl M. (1752-1828) Austrian gen surrounded by F at Ulm on upper Danube and forced to surrender unconditionally to N w 23,000 men on Oct. 22, 1805, N.S.]
13. цвет фабри́чного сукна́ — [dark blue]
14. казаки́н *(obs)* — short outer coat with hooks and gathers in back; knee-length *(F casaquin)*
15. превосходи́тельство — [form of address used to maj gen and lt gen]
16. обрыва́ть/ оборва́ть — to make a crude comment; to cut smb short
17. фронт — ranks of soldiers; mil formation *(both obs)*

One, II, 2

1. сми́рна = сми́рно
2. бесшоссе́йная доро́га — unsurfaced road
3. ве́нская коля́ска *(obs)* — light, four-seater carriage
4. кроа́т *(obs)* = хорва́т — Croat [S Slavic nation then under Austria now in N Yugoslavia]
5. го-го-го-го-ство — [unclear syllables from *(obs.)* высокопревосходи́тельство, title given to full gen and above]
6. посмотри́ [он] на него́ — if [he] were to look at him
7. измаи́льский — [Измаи́л was a Turkish fortress on Danube in Bessarabia; Suvorov took it by storm in December, 1790. Kutuzov was one of Suvorov's subordinates in the battle and lost an eye there.]
8. Ба́хус — Bacchus [Gk god of wine]
9. прете́нзия — complaint
10. разбира́ться/ разобра́ться *(mil)* — to get broken down; to fall in
11. невдалеке́ — not far away
12. кара́хтер or кара́ктер *(subst)* = хара́ктер
13. жид — Jew *(obs)*; kike
14. того́ — er; uh [stalling word]
15. субальте́рн-офице́р — lowest-ranking officer in unit
16. ска́зывать *(impf; obs* or *pop)* = говори́ть *(impf)*
17. об одно́м глазу́ = в одно́м глазу́
18. подвёртка — foot-cloths; leg bands (worn in R army instead of socks)
19. австрия́к (*obs* or *dial*) = австри́ец
20. я чай = я ча́ю fr ча́ять *(impf)*
21. как амуни́цию чи́стят [австри́йцы]
22. страже́ние *(subst)* = сраже́ние
23. Бруно́во *(subst)* — Braunau
24. Бунапа́рте *(subst)* or Бунапа́рт *(subst)* = Buonaparte
25. замиря́ться/ замири́ться — to conclude peace
26. квартирье́р — billeting officer (sent on ahead of army)
27. суха́рик fr суха́рь *(m)* — dried-out bread
28. пропрём fr пропере́ть *(pf)* — to trudge or tramp a given distance
29. е́мши *(subst)* = е́вши — having eaten
30. знай — unconcernedly
31. не́мцы как коля́ски подава́ли — [To hasten the arrival of Kutu-

zov's R army fr E after N had started marching towards Austria, the Austrians sent vehicles for R to ride in]

32. ва́жно — real good; fine
33. пе́сенники вперёд — [traditional place for men who sang in chorus while marching in R army]
34. Каме́нский — Kamenskii [Миха́йл Федо́тович К. (1738-1809) R Field Marshal. Fought against Prussia (1760-1761) and Turkey (1769-1774; 1788). Named commander-in-chief against N in 1806, but left command after only six days. Retired to his estate, where his serfs killed him.]
35. "Ах, вы, се́ни мои́, се́ни,, — [R folk song. Words and one variant of melody can be found in Иван Прач, *Собрание народных русских песен с их голосами,* под ред. В. М. Беляева, М, Гос. музык. издательство, 1955, стр. 200-201. Two other versions of the music are given in Н. М. Лопатин и В. П. Прокунин, *Сборник русских народных лирических песен,* М, Мамонтов, 1889, 2 тома, II, 66-67. The most frequently encountered treatment of this song is is in the Shrovetide Fair scene of "Петру́шка,, (1911) by Игорь Фёдорович Страви́нский (1882-1971).]
36. ло́жечник — [a man who plays ло́жки (pl), a wooden R folk-instrument w inset bells.]
37. в но́гу — in step *(mil)*
38. похру́скиванье = похру́стывание — rattling
39. перебива́ть/ переби́ть — to move *(obs);* to kill many of; to fluff up *(a bed)*

One, II, 3

1. Франц — Franz [(1768-1835). Franz II, last Holy Roman Emperor who, in 1804, took title of Franz I, Emperor of Austria]
2. Лех — Lech [Right tributary of Danube in G. Augsburg in Bavaria is on Lech]
3. Ulm — [City and fortress on Danube in Württemberg, marking upper limit of navigability of Danube. Then part of Bavaria.]
4. [граф] Ностиц — Count Nostitz [Austrian gen who commanded Croats in 1805]
5. из ря́ду вон выходя́щий — outstanding
6. под руко́й — at hand
7. нейдём = не идём

8. о́рден Мари́и Тере́зии — [Austrian medal that came in several classes]
9. Штраух — Strauch [Austrian gen in charge of food and supplies for allied army during 1805 campaign]
10. расходи́ться/ разойти́сь — to pass by smb

One, II, 4

1. поднима́ть/ подня́ть на́ ноги — to raise the alarm
2. толкону́ть *(pf, pop)* or толкану́ть = толкну́ть *(pf)*
3. на во́дку — a tip *(money)*
4. така́я [хоро́шая] бу́дет ло́шадь
5. что ба́рин — what about your master
6. ко́фей *(obs)* = ко́фе
7. ме́нтик — [short hussar's jacket with lace and loops, trimming and several rows of buttons. Worn as cape.]
8. чикчи́ры or кички́ры *(obs)* — [narrow cavalry breeches with leather at knees and seat. Worn by uhlans.]
9. Лавгу́шка — [Thus LNT shows Denisov's using back of throat "r" throughout *W & P*]
10. фре́йлен or фре́йлейн — *Fräulein* (G) = Miss
11. как ты пое́хал, так и пошло́ — when you left, then it began
12. се́мпель — *simple (F);* ordinary undoubled bet
13. паро́ль = пароли́ — *paroli (F);* doubled bet
14. хоть бы — if only *(a wish);* I wish; hopefully
15. подъе́здок — reserve horse
16. кому́ ж быть — who should it be; who else can it be?
17. да нет! — why, no!
18. окромя́ *(pop)* = кро́ме
19. запорю́ fr запоро́ть *(pf)*
20. подстёгивать/ подстегну́ть — to buckle on
21. спусти́ть шку́ру с кого́-то *(pf, pop)* — to give smb a good thrashing
22. немно́го не заста́ли — [you] didn't miss finding him by much
23. [никому́] до э́того де́ла нет — it is no one else's business

One, II, 5

1. выслу́живаться/ вы́служиться — to attain a given rank in the service *(obs)*
2. штаб-ро́тмистр *(obs)* — [cavalry equivalent of штабс-капита́н see Appendix Four. Also written штабс-ро́тмистр]
3. в том де́ло — that is the point
4. оса́живать/ осади́ть — to cut smb short
5. бе́з году неде́ля *(ironic)* — a rookie; still new
6. пра́вда ма́тка — plain truth
7. ва́ша во́ля — as you like
8. уж там боле́знь не боле́знь — whether he is sick or not
9. опя́ть в полк [меня́] вы́слали
10. ка́ша — a mess *(fig)*

One, II, 6

1. Линц — Linz [Town in Upper Austria, on Danube, just W of where Traun Rv flows into Danube]
2. Энс — Enns [Town in Austria on Enns Rv nr where it flows into Danube]
3. сю *(f, acc, sing)* fr сей
4. труба́ — *(here)* telescope
5. доппелькю́мель = *G Doppelkümmel* — double Kummel [German liqueur]
6. кто . . ., кто — some . . ., some
7. сиде́ть по-туре́цки — *lit:* to sit Turkish-style *fig:* to sit w one's legs tucked up
8. пробира́ть/ пробра́ть — to penetrate
9. так и есть — so it is
10. что они́ ме́шкают — what are they delaying for
11. нут-ка = ну-тка — well then
12. куда́ донесёт — where [it] will carry to
13. хвати́ть *(pf)* — to hit [as of a shell]

One, II, 7

1. смеючись *(pr, deep)* — laughing
2. фуршта́тский fr фуршта́т — supply train *(mil)*
3. нет, что́бы подожда́ть — you can't wait

4. запружáть *(impf, obs)* = запрýживать
5. кутáс — [brush worn to decorate shako at time of *W & P*]
6. взбрызг — splash; spurt
7. отли́чный — different
8. мелиóн *(subst)* = миллиóн
9. тапéрича *(subst)* = тепéрь
10. полыхнýть *(pf, pop)* — to hit
11. то-то онó — it sure is; that's what it is
12. холóдная — a dud; a shell that fails to explode [See Appendix Seven]
13. испужáлся *(subst)* = испугáлся
14. форшпáн — long wagon *(G-Vorspann)*
15. на пáре — with a pair *(of horses)*
16. вы́мем *(pop)* = вы́менем *(instr)* fr вы́мя *(nt)*
17. колбасá — [slang for a G]
18. то-то чéрти! — what devils [G are] !
19. вот бы тебé к ним стоя́ть — if only you were quartered w them
20. видáли — we've seen it before
21. прёшь fr перéть *(impf)* — to make one's way
22. подожжёт *(pf, ft)* fr поджигáть/ поджéчь
23. фатáет *(subst)* = хватáет
fr хватáть *(impf)* — to reach; to aim
24. подбáдривать (ся) *(impf)* — to encourage
25. вальтрáп — [type of pail used to hold saddle or sweat clothes to keep them clean of dust and dry in rain. Hussars used it]
26. тáшка — [leather case worn by Hussars, mostly for decoration, and attached by straps to waist; sabretache]
27. отчуждённость *(f)* — alienation; antagonism
28. Поднóвинское — [Amusement park of the time located on Novinskaia St. (later Blvd), along Sadovaia Street in M. For a picture of it towards end of 18th century, see *Istoriia Moskvy,* II, 572.]
29. перехóд — a day's march
30. повы́тереться *(pf, subst)* — to get rubbed away
31. то-то бы тебя́ на коня́ посади́ть *(subst)* = éсли бы посади́ли тебя́
32. бýде *(subst)* = бýдет

One, II, 8

1. спира́ться/ сопере́ться — to be pressed
2. капо́т — overcoat *(mil); (F capote)*
3. тро́нутый *(pop)* — slightly hurt
4. сби́тая фигу́ра — sturdy figure
5. ефе́с — hilt *(of sword)*
6. скучли́вый *(obs,* or *pop)* — showing boredom
7. фланкёр *(obs, mil)* — flanker
8. то . . . то — first . . . then
9. Багратио́н — Bagration [князь Пётр Ива́нович Б. (1765-1812), Prince of the Georgian ruling house. Gen in R Army. Commanded Kutuzov's rear-guard in 1805. In 1812, he was at first in charge of Second W army. Killed at Borodino.]
10. кто ве́лено *(G accent)* = кому́ ве́лено [Schubert uses -айт for -ать to show inf, uses nom for other cases, and the pl зажгу́т for sing зажжёт after кто]
11. вы́жму *(ft, pf)* fr выжима́ть/ вы́жать — to wring out
12. уже́ не — no longer
13. как бы ему́ не отста́ть — lest he fall behind
14. Влади́мир с ба́нтом — Order of St Vladimir [R order founded by Catherine II in 1782. It had 4 classes, all of which had sash.]
15. поря́док — way of doing things; course; way
16. по ком — smb at whom
17. жгут — tightly-packed straw or hemp
18. маку́ша = маку́шка
19. руба́ть *(impf, pop)* = руби́ть
20. руба́й в пе́си — to cut them up to heck [a phrase taken by LNT fr an article by Denis Davydov about the 1805 campaign. Davydov says phrase was used by R officer of Hungarian origin, whose R was none too good. Meaning of phrase is not too clear.]
21. реля́ция *(obs)* — *lit:* details accompanying citation for a medal; *fig:* combat story

One, II, 9

1. тя́жесть *(f)* — heavy things
2. Ламбах — Lambach [Town on Traun Rv in Upper Austria]
3. Амштеттен —Amstetten — [Place on Ips Rv, a S tributary

of Danube, in Lower Austria. F vanguard under Murat attacked Bagration's detachment there, Nov. 5, 1805, O.S.]

4. Мельк — Mölk or Melk [Town in Lower Austria, on Danube, towards Vienna fr Lambach and Amstetten]
5. Мортье́ — Mortier [Edouard-Adolphe-Casimir M. (1768-1835) F marshall fr 1804 on. Corps commander in 1805. Made Duke of Treviso in 1808. Commanded Young Guard in R in 1812. F ambassador to StP, 1830.]
6. он атакова́л Мортье́ — [Battle of Dürrenstein, a town on Danube towards Vienna fr Melk or Mölk, November 11, 1805, N.S. With this battle, Kutuzov upset N's plans for the campaign.]
7. Кремс — Krems [Town on Danube in Lower Austria, just above Dürrenstein, on way to Vienna]
8. Шмидт — Schmidt [Heinrich S., or Heinrich Sebastian von S. (1743-1805). *Feldmarschall-Lieutenant* in Austrian army, recalled to active service in his sixties and attached to Kutuzov's R army in Austria. Killed at Dürrenstein on November 11, 1805, N.S. For his career, see Constant von Wurzbach, *Biographisches Lexikon des Kaiserthums Oesterreich,* Dreissigter Theil, Wien, 1875, pp. 252-256.]
9. Брюнн — Brünn [Now Brno in Moravia, Czechoslovakia]
10. До́хтуров — Dokhturov [Дми́трий Серге́евич Д. (1756-1816) R Gen. Veteran of 1805-1807 campaigns. In 1812, commanded II inf corps defending Smolensk. At Borodino, commanded nr Raevskii redoubt, and took over R left after Bagration fell. Present at Tarutino, Maloiaroslavets, Leipzig, and other battles.]
11. про́воды *(pl)* — a sendoff; seeing smb off or out
12. задрёмывать *(impf)* — to start dozing off
13. хара́ктерный — showing character
14. вы́ход — appearance *(of a dignitary)*

One, II, 10

1. в чём бы ни — in whatever
2. циркуля́р — written directive
3. распуска́ть/ распусти́ть скла́дки ко́жи — to smooth his wrinkles out
4. подбира́ть/ подобра́ть ко́жу — to pucker the skin
5. августе́йший *(obs)* — most august *(used for royalty)*
6. осчастли́вить *(pf)* — to make happy

(7). Пра́тер — Prater [large amusement park in

Vienna]

8. спусти́ть ко́жу со лба — to smooth the wrinkles out on his forehead
9. Карл — Karl [K.-Ludwig-Johann (1771-1847). Austrian archduke. President of *Hofkriegsrath.*]
10. одержи́ вы = е́сли бы вы одержа́ли
11. Шенбрунн — Schönbrunn [Austrian Emperor's palace on outskirts of Vienna]
12. Врбна — [Count Rudolf Vrbna (1761-1823) Austrian emissary sueing N for peace in 1805]
13. Murat — [Joachim M. (1767-1815). F gen and husband of N's sister Caroline. Made marshall in 1804. Won distinction w cavalry at Austerlitz in 1805. Named King of Naples in 1808. Commanded F cavalry in R in 1812. Executed in Italy after Waterloo.]
14. Ауэрсперг — [Prince Auersperg von Mautern (1740-1822). Austrian Field Marshal. Tricked by Murat into giving up intact Thabor Bridge over the Danube near Vienna, thus allowing F to take the city without further ado.]
15. большо́й колпа́к — big shot (*ironic,* fr *F gros bonnet,* w pun on *R* колпа́к — simpleton)
16. берли́нское свида́ние Алекса́ндра — [Tsar Alexander signed a secret treaty w Prussia in Berlin in Oct. 1805 for Prussia to fight F. After Austerlitz, Prussia reneged on it.]
17. Campo Formio — [F-Austrian peace treaty of October 1797. Austria ceded Netherlands to F and made other major concessions to get peace]
18. Сарди́нское вели́чество — [Sardinia included also Savoy, and Liguria, w Turin the capital, but F took mainland parts of Kingdom during Revolution and under N. (Genoa is capital of Liguria.) In 1861, King of Sardinia became King of united Italy.]
19. слы́шать *(impf)* — to sense; to feel (*not* just to hear!)

One, II, 11

1. свой [челове́к] — one of the in-group; one of the boys; a good friend
2. Демосфе́н — Demosthenes [(ca. 384 B.C.-322 B.C.) Gk orator who opposed Philip of Macedon and practiced speaking w pebbles in his mouth to perfect enunciation.]

3. бра́ться/ взя́ться за вас — to take you in hand

One, II, 12

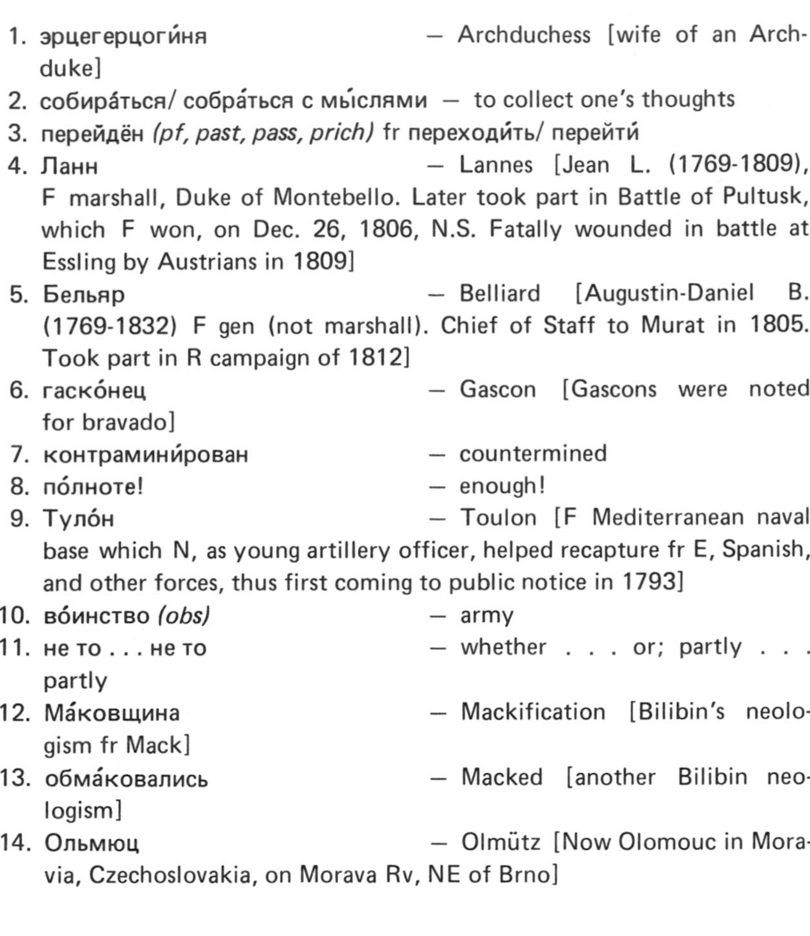

1. эрцгерцоги́ня — Archduchess [wife of an Archduke]
2. собира́ться/ собра́ться с мы́слями — to collect one's thoughts
3. перейдён *(pf, past, pass, prich)* fr переходи́ть/ перейти́
4. Ланн — Lannes [Jean L. (1769-1809), F marshall, Duke of Montebello. Later took part in Battle of Pultusk, which F won, on Dec. 26, 1806, N.S. Fatally wounded in battle at Essling by Austrians in 1809]
5. Бельяр — Belliard [Augustin-Daniel B. (1769-1832) F gen (not marshall). Chief of Staff to Murat in 1805. Took part in R campaign of 1812]
6. гаско́нец — Gascon [Gascons were noted for bravado]
7. контрамини́рован — countermined
8. по́лноте! — enough!
9. Туло́н — Toulon [F Mediterranean naval base which N, as young artillery officer, helped recapture fr E, Spanish, and other forces, thus first coming to public notice in 1793]
10. во́инство *(obs)* — army
11. не то . . . не то — whether . . . or; partly . . . partly
12. Ма́ковщина — Mackification [Bilibin's neologism fr Mack]
13. обма́ковались — Macked [another Bilibin neologism]
14. Ольмюц — Olmütz [Now Olomouc in Moravia, Czechoslovakia, on Morava Rv, NE of Brno]

One, II, 13

1. Эцельсдорф — Hötzelsdorf [Village in Lower Austria, about 80 km NW of Vienna and about 30 km WSW of Znaim (see entry 11 below in this chapter)]
2. поку́да хвата́л слух — wherever the ear could reach
3. ковро́вый — carpet-like *(in weave)*
4. ле́карский *(obs)* — doctor's

5. в лепёшку расшиба́ть/ расшиби́ть — to squash [you] into a pancake
6. шлю́ха *(coarse, pop)* — trollop
7. те = тебя́
8. де́лайте как зна́ете = де́лайте как хоти́те
9. приве́сть *(obs)* = привести́ *(pf)*
10. [нам] ху́же прихо́дится — [we] are getting worse
11. Цнайм — Znaim (Now called Znojmo). [Town about 60 mi NNW of Vienna, now in Czechoslovakia.]
12. перевью́чивать/ перевью́чить — to overload
13. Боге́мские леса́ — Bohemian forest (on what is now W G-Czechoslovak border)
14. Вейротер — Weyrother [Franz von W. (1754-1806). Austrian gen, mil theoretician, and Chief of Austrian staff in 1805. Served w R against N in 1812.]
15. Ки́евский гренаде́рский [полк] — [R regt of heavy infantry]
16. Подо́льский [полк] — [R regt of light infantry]
17. высокоблагоро́дие — [honorific form of address, used w ваше etc., for ranks 6, 7, and 8 of tsarist civil and mil svc]
18. сбо́рка — crease
19. вы́текший глаз — lost eye [an eye fr which the liquid of eyeball has flowed out, leaving the eye sunken and blind]

One, II, 14

1. Бу́ксгевден — Buksgevden or Buxhöwden [Фёдор Фёдорович Б. (1750-1811) Gen in R svc. Took part in Austerlitz. Commanded corps at start of 1806-1807 campaign. Took main command of army from Bennigsen after Tilsit in 1807.]
2. предупрежда́ть/ предупреди́ть — to anticipate
3. уси́ленный марш — forced march
4. отста́лый — straggler
5. Голлабрунн — Hollabrünn [Place where Vienna-Znaim road Murat was advancing on crossed road from Krems, which Kutuzov was retreating along]
6. сколь = наско́лько
7. как . . . так — both . . . and

One, II, 15

1. Грунт — Grunth [Village on Vienna-

Znaim road nr Schöngraben]

2. кре́стик — medal
3. собью́тся *(pf, ft)* fr сбива́ться/ сби́ться [в ку́чу] — to bunch up; to get confused
4. разу́мшись *(subst)* = разу́вшись
5. выходи́ть/ вы́йти — to come out; to succeed; to have as the result; to work out; to look out on *(a view);* to run out *(of supplies);* to be published
6. пру́тья *(nom, pl)* fr прут
(7.) мушкатёр *(obs)* = мушкетёр
8. аж — so that
9. хранцу́з *(subst)* = францу́з
[10]. послу́хай *(subst)* = послу́шай
11. не пророни́ть ни . . . сло́ва — not to miss . . . even a word
12. что он [говори́т]
13. чёрт его́ дери́! [fr драть *(impf)*] — damn him!
14. кари, мала — [nonsense syllables representing sounds of F to Sidorov's ear]

One, II, 16

1. Шенграбен — Schöngrabern or Schöngraben [Village in Lower Austria on old Vienna-Znaim road nr Hollabrünn. Here on Nov. 4/16, 1805, Bagration's R rearguard of about 5,000 men fought against Murat's F forces of 30,000. Battle is also called Hollabrünn, but not by LNT.]
2. ручью́ fr руче́й
3. во́дочка fr во́дка
4. травни́к *(obs)* — herb liqueur

One, II, 17

1. францу́зские два ко́нные *(obs)* — францу́зских два ко́нных
2. Лемарруа́ — Lemarrois [Jean-Léonard-François L. (1776-1836) F gen. Adjutant to N in 1805]
3. стро́иться *(impf)* — to fall in *(mil);* to be built
4. разбира́ть/ разобра́ть — to take [one's own weapon from the stack]
5. восто́чный акце́нт — oriental accent [Bagration's basic

language was not R but Georgian]

6. энглизи́рованная (or англизи́рованная ло́шадь) — dock-tailed horse (which holds its stump upright)
7. ста́тский *(obs)* = шта́тский — civilian
8. ауди́тор *(obs)* — [Civilian attached to army who supervised baggage train and aided billeting officer during campaigns; at other times he assisted investigator and public prosecutor at courts-martial]
9. камло́т *(obs)* — camlet [thick woolen cloth with admixture of silk or cotton]
10. фуршта́т — mil supply unit; wagon-train
11. шлёп! — smack! *(onomotopoetic sound)*
12. фейерве́ркер *(obs)* — artillery sergeant
13. спотыкну́ться *(pf, obs)* = споткну́ться *(pf)*
14. как раз — just; exact
15. брандску́гель *(obs)* — incendiary shell

One, II, 18

(1.) стклянка *(obs)* = склянка
2. по́лка — powder-pan [the part of a flintlock into which gunpowder was poured]
3. цепь *(f)* — line *(mil)*; front line
4. сла́бый на вид — weak-looking
5. карре́ or каре́ — square [formation used by infantry to defend against cavalry attacks]
6. фрунтово́й *(obs)* = фронтово́й [See One, II, 1 for фронт]
7. поддава́ть/ подда́ть за́дом — to do sth energetically
8. переменя́ть/ перемени́ть но́гу — to get in step
9. с Бо́гом! *(obs)* — good luck!
10. Тьер — Thiers [Louis-Adolphe T. (1797-1877). F historian, statesman, and journalist, most famous as first president of F Third Republic (1871). Author of *Histoire du consulat et de l'empire* (History of the Consulate and of the Empire, 1840-1855). For ways in which LNT "psychologized" and "discredited" Thiers in *W&P*, see Shklovskii, pp. 139-140, and 175-180.]

One, II, 19

Note: The G colonel says -айть for -ать in his infinitives and frequently uses grammatical forms which do not agree w each other in gender, case, and/or number.

1. Азо́вский полк — [a R heavy inf regt]
2. в чи́ном *(G accent)* = в чи́не
3. к спе́ху — in a hurry
4. в двух руже́йных вы́стрелах — two rifle shots' length distance
5. руже́й *gen pl* of ружьё
6. поскоре́е бы — let it come quickly
7. поддава́ть/ подда́ть за́дом — to move the lower part of the body sharply upwards *(said of animals)*
8. перебива́ть/ переби́ть в гало́п — to break into a gallop
9. руба́ть/ рубану́ть — to cut sth w gusto, using sth sharp; to slash
10. за секу́нду — a second before
11. на-переве́с *(obs)* — bent forward
12. что было си́лы — with all his might

One, II, 20

1. во что бы то ни ста́ло — whatever it cost
2. ни в чём не заме́ченный — above suspicion of any blame
3. засумя́тились = по́дняли сумато́ху
4. подкри́кивать/ подкри́кнуть — to accompany sth w shouting
5. вот так-так! — that's it!
6. носогре́лка = носогре́йка — short pipe *(for smoking)*
7. благоро́дие *(obs)* — [title used in addressing grades 9 through 14 of tsarist civil or mil svc]

[8.] ну́мер *(obs)* = но́мер

9. выдава́ть/ вы́дать — to betray
10. за что они́ меня́ [распека́ют] — what are they bawling me out for
11. драть *(impf only, coll)* — to take off; to run away
12. единоро́г — [long howitzer used for high-angle fire; the unicorn depicted on it gave it its name]

One, II, 21

1. подложи́ шине́ль — put a cloak under [him]
2. подстели́ fr подстила́ть/ подостла́ть
3. окровяни́ть = окровени́ть *(pf, pop)*
4. укла́дываться/ уложи́ться — to subside
5. отби́лся от ро́ты — I got separated fr my company
6. проце́нта = проце́нт — interest *(on a loan)*
7. ну, вас — oh, go on w you
8. дровору́б — woodcutter
9. бата́льный ого́нь — running fire
10. мы вме́сте немно́го не съе́хались — we didn't miss [meeting] each other by much
11. сбива́ть/ сбить с то́лку — to confuse

One, III, 1

1. смотря́ по обстоя́тельствам — depending on circumstances
2. в си́ле — in power
3. ве́даться *(impf)* — to have business or to associate w smb
(4.) 30 т[ы́сяч]
5. не сде́лай он того́ = е́сли бы он э́того не сде́лал
6. перебира́ть па́льцами *(impf)* — to finger
7. хоть за́втра брось — give it up even tomorrow
8. так-так — yes, indeed; very well
9. счёт — a bill; an account
10. ряза́нский — fr [holdings in] Riazan' (province or *guberniia* just SE of M)
11. сочтёмся *(pf ft)* fr счита́ться/ счe̋сться — to settle accounts
12. отводи́ть/ отвести́ ду́шу — to unburden one's heart
13. име́ть ви́ды на — to count on
14. Вине́с — Vigneux [F painter of miniatures who worked in Paris fr 1799 to 1814. Zaidenshnur suggests that LNT may have put the mistaken "s" on the name because he found it so spelled in R memoirs. For Vigneux, see Hans Vollmer *et alii*, eds., *Allgemeines Lexikon der bildenden Künstler*, Leipzig, 1926, XXIV, 353, and E. Bénézit, *Dictionnaire des peintres, sculpteurs, dessinateurs et graveurs*, Paris, Gründ, the most recent edition is 1976.]

15. скрып *(obs)* = скрип
16. друго́е де́ло — sth else
17. да, хороша́ — yes, she's pretty
18. противу- *(obs)* = противо-

One, III, 2

1. сто́лький *(obs)* — so much
2. Христо́с с ним = Бог с ним
3. Лёлин *poss adj* fr Лёля, *dim* of Эле́н (Еле́на)
4. поха́живать/ походи́ть — to walk up and down
5. Вязми́тинов — Viazmitinov [Граф Серге́й Кузьми́ч В. (1748-1819). Administrator. Vice President of War Collegium, Governor Gen of StP, 1805, 1812, and 1816.]
6. соте́ *(indecl)* — sauté
7. что за [глу́пость] — what [silliness] ; what kind of
8. углублённый — submerged
9. Пари́с — Paris [the Trojan whose taking of Helen started the Trojan War in the *Iliad*]
10. Вот Еле́на Васи́льевна, так та — Now, Elena Vasil'evna, she...
11. усво́иваться *(obs)* = усва́иваться
12. Бог да благослови́т вас — May God bless you

One, III, 3

1. Мари́ *(indecl)* — Marie *(F form of name)*
2. в тот день как прие́хать = в тот день когда́ прие́хал
3. отсове́тывать *(impf, obs)* = отсове́товать *(pf)*
4. дво́рня — *(here)* serfs' quarters
5. прешпе́кт *(obs)* = проспе́кт
6. сла́ва тебе́ го́споди = сла́ва Бо́гу
7. закида́ть доро́гу [сне́гом]
8. ве́шать/ пове́сить нос — to become depressed
9. определя́ть/ определи́ть — to get smb a position *(obs)*
10. колле́гия — govt dept or bureau *(obs)*
11. обтя́нутый — pulled down
12. не раз — more than once
13. ведённый fr вести́ *(impf)*
14. па́пенька их — his daddy *(obseq form uses pl)*
15. проволо́к *(m, past, pf, sing)* fr

проволáкивать/ проволóчь — to drag along
16. масакá — a dark red color
17. подёрнуть *(pf, pop)* — to pull lightly
18. образнáя *(obs)* — small chapel room with icons
19. пóмысл *(obs)* = пóмысел

One, III, 4

1. припомáженный fr припомáдить *(pf)* — to smooth down hair with hair tonic
2. вовлеклá *(f, past, pf, sing)* fr вовлекáть/ вовлéчь *(past, pass, prich:* вовлечён)
3. когдá вы́йдет [зáмуж] за меня́
4. жить в дéвках — to live as an unmarried woman
5. убирáться/ убрáться — to have one's hair done
6. для милá [ми́лого] дружкá [дрýга] семь вёрст не окóлица — one goes far out of one's way for a dear friend
7. Потсдáм — Potsdam [site of Frederick the Great's palace a few miles fr Berlin]
8. нас с твои́м отцóм — your father and me
9. я перешёл в áрмию — [the Guards were not part of the army]
10. оди́н-на-оди́н — alone with him
11. мне хоть зáвтра — it can happen tomorrow,as far as I'm concerned
12. взведённый *(past, pass, prich)* fr взводи́ть/ взвести́ — to lead up; to bring up
13. ввечерý *(obs)* = вéчером

One, III, 5

1. чéшется fr чесáться *(impf)*
2. фр — [sound of snorting]
3. обрóсший fr обрастáть/ обрасти́
4. пропози́ция *(obs)* — marriage proposal
5. для мои́х прекрáсных глаз — for my pretty face *(F pour mes beaux yeux)*
6. придáнное = придáное
7. расположéние — good will; favor
8. загибáть/ загнýть нóгу — to bend one leg high over the

other while sitting w one's legs crossed. [Sitting w legs crossed is still considered rude in R.]

One, III, 6

1. произведён *(m, pf, past pass prich, short form)* fr производи́ть/ произвести́ — to promote
2. отерла́ *(f, pf, past, sing)* fr отира́ть/ отере́ть = обтира́ть/ обтере́ть — to wipe off
3. пригота́вливать *(impf)* = приготовля́ть/ пригото́вить
4. пе́рсик — *lit:* peach; *fig:* sugar-plum, honey-bun
5. отстава́ть/ отста́ть — to leave alone
6. востру́шка *(coll)* — alert, smart girl
7. ню́ня *(coll)* — a whiner
8. разбега́ться/ разбежа́ться — to gather speed while running
9. выходи́ть/ вы́йти в кого́ — to take after smb
10. штиль *(m, obs)* = стиль *(m)*
11. обзаведе́ние — providing w necessary things; fitting out
12. вели́кий князь — grand duke [son of tsar]
13. Константи́н Па́влович — Konstantin Pavlovich [(1779-1831). Paul I's second son, heir to the throne of Alexander I (who had no legitimate children) at time *W&P* takes place. Commanded guards in 1805. Took part at Austerlitz. Inspector-Gen of R Cavalry from 1797 to death. In 1825 he renounced his rights to the throne voluntarily, thus enabling younger brother to become Tsar Nicholas I.]

One, III, 7

1. боева́я а́рмия — army in the field
2. Изма́йловский полк — [Life-Guard Regt of heavy inf, formed in 1730]
3. затёртый — soiled; worn
4. петизанфа́н, але́ куше́ дорми́р — *petits, enfants, allez coucher dormir (bad F w R accent)* — Children, go sleep in bed
5. сме́иваться *(impf, obs* or *pop, many-x)* — to laugh

(6.) отсторони́ть (ся) *(pf, obs)* = отстраня́ть (ся) / отстрани́ть-(ся)

7. арме́йщина — soldiers *(ironic)*

8. Гео́ргиевский крест — Medal of St. George [R medal given in 4 classes. Order founded by Empress Catherine II in 1769.]
9. пробива́ться/ проби́ться — to struggle; to make do
10. Алекса́ндр Па́влович — [the tsar]
11. хвати́ть *(pf)* — to drink as much (alcohol) as one wishes
12. назначе́ние — destination
13. чёрта ли мне в письме́ — what the dickens is the letter to me
14. немчура́ *(pej, pop)* fr не́мец
15. Гали́ция — Galicia [Area then in Austria, now in SW USSR, Ukr SSR, around Lvov (Lemberg)]
16. Арна́ут — Arnaut [orig. Albanian soldiers in Turkish army; the name was given in R to ethnic Albanians living in R Bessarabia. Used pej here.]
17. о́тче наш *(OCS)* — Our Father [Lord's Prayer; *cf.* Matthew 6:9-14; Luke 11:2-5. Berg distorts correct forms, "Отче наш иже еси на небесех". *(OCS)*.]
18. в ли́цах — by visual demonstration
19. пуши́ть *(impf)* — to rebuke; to scold
20. сви́хивать/ свихну́ть — to dislocate
21. предположе́ние — intention; plan
22. фура́жное — forage allowance *(money)*
23. удосто́ивать *(impf)* = удоста́ивать/ удосто́ить
24. на днях — in a few days

One, III, 8

1. подра́гиваться *(impf)* — to tremble; to quiver
2. па́льник — linstock
3. подпёртый *(past, pass prich)* fr подпира́ть/ подпере́ть
4. флю́гер *(obs)* — guidon carried on a lance
5. затрепа́ться *(coll, pf)* — to start fluttering
6. генера́л-марш — forward march signal (given by bugles)
7. четвероуго́льник *(obs)* = четырёхуго́льник
8. наде́тый с по́ля — [three-cornered (or cocked) hat worn w both peaks on a line w one's ears. Maude points out (p. 1222 of *War and Peace,* New York, Norton Critical edition, ed. by George Gibian,1966) that the so-called three-cornered hat had lost one of its corners by 1805 and had only two peaks left.]

9. гео́ргиевское зна́мя — [banner of St. George given as unit citation]
10. что бы́ло его́ сил — as much as possible
11. вызыва́ть/ вы́звать — to challenge (smb to a duel)
12. церемониа́льный марш — the march past the reviewing officers at a parade, accompanied by band-music
13. замо́к эскадро́на — *lit:* the lock of a squadron (i.e. the man, generally a non-com, who rode alone after the last rank of the squadron to bring up the rear)
14. переменя́ть/ перемени́ть но́ги — to move his legs
15. зава́ливать/ завали́ть — to bend
16. Эссен — Essen [Ива́н Ива́нович Э. (1759-1813). Gen in R army. Commanded army corps; his forces were 40 miles fr Austerlitz battlefield and did not take part.]
17. Пру́ссия — [After the R-Prussian convention of Nov. 3, 1805, N.S., the Prussians were committed to entering war against F, should F not agree to peace terms laid down by E and R. However, after Austerlitz (Dec. 2, N.S.), Prussia reneged on this and signed a treaty w F.]

One, III, 9

1. на вы́тяжке or навы́тяжке — at attention
2. затя́гивать/ затяну́ть — to lace tight
3. Долгору́ков — Dolgorukov [Perhaps князь Пётр Петро́вич Д. (1777-1806). Adjutant Gen and favorite of Alexander I in 1805.]
4. Шварценберг — Schwarzenberg [Karl-Philipp, Prince von S., Duke of Kruman (1771-1820). Austrian Field Marshal. Vice-President of *Hofkriegsrath* in 1805. In 1808 he was Minister to StP. In 1812 he commanded Austrian auxiliary corps. Commanded allied forces at Battle of Leipzig in 1813. Referred to earlier in One, II, 9.]
5. отчётливость *(f)* — precision
6. Буонапа́рте потеря́л свою́ латы́нь — Buonaparte is completely baffled (Gallicism. *F: Buonaparte a perdu son Latin.*)
7. традиридира — [nonsense syllables]
8. "мой брат" — [i.e. князь Миха́йл Петро́вич Долгору́ков (1770-1808). R colonel who visited Paris in 1800 to arrange for exchange of war prisoners.]
9. Марко́в = Морко́в — Morkov [граф Арка́дий Ива́но-

вич М. (1747-1827). R envoy in W Europe, spent 1801-1803 in Paris fr which he was recalled at N's request.]

10. Чарторúжский — Czartoryski or Chartorizhskii [Prince Adam C. (1770-1861). Polish statesman in R service as Minister of Foreign Affairs, 1804-1806. Favorite of Alexander I.]

One, III, 10

1. альзáсец — Alsatian
2. алё *(subst)* = алló
3. дивизиóн — 2 squadrons
4. рóздан *(past, pass, prich)* fr роздáть *(pf, obs)* = раздавáть/ раздáть
5. Аустерлиц — [One of N's major victories fought Nov. 20/Dec. 2, 1805, betw 70,000 F and 90,000 allies (Austrians and R). All three Emperors were present. Two days later N granted Austria's request for an armistice, thus ending his campaign in victory. Austerlitz is now in Czechoslovakia, lying several miles E of Brno (Brūnn). Austerlitz is now called Slavkov u Brna.]

One, III, 11

1. Вишау — Wischau (Vyskov) [Town about 15 mi E of Brūnn]
2. Вилье or Виллие — Villiers or Vill'e or Villie [барóн Яков Васúльевич В. (1765-1854) Scottish immigrant to R. Personal Physician to Alexander I and President of R Medical-Surgical Academy, 1809-1838).]
3. Саварú — Savary [Henri Jean-Marie-René S., Duke of Rovigo (1774-1833) F gen, Adjutant and confidant of N's from 1800. Commanded a division in campaigns of 1805-1807.]
4. зýбьями fr зýбья fr зуб — cog *(this pl is used in this meaning)*
5. уравномéренный = равномéрный
6. óбер-гофмáршал — [senior household official to the Emperor; grand marshal *(non-mil)* of the Court]
7. граф Толстóй — Tolstoi [Николáй Алексáндрович Т. (1765-1816)]
8. кунктáтор — cunctator [*L*-procrastinator. Nickname of Roman gen who finally defeated Hannibal.]
9. Вимфен — Wimpffen [Max W. (1770-1851),

Austrian gen on Kutuzov's staff at Austerlitz. Captured there by F.]

10. Ланжеро́н — Lanzheron or Langeron [Count Alexandre L. (1763-1831), F Royalist emigré entered R svc in 1790. Was gen by 1805.]
11. Лихтенште́йн — Lichtenstein [Johann-Joseph, Prince von L. (1760-1836) Austrian Field Marshal. After Austerlitz, he conducted talks w F leading to peace at Pressburg (Bratislava).]
12. Гогенлое — Hohenloe [Perhaps Friedrich-Ludwig Prince of H.-Ingelfinger (1746-1816), Prussian gen who fought at Austerlitz]
13. Прш . . . — Prz . . . [Ignacy Przebyszéwski (1755-?). Polish gen in R svc. Commanded third column at Austerlitz, where F took him and his troops prisoner. Later in R, court-martialed, degraded to the ranks for one month, and discharged from the R army.]
14. Милора́дович — Miloradovich [граф Миха́йл Андре́евич М. (1771-1825), R gen at Austerlitz. Much more active in 1812-1813, when he commanded at various times both vanguard and rear-guard. Later named commander of guards and governor general of StP. Died of wounds inflicted in Decembrist uprising.]
15. Аракче́ев — Arakcheev [граф Алексе́й Андре́евич А. (1769-1834), Favorite of Alexander I. Inspector of artillery in 1803. In Alexander's retinue at Austerlitz. Minister of War (1808-1825). Most influential after 1812. Notorious for cruelty.]

One, III, 12

1. запряжённый *(pf, past, pass, prich)* fr запряга́ть/ запря́чь
2. Остралиц — Ostralitz [village just SW of Austerlitz]
3. Кобельниц – Kobelnitz — [Village about 6 mi W of Austerlitz]
4. Сокольниц – Sokolnitz — [Village about 2 mi S of Kobelnitz]
5. Тюра́сский лес — Thuerassa Woods [just W of Austerlitz]
6. Шлапаниц — Schlappanitz or Schlapanitz [Village about 2 mi N of Kobelnitz]
7. Беловиц — Bellowitz [Village about 1 mi N of Schlappanitz]
8. а вы всё ещё про э́ти глу́пости [говори́те]

9. лека́рка *(pop)* — quack doctor
10. Тит, ступа́й молоти́ть — [Speaker may have in mind folk dialog which he uses to tease Tit: "Тит, ступа́й молоти́ть!"— Брю́хо боли́т. "Тит, поди́ кисе́ль есть!" —А где моя́ больша́я ло́жка? Cf. В. Даль, *Пословицы русского народа,* М, ГИХЛ, 1957 стр. 256.]
11. ну те к чо́рту! — go to the devil!

One, III, 13

1. ло́зунг — password
2. *une tache (F)* — a spot
3. На . . . ташка — [Pun on "Take . . . ташка" and sister's name. Here LNT approaches 20th century stream of consciousness.]
4. наступи́ть — [puns w тупи́ть нас]
5. Тверска́я — [a main street of downtown M at that time]
6. Гу́рьев — Gur'ev [An anachronism. Михаи́л Васи́льевич Г., old Muscovite and надво́рный сове́тник, bought the building at No. 37, Тверская only in 1839. In 1805, the building belonged to князь А. А. Прозоровский.]
7. зажёгся, зажгли́сь *(pf, past)* зажига́ться/ зажéчься
8. кто ё зна́ет *(subst)* = кто его́ зна́ет
9. мо́же *(subst)* = мо́жет [быть]
10. не могу́ знать — I don't know *(mil)*
11. слу́шаю-с — yes, sir *(mil)*
12. прое́зженный *(obs)* — well traveled

(13.) расстро́ивать *(impf, obs)* = расстра́ивать/ расстро́ить

One, III, 14

1. долженствова́ть *(impf, obs, bookish)* — to be obliged to; to have to
2. отбива́ть/ отби́ть дробь нога́ми — to stamp their feet
3. влеко́м *(pr pass prich)* fr влечь *(impf)*
4. на душе́ — in his heart; at heart
5. ку́рские — [Kursk Regt of heavy infantry]
6. во́йски *(subst)* — [Speaker treats *nt pl* word войска́ as if it were *f sing*]
7. вечо́р *(obs* or *dial)* —last night

8. Москвá — [as many people as in M]
9. что стáли-то *(obs)* = почемý остановúлись
10. аль *(obs or dial)* = úли
11. нет, не слыхáть *(impf)* — no, not a sound
12. тафа-лафа — [Sounds of G to a R who does not understand them. Perhaps fr G *Teufel* — devil]
13. пáдать дýхом *(impf)* — to lose spirit
14. Гольдбах — Goldbach — [Rivulet W of Pratzen Heights, (which were W of Austerlitz). The stream, at start of battle, separated F positions on SW fr Austrians and R on NE.]

One, III, 15

1. могýщий *(pr, act prich)* fr мочь *(impf)*
2. развёртывать/ развернýть — to deploy; to extend
3. к ногé — [at] order arms *(mil)*
4. подначáльственный — subordinate
5. прогалопúровать *(pf)* — to gallop [a given distance]
6. отдохновéнный — relaxed
7. Волкóнский — Volkonskii [Пётр Михáйлович В. (1776-1852), светлéйший князь, Field-Marshal, Minister of Court and of Crown Landed Property. In 1805, served as gen on duty with Buxhöwden and Kutuzov both. In 1812, was in tsar's retinue. Headed main headquarters in 1813-1814.]
8. Стрóганов — Stroganov [граф Пáвел Алексáндрович С. (1774-1817) Lt gen, senator, and confidant of Alexander I. Accompanied tsar in 1805 campaign, concentrating on diplomatic contacts with Austrians, Prussians and British.]
9. Новгорóдский [кирасúрский] полк — [regt. of heavy cavalry, or cuirassiers]
10. Апшерóнский полк — [regt. of heavy infantry]
11. надéтый набекрéнь и с пóля — [cocked hat worn tilted over one ear with both peaks on the sides of one's head (not front and back).]
12. марш-марш *(obs)* — very rapid march
13. Мáрсово пóле — Field of Mars [large parade ground in StP, now a park. So called since 1818 when the former Царúцын луг was renamed.]

One, III, 16

1. карабине́ры — [In Alexander's time, these were the best cavalry marksmen in a squadron. They protected its flanks with their carbines.]
2. повлекла́ *(pf, past)* fr влечь/ повле́чь
3. подпра́порщик *(obs)* — platoon guide and standard-bearer *(a non-com)*
4. сби́тый на́бок — knocked to one side
5. ко́лет *(pr)* fr коло́ть *(impf)*

One, III, 17

1. ма́ло того́ — moreover
2. Ува́ров — Uvarov [граф Фёдор Петро́вич У. (1773-1824). R gen. Commanded Horse Guard Regt in 1805 at Austerlitz. At Borodino, in 1812, U. took R I Cavalry Corps around F left, almost to F rear. This diversion saved Raevskii redoubt for a few hours and forestalled F attack against weakened R left. U. was aided by Platov's Cossacks.]
3. расплыва́ться/ расплы́ться — to spread
4. лейб-ула́ны — Uhlans (lancers) attached to the monarch or his court
5. скок — gallop
6. кавалерга́рд — horse-guardsman
7. во весь мах — at a full gallop
8. что было мо́чи — as fast as possible
9. пяти́вершко́вый — 5 *vershoks* high [a *vershok* is 1.75 inches. The base presumed is 2 *arshins,* or 56 inches. Thus the horse stood almost 65 inches (or just over 16 hands) high.]
10. прикла́дывать/ приложи́ть у́ши — to prick up its ears
11. вот как — so that's it; you don't say; really!
12. коле́т — cavalry man's tunic [Worn with hooks around neck and shoulders]
13. пропада́й всё — the hell w it all

One, III, 18

1. Гостиерадек — Hosjeradek [Village about 5 mi

SW of Austerlitz and just E of Pratzen heights.]

2. во весь дух — at full speed
3. другóй кто — someone else
4. преблéдный — very pale
5. с другúм как — with anyone except
6. сползáться/ сползтúсь — to crowd together while crawling
7. фон-Толь — Fontoll' or von Toll [граф Карл Фёдорович Ф-Т. (1777-1842). Took part in campaigns of 1805-1809. A colonel in 1812, took part in most battles. Helped suppress Polish rebellion in 1830.]
8. фýрман *(obs)* — driver *(G Fuhrmann)*
9. Аугест — Augezd [Village about 2 mi SW of Hosjeradek, and about 6 mi SW of Austerlitz]
10. морáвы — Moravians [Czechs of that area]
11. втеснáться/ втеснúться — to squeeze in
12. что стал *(obs)* = почемý остановúлся
13. потоплáть/ потопúть — to push to the bottom; to drown

One, III, 19

1. сондúрование *(obs)* fr зондúровать *(impf)*
2. Рéпнин — Repnin [граф Николáй Григóрьевич Р. (1778-1833) R officer. In 1805 commanded 4th squadron of Horse Guards Regt. Led famous attack at Austerlitz which left only 18 men unwounded. He sustained chest contusions, bullet in head, and was captured. In 1812, he commanded 9th cav div. Later adj gen.]
3. Сухтéлен — Sukhtelen [граф Пáвел Петрóвич С. (1788-1833) In 1805 S was cornet (lowest commissioned grade in cavalry) of Horse Guards Regt. Captured at Austerlitz. Returned to R in 1806. Later rose to Lt. gen and Adj. gen.]
4. Ларрéй — Larrey [Dominique-Jean, Baron Larrey (1766-1842) Distinguished army surgeon. N's personal physician, who was with him on all his campaigns.]

(5.) лáдонка *(obs)* = лáданка

TWO, I, 1

ТОМ ВТОРОЙ, ЧАСТЬ ПЕРВАЯ, ГЛАВА ПЕРВАЯ

1. Воро́неж — Vorónezh [City and province on Voronezh Rv a few miles before it falls into Don Rv. About 365 mi S of M. Province was famous for its horses.]
2. кала́ч — [A signboard w a roll depicted on it would hang outside bakeries to attract customers]
3. столб — lamp post
4. покро́мка — selvage [edge of a woven fabric]
5. ба́тюшки све́ты! — good heavens!
6. ми́лости прошу́ — welcome; let me welcome you
7. перехва́тывать/ перехвати́ть — to get hold of sth before the person does for whom it was intended; to intercept sth; to grab w other hand or in another place *(coll)*
8. до деся́того ча́са — until it was past nine
9. предше́ствующая ко́мната — the room next to it
10. вали́ться *(impf)* — to be tossed around carelessly
11. раздува́ть/ разду́ть пла́тье — to let one's dress out wide (before sitting down)
12. ме́тина *(pop)* — mark
13. разожгла́ *(pf)* fr разжига́ть/ разже́чь
14. ну, так дру́жны́ — we're such good friends
15. совсе́м не то — not right at all
16. она́ ему́ показа́лась ещё лу́чше — she seemed even prettier to him
17. Duport — [Louis Duport (1782-1853) F ballet dancer who moved to StP in 1803]
18. округля́ть/ округли́ть sth — to put sth into a circle; to round
19. я пойду́ в танцо́вщицы — I'll be a dancer (note *nom pl*)

Two, I, 2

1. солда́тский Гео́ргий — the Order of St. George given to a mil man
2. Англи́йский клуб — E Club [this was a social club

where R aristocrats would gather, as E do, to talk, to play cards, etc. Founded in 1770. Located then at 15 Strastnoi Bul'var. In real life, a dinner was organized there for Bagration by, among others, LNT's grandfather. (Cf. *Istoriia Moskvy* III, 53.)]

3. поéздка *тудá* — [i.e. to a house of prostitution]
4. спáржа — [a luxury in R]
5. рéдко кто — the person was rare, who
6. на ширóкую рýку — generously and luxuriously
7. тортю́ — [an elegant dish baked and served in a turtle shell]
8. холóдных [блюд]
9. майонéз — mayonnaise *(nowadays, but not here); (here)* either 1) a cold dish of fish, game or vegetables served w mayonnaise, or 2) *(and more likely)* a meat, fish, or game course in aspic. [Karlinsky has pointed this out; recipes for this last can be found in Molokhovets, pp. 159 ff.]
10. кóли не уступáют — if they don't come down in price
11. антрé = *entrée (F)* [dish served at start of dinner, generally without sauce]
12. отцы́ мои́ — what more can we do [interjection expressing confusion and/or need for assistance]
13. наряжáть/ наряди́ть бáрщину — to put [serfs] on corvée
14. волóк *(m, past, sing)* fr волóчь *(coll, impf)* — to drag
15. вы́холиться *(pf)* — to be cared for
16. наш брат — the likes of us
17. Разгуля́й — [M street]
18. Илю́шка Цыгáн — [Илья́ Осипович Соколóв, who directed a M gypsy chorus for forty years, and was sung about by Davydov and Pushkin.]
19. завести́ глазá *(pf)* — to squint *(in pain)*
20. Ростóпчин, or Растóпчин — Rostopchin or Rastopchin [граф Фёдор Васи́льевич Р. (1763-1828). Favorite of Paul I. Later, fr 1812 to 1814, Governor Gen of M. We shall see much of him in Volume Three below.]
21. Долгорýкий or Долгорýков — Dolgorukii or Dolgorukov [граф Юрий Влади́мирович Д. (1740-1830). R gen chosen in 1806 to be chief of militia of seventh district.]
22. Валýев — Valuev [Пётр Степáнович В. (1743-1814). Archeologist. Chief of Kremlin Dept and Armory.]
23. Вя́земский — Viazemskii [князь Андрéй Ивáнович В. (1750-1807). Rank 4 civil servant. Father of writer,

Пётр. Son was Pushkin's friend.]

24. говори́ть с чужо́го го́лоса — to repeat sth blindly
25. италья́нский похо́д — [Suvurov's brilliant campaign against F in N Italy in 1799, when R formed part of Second Coalition against F]
26. Вольте́р — [Voltaire supposedly said the same thing about God]
27. сати́р — [Kutuzov was a notorious woman-chaser]
28. лепя́, лепя́ и обле́пишься — you model [w sth] and you get all smeared up w the stuff

Two, I, 3

1. [бу́дущность] за на́ми — [the future] belongs to us, is ours
2. Нары́шкин — Naryshkin [Perhaps Алекса́ндр Льво́вич Н. (1760-1826). Chief of Imperial Theaters, 1799-1819.]
3. Суво́ров закрича́л петухо́м — [this was one of the generalissimus's more unusual idiosyncrasies]
4. геро́йствовать *(impf)* — to show heroism
5. старшина́ — senior representative
6. Беклешо́в — Bekleshov [Алекса́ндр Андре́евич Б. (1745-1808). Governor-Gen of M, 1804-1806.]
7. протолка́ть *(pf)* — to push one's way through
8. сам сочини́тель взял стихи́ — [Никола́й Петро́вич Нико́лев (1758-1815) wrote the verses following]
9. та́ко *(obs)* = так
10. Тит — Titus [Flavius Vespasian Titus, (41-81 A.D.) Roman Emperor (79-81 A.D.). He genuinely tried to better the lot of his people.]
11. ку́пно *(obs)* = совоку́пно
12. Рифе́й — Rhipheus [any northern mountain range]
13. Алки́д — Alcides (Hercules)
14. по́льский or польско́й *(obs)* — P national dance (which usually opened a festive occasion, such as a ball); a polonaise
15. "Гром побе́ды раздава́йся" — [verses by Гаври́ла Рома́нович Держа́вин (1743-1816) fr "Хор для кадри́ли." Set to music by Осип Анто́нович Козло́вский (1757-1831) and first performed in Potemkin's StP palace in 1791 after capture of Izmail. For music

see Alexander Tcherepnin, *Russische Musik—Anthologie,* Bonn, M.P. Beliaeff, 1966, p 45.]

16. росс *(obs; poetic)* = ру́сский
17. уга́щивать (*obs* or *pop, many-x*) — to treat
18. скоро́мный — [food one could not eat on days when there was a church fast, such as during Lent]
19. П. И. Куту́зов — Kutuzov [Па́вел Ива́нович К. (1767-1829). Important political figure, senator, and writer of odes. From 1810 on, he was warden of M University.]
20. Апра́ксин — Apraksin [граф Степа́н Степа́нович А. (1757-1827) Gen-of-Cavalry. Governor Gen of Smolensk, 1804-1812.]

Two, I, 4

1. [ему́] было не до э́того — [he] wasn't interested in that; [he] had no time for that
2. Соко́льники — Sokol'niki — [then a pine forest outside of M. Now a park in NE M.]
3. страх прошёл — the fear has passed
4. как бы то́лько [медве́дь] не ушёл — if only [the bear] didn't get away
5. попадёт *(ft, pf)* fr попада́ть/ попа́сть
6. барье́р — barrier [the duelling area was marked off by the seconds. Each duellist then advanced towards the other, but could go only as far as his own barrier. There were some yards (ten paces in this duel) between the two barriers, which were lines marked by the swords stuck into the ground. Each duellist could fire at any time. However, if he missed, he had to continue up to his barrier and wait for his opponent to shoot fr other barrier. See Nabokov's notes in his commentary to Pushkin's *Eugene Onegin,* III, 43-45.]
7. иста́ять *(pf)* — to melt completely

Two, I, 5

1. подбира́ть/ подобра́ть [под себя́] но́ги

Two, I, 6

1. перерабо́тывать *(impf, obs)* = перераба́тывать *(impf)* — to rework; to chew over
2. Робеспье́р — Robespierre [Maximilien Robespierre (1758-1794). F lawyer who led Jacobin extremists during Revolution. Started Reign of Terror in 1793 to rid revolution of its alleged enemies. Finally, the Convention overthrew him, tried him, and had him guillotined.]
3. жив и живи́ — live if you're alive
4. Молье́рово *(poss, adj)* — Molière's [The quotation comes fr *Les Fourberies de Scapin* (*Scapin's Pranks,* 1671), and is spoken by Géronte. Jean Baptiste Poquelin Molière (1622-1673) was the great F playwright.]

Two, I, 7

1. отретирова́ться *(pf, obs)* — to withdraw
2. ретира́да *(obs, mil)* — withdrawal
3. льщу fr льстить *(impf)*
4. ко́их *(obs)* fr кой *(obs)* = кото́рый
5. от разма́ха — *(here:)* from inertia
6. разреше́ние — delivery; giving birth

(7.) розы́скивать *(impf, obs)* = разы́скивать

Two, I, 8

1. фри́штик *(obs)* — breakfast *(G Frühstück)*
2. друга́я неде́ля — a second week
3. подхва́тывать/ подхвати́ть — to chime in
4. ба́бушка — *(here)* = [повива́льная ба́ба]
5. вам деви́цам про э́то зна́ть не сле́дует — [i.e. single girls ought not to be present at childbirth]
6. утиша́ть/ утиши́ть (*obs* or *pop*) — to quiet down
7. княжо́вый *(obs, poss adj)* — the young prince's
8. уго́дник = свято́й уго́дник — a saint *(depicted on an icon)*
9. брать/ взять своё — to claim its own; to win out
10. подста́ва *(obs)* — relay; horse sent ahead beforehand for use later
11. зажо́ра — water collected under snow

12. пря́дка fr прядь
13. Кишинёв — Kishinev [Province capital of Bessarabia on SW R frontier in LNT's day. However, in 1805 this area was still part of Ottoman Empire. R did not annex it until Treaty of Bucharest in May 1812.]
14. до́хтур *(subst)* = до́ктор
15. выставля́ть/ вы́ставить ра́мы — to remove the second window-frame [R windows open in and out. A second set of outer windows is added for the winter and removed in the spring.]
16. затрепа́ть *(pf)* — to start blowing
17. свеча́ текла́ — the candle was guttering (losing molten wax near the wick)

Two, I, 9

1. изно́жье (*obs* or *dial*) — foot of the bed
2. ма́мушка — wet nurse
3. помя́тый — having an uneven surface as a result of use or abuse
4. вощечо́к fr воск — [Maude explains that the priest cuts off a bit of the child's hair and joins it with wax from the candle. If the waxed hair sinks, the result augurs bad luck.]

Two, I, 10

1. сыно́в *(poetic)* = сынове́й
2. переда́вливать/ передави́ть — to crush *(many or all)*
3. Ио́гель — Iogel' or Jogel [Dancing-school owner in M who catered to high society]

Two, I, 11

1. и то — and even so; that's it; that's right
2. на но́гу — on a footing; on a basis
3. *pas de châle (F)* — shawl dance [F dance favored by R aristocratic women]
4. е́сли что ска́зала — once she has said sth

Two, I, 12

1. вы́де́лывать/ вы́делать — to perform; to produce
2. Горчако́в — Gorchakov [A well-known family of princes, which included LNT's grandmother]
3. езжа́ть *(obs)* = е́здить *(impf, many-x)*
4. танцо́вывать *(coll, impf, many-x)* fr танцева́ть *(impf)*
5. дочеса́ть *(pf)* — to finish combing *(hair);* to finish scratching
6. уво́льте — spare me
7. Ва́ська — [A traditional name for a tom-cat in R)
8. подщёлкивать/ подщелкну́ть — to click sth (softly or in time to music)

Two, I, 13

1. домечу́ fr домета́ть *(pf)* — to finish dealing at cards [The dealer at bank, macao, etc. first dealt the cards fr one deck to the players. Then, he would place the cards fr a second deck on the table as indicated below.]
2. ста́вить/ поста́вить — to bet
3. разо́рванная коло́да — an unsealed deck of cards
4. проме̃тывать/ промета́ть — to deal cards for a while
5. сочтёмся *(ft, pf)* fr счита́ться/ сче́сться
6. пре́жде на пра́во, чем на ле́во — [If a card came up first on the right, the dealer won; if on the left, his opponent won. For a good, short description of Russian faro, see Nabokov's notes to *Eugene Onegin,* III, 258-260]
7. опроки́дываться/ опроки́нуться — to lean back; to settle back
8. мечи́ *(impv)* fr мета́ть *(impf)*

Two, I, 14

1. у́гол — [a corner of the card bet on was turned down]
(2.) пе *(obs)* — to bet double or nothing
3. мама́ — *maman (F)* = mama
4. итти́ угло́м — to bet an у́гол *(¼ of wager)*
5. чёрные мужчи́ны — swarthy men

6. ро́знить (*impf, obs,* or *pop*) — to make up the difference

Two, I, 15

1. брать/ взять акко́рд — to play a chord
2. Коко́ fr Ко́ля fr Никола́й [This doubling of first syllable to make a nickname is very F]
3. дружо́к *(aff)* fr друг — my dear fellow
4. за ва́ми [о́чередь] — your turn
5. вот она́ я — that's the sort of girl I am
6. на три те́мпы — into a beat of three
7. Oh, mio crudele affetto [See Appendix Seven.]
8. si — [R follow Italian system of *do re mi fa* etc. based on the scale of "c" so that *"si"* is "b" to us]

Two, I, 16

1. говори́ть де́ло *(impf)* — to talk business; to talk seriously
2. мосьё — monsieur
3. а так — as it is; for no particular reason; just so

(4.) роспи́ска *(obs)* = распи́ска

Two, II, 1

1. Торжо́к — Torzhok [Stage coach stop on Tvertsá Rv on old main road fr StP to M. It is about 150 mi fr M and was famous for fine gold embroidery work done on velvet and leather.]
2. смотри́тельша — wife of смотри́тель
3. свёртываться/ сверну́ться — to move to one side; to lose its thread (Maude)
4. курье́рские [ло́шади] *(obs)* — courier horses [Horses or troikas sometimes reserved for official use. The user could, at the next station, have another relay without delay. This was a comparatively fast way to travel.]
5. проезжа́ющий *(obs)* -- traveler
6. приби́ть *(pf)* — to thrash; to beat unmercifully

7. счёл *(past, pf)* fr — считáть/ счесть
8. разрéзанная до половúны кнúга — [In F books to this day, the reader often has to cut the pages for himself]
9. Mme Suza — [Adélaide Filleul, first Countess Flahault, then Marquise de Souza-Botelho (1761-1836) F writer and mistress of Talleyrand. Her novels were popular at start of 19th century. LNT may have in mind *Émilie et Alphonse* (Hambourg, 1799).]
10. Адáмова головá — death's head
11. разбирáть/ разобрáть — to put in order
12. недокýсанный — incompletely bitten
13. заложúть [странúцу] *(pf)* — to put a bookmark (on a page)

Two, II, 2

1. как ни — however; in any way
2. государь мой *(obs)* — my dear sir
3. масóнство — masonry; freemasonry [The masons were and are a secret fraternal order preaching charity, obedience to laws of the land, etc. In R, they reached the zenith of their influence at the end of the 18th and the start of the 19th centuries (See Leon Stilman's introduction to N.M. Karamzin, *Letters of a Russian Traveler,* tr by Florence Jonas, N.Y., 1958, pp 7-15, for sth on masons in R towards end of 18th cent.) Catherine II was against them. During the period of *W&P,* they were tolerated but kept under police surveillance. However, the later, pre-Decembrist, secret political societies were connected with masons. All secret societies, including masons, were ordered dissolved in 1822.]
4. назначéние э́тих часóв — [The metaphor of God as a watchmaker and the world as his watch was a favorite one in 18th-century Europe]
5. что лóшади? — how about the horses?
6. сдáточные *(pl)* — post-horses changed at posting stations; exchange horses
7. тóкмо (*obs* or *pop*) = тóлько
8. мартинúст — [Follower of system set forth by Louis-Claude de St. Martin (1743-1803), the so-called unknown philosopher, a mystic. He believed that goodness was based on sincerity and wrote a book *Des Erreurs et de la vérité* (*Of Errors and Truth,* 1773). Martinism led to a split in R masonry over how closely to affiliate w European masonic lodges.]
9. Нóвиков — Novikov [Николáй Ивáнович

H. (1744-1818). Writer and magazine editor. He became a mason in 1775 and published many books in R from 1779 to 1792. A leading figure in cultural life during the reign of Catherine II.]

Two, II, 3

1. Фомá Кемпи́йский — Thomas à Kempis [G monk (1379 or 1380-1471) and mystic. Often considered author of *Imitation of Christ.*]
2. В начáле бе слóво и слóво бе к Бóгу = В начáле бы́ло Слóво и Слóво бы́ло у Бóга — "In the beginning was the Word, and the Word was with God." (John 1:1).
3. ри́тор — rhetor [the mason who serves as guide to the new member. In Gk, the word connotes one who teaches eloquence.]
4. нéкоего *(gen)* fr нéкий
5. приуготовля́ть *(impf, obs)* = подготáвливать *(impf)*
6. хрáмина *(obs)* — building; room
7. неподвéрженный — not subject to
8. объедéние — gluttony

Two, II, 4

1. предвéчный — eternal; everlasting
2. стрáждущий (*OCS* or *obs*) = страдáющий
3. кáменщица — wife of a freemason
4. береги́сь fr берéчься *(impf)*
5. огнь *(obs, poetic)* = огóнь *(m)*
6. дéлание fr дéлать *(impf)*
7. обря́щешь *(2nd sing)* fr обрести́ *(pf)*

Two, II, 5

1. жи́рный телéц — the fatted calf [which is killed to welcome the Prodigal Son home. See Luke 15:11-32.]

Two, II, 6

Note: Alexander's manifesto announcing a new war w F came out Nov. 16/28, 1806. This superseded the armistice of Nov. 22/Dec. 4, 1805 and the Treaty of Pressburg (Bratislava) betw Austria and F of Dec. 26, 1805, N.S., under which treaty, R troops had left Austria. In 1806, Prussia was R's ally, but Prussia was soon conquered by F. This war ended w armistice and then Treaty of Tilsit betw F and R of June 25/July 7, 1807.

1. Мара́т — Marat [Jean Paul M. (1743-1793). F Revolutionary leader noted for extremism w which he hounded moderate Girondists. Assassinated in bathtub by Charlotte Corday.]
2. устро́ивать *(impf, obs)* = устра́ивать
3. Иена и Ауэрштет — Jena and Auerstedt or Auerstadt. [On Oct. 14, 1806, N.S. N defeated the main Prussian army at Jena, on the Saale Rv in Thuringia (now in E G). That same day, Marshall Davout defeated another Prussian force at Auerstedt, NE of Weimar, also now in E G. These battles almost knocked Prussia out of the Third Coalition against the F, who occupied Berlin only 11 days later. R was thus left in the lurch, esp because she was also fighting against Turkey; but the war between R and F continued.]
4. Бонапа́ртию (as if name were Бонапа́ртий)
5. *Tu l'as voulu, Georges Dandin (F)* — You wanted it, Georges Dandin. [Georges Dandin, hero of play *Georges Dandin, ou le Mari confondu* (Georges Dandin, or the Fooled Husband) written in 1668 by Molière. The phrase has become set, with implications of "you asked for it."]
6. Глогау — Glogau [City on Oder Rv, then in Prussia, which N would capture on Nov. 2, 1806, N.S. Now in P, called Głogów.]

Two, II, 7

1. *pour le roi de Prusse (F)* — [A timeworn pun in F, meaning *lit*: for the King of Prussia, and *fig*: for trifles.]
2. NN, SS — X, Y [Used when narrator does not wish to give names]

Two, II, 8

1. грудно́й [ребёнок] князь Никола́й
2. полови́на — rooms in a house *(obs)*
3. лысого́рский fr Лысы́е Го́ры
4. отделя́ть/ отдели́ть — to give an heir part of his inheritance w right to manage it independently *(obs)*
5. переплетённый *(pf, past, pass, prich)* fr переплета́ть/ переплести́
6. то то, то друго́е сре́дство — now one means, and now another
7. Бенигсен — Benigsen, or Bennigsen [граф Лео́нтий Лео́нтьевич Б. (1745-1826), генерал-от-кавале́рии. He had battled the F at Pultusk in Warsaw Province on the Narew Rv on Dec. 26, 1806, O.S. and was named commander-in-chief of R army in 1807. In winter of 1807, he fought a bloody but indecisive battle against F at Preussisch Eylau, which he reported as a great R victory. In 1812, he served first w Alexander I, and then headed R gen staff. He took part in battles at Borodino and Tarutino. In 1813, he commanded R army in Poland. In 1814, B. was w R army which helped take Paris. He had been a chief conspirator in palace assassination of Paul I in 1801.]
8. викто́рия *(obs)* — victory
9. Корче́вский fr Корчева — [district town in Tula Province]

[10.] туды́ (*obs* or *pop*) туда́

11. неме́для = неме́дленно

Two, II, 9

1. Пре́йссиш Эйлау — Preussisch Eylau or Eylau. [Town nr Kõnigsberg, then in Prussia, now in USSR. On Janu 26-27/ Feb 7-8, 1807, N fought an indecisive battle here w R under Benigsen. Now called Bagrationovsk.]
2. *ab ovo (L)* — *lit*: fr the egg; *fig*: fr the beginning
3. враг ро́да челове́ческого — [N]
4. Прозо́ровский — Prozorovskii [князь Алекса́ндр Алекса́ндрович П. (1732-1809), R field-marshal. Commanded R army against Turks, 1808.]

(5.) су́точный прика́з — order of the day *(mil)*

6. кор д'арме́ *(Gallicism)* = *corps d' armée (F)* — army corps
7. пособля́ть/ пособи́ть *(pop)* — to help; to relieve
8. Остерма́н — Osterman [граф Алекса́ндр

Ива́нович Остерман-Толстой (1770-1857). R gen. Took part in wars of 1805-1809. In 1812, he commanded 4th Army Corps of 1st Western Army. Took part in Borodino and 1813 campaign in Europe.]

9. го́шпиталь *(f, obs)* = го́спиталь *(m)* [gender has changed]
10. Остроле́нка — Ostrolenka [District town of Łomza Province on Narew Rv in Poland, then part of R.] (P Ostrołęnka)
11. всепо́дданнейший *(obs, book)* — most humble
12. разглаше́ние — noise, stir, uproar
13. ма́ло ли чего — who knows what else

Two, II, 10

1. Опеку́нский Сове́т — [A state establishment in charge of M foundling hospital. In 1808 the Ссу́дная ка́сса, or Loan Office, was attached to it, w authority to lend money on mortgaged real estate, buildings, etc. This is thus a bit anachronistic.]
2. княжо́н *(gen pl)* fr княжна́
3. богоуго́дное заведе́ние — charitable institution
4. расходи́ться/ разойти́сь — to be spent *(of money)*
5. цепля́ть *(impf, obs* or *coll)* — to catch hold of
6. Кострома́ — Kostroma [Province on upper Volga about 230 mi NE of M, and about 70 mi downstream fr Iaroslavl'. On Kostroma Rv.]
7. Пётр и Па́вел — Peter and Paul [June 29, O.S. is the name-day of the apostles, Peter and Paul, celebrated together, in the R Orthodox Church]
8. ребя́тница *(dial)* — nursing, peasant mother

Two, II, 11

1. отштукату́рить *(pf)* = штукату́рить/ оштукату́рить
2. э́того ма́ло — that is [too] little
3. выроста́ющий *(obs)* fr выраста́ть/ вы́расти
4. предводи́тель дворя́нства — marshall of the nobility [Each province and its constituent districts had elections of the gentry in which a marshall was chosen. He conducted their affairs as an "estate."]
5. протоколи́ст — minor clerk
6. Юхнов — Iukhnov [District town in Smo-

lensk province, where Kunov Rv empties into Ugru Rv]

7. брей fr брить *(impf)* — [A landowner shaved half the head of a serf being sent for mil service so as to facilitate identification should the serf seek to flee]

Two, II, 12

1. Гердер — Herder [Johann Gottfried von H. (1744-1803). G philosopher. Author of *Ideen zur Philosophie der Geschichte der Menschheit* (Outlines of a Philosophy of the History of Man, 1784-1791). A leader in G *Sturm und Drang,* he opposed 18th cent. rationalism.]

Two, II, 13

1. Ма́шин *poss adj* fr Ма́ша
2. бо́жьи лю́ди fr бо́жий челове́к (*obs* and *pop*) — *lit*: a godly man; *fig*: a wandering beggar who asked alms in God's name.
3. попива́ть *(impf)* — to sip unhurriedly
4. Ки́ев — [Kiev was famous for its many old churches and was even called the Jerusalem of Russia]
5. рожество́ (*native R form, for the more common* Рождество́*)*
6. у уго́дников сообщи́ться святы́х небе́сных та́ин — to take communion (common error, for приобщи́ться) with the holy, heavenly sacraments at the saints' shrines. (Perhaps referring to the famous Ки́ево-Пече́рская Ла́вра.)
7. Коля́зин = Каля́зин — Koliazin or Kaliazin [District town in Tver province]
8. благода́ть *(f, rel)* — state of grace; grace *(rel)*
9. корми́лец — [aff form of addressing a man, *obs* and *pop.*]
10. взыска́ть *(pf, obs)* — to reward; to bring forward
11. юро́дивый — a beggar or lunatic who allegedly possesses gift of prophecy
12. что хо́чешь . . . не по своему́ ме́сту — why are you walking around in the wrong placc
13. пресвято́й — most holy
14. Го́споди Иисусе Христе́ *(old vocative case)* — Oh Lord, Jesus Christ
15. так-то — so this is how things are *(used to sum sth up)*

16. анара́л *(subst)* = генера́л
17. ма́тушка Пече́рская — [allegedly wonder-working icon of Mary dating fr 14th cent and moved later from Kiev Cave Monastery (which gave the icon its name) to the Voznesenskii (Ascension) Monastery in Nizhnii-Novgorod (now called Gor'kii) on the Volga]
18. кра́ска — blush; flush
19. я так то́лько [шути́л] — I was only joking
20. ты не дума́й [об э́том]

Two, II, 14

(1.) ла́дон = ла́дан — incense
2. суха́рик fr суха́рь *(m)*
3. вы́пусти — if you let out *(note this use of impv)*
4. годово́й — one-year old

Two, II, 15

1. Пова́рский — on Povarskaia St [in M, where Rostovs lived]
2. безуря́дица — disorder; confusion
3. треть [го́да] — every four months
4. Пулту́ск — [Polish town on Narew Rv nr Warsaw. F and R armies fought here on Dec. 14/26, 1806 w inconclusive results.]
5. Бартенштейн — Bartenstein [Town then in E Prussia nr Koenigsberg]
6. Пла́тов — Platov [граф Матве́й Ива́нович П. (1751-1818). R gen. Ataman of Don Cossacks. Later, a major figure in campaigns of 1812 and 1813. At Borodino, he attacked rear of left flank of F army. After Borodino, his light Cossack forces defended Mozhaisk for two days. During F retreat fr M, his forces almost captured N at Maloiaroslavets, nr M.]
7. Удино́ — Oudinot [Charles-Nicolas O. (1767-1847). F marshall, and Duke of Reggio. Commanded F grenadier corps in 1806-1807.]
(8.) до тла = дотла́
9. ро́степель *(f, dial)* — thaw
10. непрое́здный *(coll)* — impassable

11. проро́сший *(pf, past, pass)* fr прорасти́ *(pf)*
12. Алёша-пройдо́ха — [braggart hero of folk tales]
13. Мико́лка попо́в батра́к — Mikolka the priest's hired hand [folk-tale hero who arranges own affairs while working for priest]
14. сва́йка — [R game. A nail or spike (the сва́йка) is thrown to make it stick in ground inside a circle.]
15. де́лывать *(impf, many-x)* fr де́лать *(impf)*

Two, II, 16

1. сход — descent
2. перека́тываться/ перекати́ться — to sound first louder then softer in the distance
3. угре́ться *(pf, pop)* — to warm up
4. заса́живать ре́дьку *(impf)* — to drive the spike into the ground at сва́йка, thus making loser pull it out and serve it
5. радёшенек *(coll)* = о́чень рад
6. отбива́ть/ отби́ть — to take by force; to beat out rhythmically; to break off

(7.) в во́лю = вво́лю — to one's heart's content

8. о́бер-вор — [Denisov's neologism based on о́бер, "senior," and вор.]
9. комиссионе́р — commission merchant; clerk
10. распротако́й-сяко́й — so-and-so; blankety-blank
11. ката́ть *(impf, pop)* — to beat; to hit
12. фо́рменный — formal *(obs)*
13. обер-провиа́нтмейстер *(obs)* — chief mess officer

Two, II, 17

1. Фридла́ндское сраже́ние — Battle of Friedland [Here, in E Prussia, N defeated R army under Bennigsen on June 2/14, 1807. Town now in U.S.S.R. and called Pravdinsk.]
2. зага́женный fr зага́дить *(pf)* — to befoul
3. разо́бранный забо́р — a pulled-down fence
4. тре́пемся *(subst)* = тре́племся fr трепа́ться *(impf, coll)* — to hang around
5. перемере́ть *(pf, coll)* — to die off
6. сли́шком or с ли́шком — more than; and more
7. Моли́тен — Moliten [Place then in E

Prussia]

8. при́толка *(coll)* = при́толока — lintel
9. придыша́ться *(pf, coll)* — to get used to a smell *(gen unpleasant)*
10. па́мять *(f)* — consciousness
11. обстри́жен *(past, pass, prich)* fr обстри́чь *(pf, coll)* = остри́чь *(pf)* — to cut hair short
12. остри́чь в ско́бку — to cut one's hair on a line from forehead to temples to back of head
13. зака́ченный *(past, pass, prich)* fr закати́ть глаза́ *(f)* — to roll one's eyes up (so that pupils are beneath upper lids)
14. испи́ть *(pf)* — to have a drink
15. отбива́ть/ отби́ть шаг — to walk w measured step
16. здра́вия жела́ю! — good day, sir! *(formula for soldiers to respond to senior officer's greeting)*

Two, II, 18

1. опу́хлость *(f)* — swelling; swollen quality
2. по мне — in my opinion
3. выводи́ть/ вы́вести на чи́стую во́ду — to expose; to show up
4. что и говори́ть — it must be admitted
5. рука́ — a person connected w matter in question; a connection

Two, II, 19

1. Тильзит — Tilsit [Port town of Niemen Rv, then in E Prussia. Here N met Alexander I on a raft in river on June 13/25, 1807. Two days later, the two Emperors concluded a preliminary peace treaty. At Tilsit, R recognized the Grand Duchy of Warsaw and promised secretly to be F ally against E. Town now in U.S.S.R. and called Sovetsk.]
2. не во́ время or не во́время — at a bad time

Two, II, 20

1. Почётный легио́н — Legion of Honor [F medal given

in any of 5 classes. Order founded by N in 1802.]

2. [о́рден] Андре́я — [Order of St. Andrew the First-Called (Apostle). Founded by Peter I in 1698. Highest of R orders, it came in only 1 class.]
3. Преображе́нский полк — Preobrazhenskii Regt. [One of two oldest Guards infantry regts. in R Empire. Formed by Peter I in 1698, along w Semënovskii Regt.]
4. кого́ вам [уго́дно]? — whom do you want?
5. камер-фурье́р — [court official in charge of servants and main tables]
6. по кома́нде — along the chain of command; through proper channels

Two, II, 21

1. преображе́нец — Member of Preobrazhenskii Guards Regt.
2. камзо́л — camisole *(type of jacket formerly worn by men)*
3. чепра́к — shabrack *(light cavalry saddlecloth)*
4. ранжи́р *(obs)* — rank
5. всё ли ещё ему́ стоя́ть — should he go on standing there
6. пенсио́н *(obs)* = пе́нсия — pension
7. [о́рден Свято́го] Гео́ргия

Two, III, 1

1. Эрфурт — Erfurt [Capital of Thuringia, now in SW part of E G. Here, fr Sept. 27, 1808, O.S. to Oct. 14, O.S. N, Alexander, and Friedrich Wilhelm III of Prussia held meetings to renew their alliance.]
2. в 1809 году́ — [In 1809, Austria fought F. R supported F. The Austrians invaded Bavaria, Italy and the Grand Duchy of Warsaw. N, aided by G allies fr the Confederation of the Rhine, beat back the invasion and took Vienna, while R took Cracow in Poland. The Peace of Schönbrunn was signed on October 2/14, 1809. Austria ceded W Galicia to Warsaw and Illyria to F.]

3. ба́рщина — corvée [The system under serfdom whereby peasants paid their dues to the landowners in labor]
4. обро́к — quitrent [The system under serfdom whereby peasants paid their dues to the landowners in money. It was considered less oppressive than *barshchina.*]
5. обсе́ять *(pf)* — to sow
6. лёгко — peaceful; happy; good

Two, III, 2

1. отра́денский *adj* fr Отра́дное — [Name of Rostov estate]

(2.) на пере́ре́з = наперере́з

3. так бы вот села́ на ко́рточки, вот как — I could just squat down, like this *(implying she will fly off or away)*
4. спать так спать — if one has to sleep, one has to sleep

Two, III, 3

1. глу́ше *comp* fr глухо́й
2. беспереме́нный — irrevocable
3. ма́ло того́, что — it's not enough that
4. быва́ло ска́жет — used to say — [The быва́ло shows the action took place repeatedly; the pf ft verb gives it immediacy.]

Two, III, 4

1. Спера́нский — Speranskii [граф Михаи́л Миха́йлович С. (1772-1839). Alexander's almost omnipotent favorite (1809-1812). Son of a priest. He accompanied Alexander to Erfurt and impressed N favorably. He initiated many ideas for important reforms, which were never given a chance. He was banished in March 1812, but allowed to make a limited comeback after 1815.]
2. Петерго́ф — Peterhof [Town on S shore of Gulf of Finland about 18 mi fr StP in which there were imperial summer palaces and parks. Name Russianized after World War II to Petrodvoréts.]
3. два . . . ука́за — [Speranskii drafted these decrees

in April and Aug. 1809. Alexander never did give R a constitution.]

4. Кочубе́й — Kochubei [князь Ви́ктор Па́влович К. (1768-1834). Minister of Internal Affairs (1802-1807). Member of tsar's secret committee and one of his favorites.]
5. *comité du salut publique (F)* — Committe of Public Safety [In F Revolution, this was executive committee of 9 appointed by National Convention. Robespierre's joining it in July 1793 led to his pre-eminence and dictatorship until he too was tried and executed in July 1794.]
6. дать ход [де́лу] — to let the action take its course
7. шепча́сь *(pr, act, deep)* fr шепта́ться *(impf)*
8. перекла́дывать/переложи́ть но́ги — to cross and uncross one's legs
9. впу́щен fr впусти́ть *(pf)* — to let in
10. ка́ре = ка́рий — brown
11. резолю́ция — written decision about an official paper

(12.) попере́г *(obs)* = попере́к — across

13. поне́же *(obs)* — because
14. зови́ — call [the next one in]

Two, III, 5

1. его́ тяну́ло — he longed for; he was drawn to
2. отпуще́ние *(obs)* — emancipation; manumission
3. Михаи́л Миха́йлович [Спера́нский]
4. Екатери́нинский — fr Catherine's time [Catherine II reigned fr 1762 to 1796]
5. пала́та — a government office
6. зо́лото челове́к — a man worth his weight in gold
7. госуда́рственный секрета́рь *(m)* — secretary of the state council
8. докла́дчик — author of a report or of reports
9. Магни́цкий — Magnitskii [Михаи́л Лео́нтьевич М. (1778-1855). In 1809, Magnitskii was a liberal. His career took wings fr 1816 to 1825 when, as a conservative, he purged Kazan' University.]
10. семинари́ст *(very cont)* — former seminary student
11. новый прика́з о придво́рных чина́х — [Speranskii's order of 1809 removed the privilege fr children of the gentry of having a *chin* in childhood.]
12. Montesquieu — [Charles de Secondat, Baron de

la Brède et de M. (1689-1755). F philosopher, political scientist and satirist. His *L'Esprit des lois* (The Spirit of the Laws, 1748), w its emphasis on checks and balances, influenced U.S. Constitution and is what Prince Andrei has in mind.]

Two, III, 6

1. пéрвое врéмя — the first period
2. пóшло [not пошлó]
3. кутéйник *(obs, pop, very cont)* — son of a priest
4. Розенкампф — Rosenkampf [барóн Густáв Андрéевич Р. (1762-1832). R jurist who served on commission for compiling the laws (1803-1822).]
5. Сенáт — Senate [Founded by Peter I in 1711, this served as a supreme court and overseer of governmental functions]
6. Code Napoléon [and] Justiniani — [The Napoleonic code was compiled by a F commission, mainly fr 1800-1804, and is a compromise betw G and Roman law. It is still very influential in Quebec, Louisiana, Latin America and W Europe. The Justinian Code, or *Corpus Juris Civilis,* was the body of civil law in the Roman Empire compiled under Emperor Justinian fr 528 to 534 A.D. R law-making projects would often start by investigating what had been done in other countries.]

Two, III, 7

1. кáменьщичество — stone-masonry
2. сочтя́ *(pr, deep)* fr счесть *(pf)* — to count
3. при кóем — along w which
4. человéков *(obs)* = людéй
5. иллюминáтство — Illuminism [The Illuminati were a secret anti-clerical society founded by a G, Adam Weishaupt, which flourished briefly after 1776. Their aim was to replace Christianity with deism, and monarchies with republics. They were connected with freemasonry. The Roman Catholic Church denounced them in 1785, and they were suppressed in Bavaria.]

Two, III, 8

1. предлежа́ть *(impf)* — to lie before; to be ahead

Two, III, 9

1. Caulaincourt — [Louis, marquis de C., Duke of Vicenza (1772-1827) F gen. Ambassador to St P (1807-1811), where he enjoyed special favor of tsar. Aide-de-camp to N in R (1812). Memoirist.]
2. Prince de Ligne — [Charles-Joseph, P. de L. (1735-1814). Freethinker fr what is now Belgium, who became Austrian field-marshal. Charming, witty, and a memoirist.]

(3.) слове́чко — wisecrack

Two, III, 10

1. Уру́сов — Urusov — [Perhaps князь Алекса́ндр Миха́йлович У. (1766-1853), member of State Council.]
2. приуготови́тельный *(obs, book)* — preliminary
3. архитекто́н *(Gk)* — architect; chief artificer
4. Адона́и *(Hebrew)* — Adonoy — Lord
5. Элои́м *(Hebrew)* — Elohim — God
6. совоку́пность *(f)* — sum total; totality
7. стегно́ (*obs* and *dial*) — thigh
8. совокупля́ть/ совокупи́ть *(obs, book)* — to combine
9. живот бе свет человеком . . . — *(OCS)* . . . "The life was the light of men. And the light shineth in darkness; and the darkness comprehended it not." [(John 1:4-5) This same passage is the source of the title of LNT'S unfinished play "И свет во тьме све́тит", published posthumously in 1911, which G.B. Shaw considered LNT's dramatic masterpiece.]
10. александри́йская [бума́га] — [special type of large, thick, smooth paper used for sketching]
11. возлета́ть *(impf, obs)* = взлета́ть/ взлете́ть — to fly up
12. да бу́дет во́ля твоя́ — Thy will be done [Matthew 6:10]
13. бу́де *(obs)* — in case; if

Two, III, 11

1. Финля́ндская война́ — Finnish War [Encouraged by N, Tsar Alexander occupied Swedish-ruled Finland in February 1808 and proclaimed the annexation of Finland on March 20/April 1, 1808. The Swedes were forced to recognize this by the Treaty of Frederikshamn on Sept. 17, 1809, N.S.]
2. на отли́чном счету́ — w an excellent reputation
3. лифля́ндский — Livonian [Livonia comprised Estonia and N Latvia, including Riga and Tallinn. It was conquered by G Livonian Knights in 13th cent. The G-speaking "Baltic Barons," including such as Berg, were largely descended fr these knights.]
4. Остзе́йский край — Baltic provinces [Estonia, Livonia, and Courland] *(G Ostsee)*
5. закла́дывать/ заложи́ть — to mortgage
6. люблю́, что [ты] позабо́тился — I appreciate your concern
7. чи́стые де́ньги — cash; ready money
8. скорогово́рка — speaking rapidly

Two, III, 12

1. ещё бы! — that's for sure! and how!
2. о́бли́тый — covered [by]
3. её никогда́ не отдаду́т [за́муж] за него́

Two, III, 13

(1.) крехте́ть *(impf, obs)* = кряхте́ть *(impf)*
2. земно́й покло́н — a bow to the ground
3. ду́шка *(pop)* — dimple on lower part of throat, in front
4. суста́в па́льца — knuckle
5. янва́рь, февра́ль — [Maude says R counted months on knuckles, excluding thumbs, with each knuckle having 31 days, and each space between them having not more than 30 days]
6. франмасо́н *(subst)* = франкмасо́н
7. куда́ ей — how can she [understand]
8. Херуби́ниевский *(poss adj)* fr Херуби́ни, now spelled Керуби́ни — Cherubini [Maria-Luigi C. (1760-1842). Italian composer who lived in Paris after 1808 where he became a major figure in music. He wrote 14 operas, became Director of Paris Conservatory in 1822.]

Two, III, 14

1. Англи́йская на́бережная — [One of fanciest streets in St P, on S bank of Bol'shaia Nevka, below Admiralty]
2. откла́дывать/ отложи́ть — to turn down
3. Таври́ческий сад — Tauric Garden [Catherine II presented Tavrida Palace to Prince Potëmkin in 1783, and crown took it back after his death in 1791. Its grounds were the Garden mentioned. On S bank of Neva, betw Summer Garden and Smól'nyi.] (Also called "Tauride.")
4. как нельзя́ лу́чше — as finely as possible
5. ды́мковый fr ды́мка — light, transparent fabric of gauze, tulle or muslin
6. ро́зан *(coll)* — rose
7. ско́ро ли вы [бу́дете гото́вы]
8. то́ка = ток
9. припома́женный *(past, pass, prich)* fr припома́дить *(pf)* — to smooth one's hair down w pomade
10. кра́ля *(pop)* — beauty

Two, III, 15

1. Ма́рья Анто́новна — [Нары́шкина (1779-1854) wife of D.L. Naryshkin and favorite mistress of tsar]
2. фармазо́н (*obs* or *pop*) — freemason
3. *Il fait à présent la pluie et le beau temps (F)* — He is ruling the roost for now

Two, III, 16

1. Елизаве́та — [Алексе́евна (1779-1826). Born Princess Louise of Baden, she married the future Alexander I at 15. She converted to R orthodoxy, and became Empress-consort in 1801.]
2. кавале́р — *(male)* dancing partner; a soldier or officer who has been decorated
3. глисса́д — glissade [dancing figure in which one foot glides along the floor]
4. убыстря́ться/ убыстри́ться *(coll)* — to quicken

Two, III, 17: none

Two, III, 18

1. вестовщи́к *(obs, coll)* — gossip
2. конституцио́нный — [By Oct. 1809, Speranskii had completed his project for reforming the R state. He proposed separation of powers and a limited franchise to elect a legislative assembly. Alexander at first seemed to approve of this new constitutionalism, but Speranskii's plan was never put into effect.]
3. госуда́рственный сове́т — [Established by manifesto on January 1, 1810, O.S. Its original purpose in Speranskii's plan was to draft laws and to advise the tsar. However, its 35 appointed members served at the tsar's pleasure and could not overrule him.]
4. Жерве́ — Zherve or Gervais [Андре́й Андре́евич Ж. (1773-1832). Speranskii's relative. Served in ministries of foreign affairs and finances.]
5. Столы́пин — Stolypin [Арка́дий Алексе́евич С. (1778- 1825) writer and senator]
6. испа́нские дела́ Наполео́на — [In 1808, F occupied Madrid and other Spanish cities. The Spanish King was forced to abdicate and N's brother Joseph was proclaimed King of Spain. E forces under Sir John Moore and Arthur Wellesley (later made Duke of Wellington) came through Portugal to Spain to fight F. This began the Peninsular War (1808-1814) in which Wellington and Spanish forces drove F out of Spain.]
7. в сапожка́х хо́дит *(obs, pop)* — costs an arm and a leg
8. обсу́живать *(impf, obs)* = обсужда́ть *(impf)*

Two, III, 19

1. бьюсь fr би́ться *(impf)*

Two, III, 20

1. нести́ расхо́ды *(impf)* — to bear the expenses
2. переймёшь *(pf, ft)* fr перенима́ть/ переня́ть
3. вака́нция *(obs)* = вака́нсия
4. филиа́ция *(book)* — development; sequence
5. Юсу́пов — [well known R aristocratic

family]
6. затро́гивать *(impf, obs)* = затра́гивать
7. Па́нин — [well known R aristocratic family]

Two, III, 21

1. отха́живать/ отходи́ть — to play [a card]
(2.) ро́бер *(obs)* = ро́ббер
3. Натали́ *(F)* — Natalie
4. взять его́ по́д руку — to take him by the arm

Two, III, 22

1. по́лно — that's enough
2. а́кты — records; documents
3. что ты не говори́шь = почему́ ты не говори́шь

Two, III, 23

1. диплома́ция *(obs)* = диплома́тия
2. поскри́пывание — light or occasional squeaking

Two, III, 24

1. разлю[би́ть] *(pf)*

Two, III, 25

1. ста́рая де́ва — old maid
2. уби́тый в Ту́рции — [R was at war w Turkey fr 1806 to 1812 over whether R ships could pass through Dardanelles and about R rights in Moldavia and Wallachia. The war ended w Treaty of Bucharest (May 16/28, 1812) under which R acquired Bessarabia.]
3. внук Вели́кой Екатери́ны — [the tsar]

Two, III, 26

1. и ему́ чтоб без ма́чехи не быть — he [Andrew] must not be without a stepmother either
2. поско́нный — hemp
3. воздыха́ние *(obs)* = вздыха́ние — sigh
4. ей на́до бы́ло итти́ стра́нствовать — [a recurrent theme in Tolstoy's life and works after 1880., e.g. "Оте́ц Се́ргий", published posthumously in 1912]

Two, IV, 1

1. библе́йское преда́ние — Genesis 3, especially 3:19
2. сни́скивать *(impf)* fr сниска́ть *(pf)*
3. ходи́ть/ идти́ по́ миру — to go begging
4. е́зженный — used for riding
5. подава́ть/ пода́ть в о́тпуск — to apply for leave
6. Анна — [Holstein Order of St. Anne, established there in 1735, and included among R orders by Paul I in 1797. Peter III (who reigned fr 1761 until his wife, Catherine II, deposed him in 1762) was the son of the Duke of Holstein-Gottorp, and of Anna Petróvna, the daughter of Peter I. The order was founded in Anna's memory. Paul divided it into 3 classes, and Alexander I added a 4th class in 1815.]
7. бить на *(impf)* — to secure; to obtain
8. па́нна — an unmarried girl of gentry class in P, Ukr or Byelorussia
9. му́зыка *(pop)* — orchestra; band
10. кача́ть *(impf)* — to toss smb in air out of enthusiasm
11. Кременчу́г — Kremenchug [Ukr town on Dnieper Rv nr Poltava]
12. совсе́м не та — [you are] not at all the same
13. ты не смотри́, что она́ весела́ — don't pay attention to her seemingly good disposition

Two, IV, 2

1. вы́борный — peasant — elder
2. зе́мский or земско́й — country — clerk
3. что́бы ду́ху твоего́ здесь не́ было — don't ever set foot here again
4. ме́ньше ва́шего = меньше вас
5. от угла́ на шесть куше́й — *(billiard term)* [куш *(F couche)* is a monetary bet. A billiard-player tries to hit the balls into the pockets fr one corner. If he succeeds, he wins six times as much as his original bet. (I thank Zaidenshnur for this explanation.)]

Two, IV, 3

1. зази́мок *(dial)* — first frost
2. зако́вывать/ закова́ть — to freeze; to cover w ice
3. укло́читься *(pf; dial)* — to blossom out; to come up
4. перели́нивать/ перелиня́ть — to shed hair *(of animals)*
5. войти́ в охо́тничье те́ло *(pf)* — to get into good shape for hunting
6. подби́ться *(pf)* — to harm the flesh of a dog's paws
7. замола́живать/ замолоди́ть — to grow overcast
8. мга *(dial)* = мгла
9. поруса́чьи or по-руса́чьи — like a руса́к *(hare)*
10. прави́ло *(hunting)* — tail of a borzoi dog or of a fox
11. по́дклик *(hunting and pop)* — to call someone w a shout
12. доезжа́чий *(hunting)* — whipper-in *(hunter's assistant, who whips in the hounds)*
13. порска́ть *(impf, nt; hunting)* — to halloo on *(hounds)*
14. гоньба́ — chasing *(an animal on a hunt)*
15. зака́з *(dial)* — game reserve
16. отъёмный — separate
17. соба́ки ничего́ — the dogs are all right
18. тще́тны ро́ссам все препо́ны — [fr cantata by P.I. Golenishchev-Kutuzov, mentioned in Two, I, 3 above]

Two, IV, 4

1. зае́зд *(hunting)* — ambush
2. Доне́ц — Don-River breed of horse
3. игре́невый — chestnut-colored, w white mane

and tail

4. меренóк = меринóк fr мéрин
5. лаз — a blind; ambush
6. гóнчая собáка — [special breed of lop-eared, big-headed dog taught to hunt in packs while barking loudly]
7. выжля́тник — master of the dog-pack
8. борзя́тник — keeper of borzoi dogs
9. чи́стое дéло марш — [speaker's own phrase, apparently to give encouragement; given in no dictionary I can find]
10. Илáгины — [It was permissible to hunt on other people's lands]
11. свали́ть стáи *(pf)* — to put together several dog-packs
12. передáвливать/ передави́ть — to run over all or many [dogs]
13. вы́жлец — hound
14. óстров *(hunting)* — patch of woods; copse
15. матерóй [волк] = матёрый
16. глáдить *(impf, hunting)* — to let a hunted animal get away by releasing the hounds too late

(17.) протрави́ть *(pf)* — to let a hunted animal get away

18. фюи́т! = фьють! — get going! away!
19. бурдáстый *(obs)* — having a dewlap
20. бирáть *(impf, many-x)* fr брать
21. снаря́д — special equipment
22. Настáсья Ивáновна — [The male fool is called by a female name]
23. оттóпать *(pf) (obs)* fr оттóпывать/ оттоптáть — to frighten a game animal away
24. я сам с усáм = я сам с усáми — I can take care of myself
25. хоть бы мужчи́не в пóру [впóру] — it would even be good enough for a man
26. помкну́ть *(pf)* — to force a game animal to flee in direction hunter desires
27. у́ймище — woods; wide space
28. улюлю́кать *(impf)* — to sic dogs on a game animal
29. гон — chasing an animal on a hunt; a chase
30. скок — bounding; running
31. лобáстый — having a large forehead

Two, IV, 5

1. влепля́ться/ влепи́ться *(pop)* — to stick to
2. измы́тый *(obs)* — hollowed out, washed away
3. нае́денный fr нае́сть *(pf)* — to feed well, or alot
4. желе́зка — iron collar [dogs, when hunting wolves, wore spiked, iron collars to protect their necks against wolf-bite]
5. во́йлок — matted hair
6. водомо́ина — gully (formed by running water)
7. попере́чь or впопере́чь *(dial)* = попере̄к
8. приспе́ть *(pf)* — to draw near
9. наддава́ть/ надда́ть — to increase speed
10. муру́гий — red-brown; dark brown (of an animal's coat)
11. ля́скнуть зуба́ми *(pf)* — gave a click w his teeth [Also ля́згнуть *(pf)*]

(12.) на утёк = наутёк

13. молоча́ fr молоти́ть *(impf)* — to strike; to hit
14. стру́нивать/ стру́нить *(pf, hunting)* — to muzzle a captured animal w a thong
15. матёрищий fr матёрый plus aug suff -ище — a big, full-grown one

Two, IV, 6

1. поро́сший *(pf, past, act, prich)* fr порастáть/ порасти́
2. насупроти́в (*obs* or *pop*) = напро́тив
3. заво́дить/ завести́ го́нчих — to loose hunting dogs fr a given place
4. волто́рна *(obs)* = валто́рна
5. подава́ть/ пода́ть го́лос *(hunting)* — to pick up the sound of a game animal and follow it
6. отве́ршок = отве́ршек — branch of a gully
7. распуши́ть *(pf)* — to make fluffy; to fluff up
8. труба́ *(hunting)* — tail of a fox; brush
9. спеть (*impf, obs* or *pop*) — to hurry after; to chase
10. виля́ть/ вильну́ть — to dodge around while running
11. звездо́й — [i.e. heads eating the killed animal and tails radiating out]
12. торочи́ть (*impf, hunting* or *mil*) — to tie sth behind the saddle w straps.

13. чумбу́р — tie-rope; tether
14. бунтова́ть *(impf)* — to rage; to show extreme annoyance
15. торока́ *(pl)* — straps behind the saddle to tie things w
16. мыша́стый — mouse-colored
17. поди́, суди́сь — try going to court
18. я его́ лиси́цей ну ката́ть — I hit him w the fox
19. уго́рь *(m)* = уго́рье *(dial)* — a slope
20. чистопсо́вая соба́ка — pureblood dog [a special breed, big in the chest, and shaggy, esp in tail]
21. что как с уше́й оборву́т — what if they get the better of; suppose they outperform
22. по дере́вне за соба́ку — each dog costs the price of a village
23. пла́ченный fr плати́ть *(impf)*
24. поме́рять *(pf)* — to try; to try on
25. полуго́рка — halfway up the hillock
26. чу́я моро́з к за́втрашнему у́тру — sensing the next day's frost
27. смычо́к *(hunting)* — rope by which hunting dogs are tied together in pairs
28. сбива́ть/ сбить соба́к — to collect the dogs in one place
29. приложи́ть у́ши *(pf)* — to fold his ears back
30. во все но́ги — at full speed
31. заложи́ться *(pf)* — to chase (of dogs)
32. отсе́сть *(pf, hunting)* — to jump up; to jump sideways
33. повиса́ть/ пови́снуть *(hunting)* — to keep same distance fr hunted animal when running in hot pursuit (said of dogs)
34. как бы — hopefully
35. вихну́ть *(pf)* — to dodge; to turn sharply
36. ды́шловый fr ды́шло — a beam (betw two horses drawing a carriage, it is attached to front axle of carriage)
37. злей = злее *(comp)* fr злой — fast
38. отпа́занчить *(pf)* — to cut off hare's paw below the ankle
39. вытя́гивать/ вы́тянуть — to outdo
40. па́занка — hare's paw
41. выма́хиваться/ вы́махаться — to grow exhausted
42. уго́нка — running down a game animal [A dog was given three chances to do this]
43. второчи́ть *(pf)* — to tie in торока́
44. держи́сь! — take care! look out!

Two, IV, 7

1. на бочькю́ or на бочкю́ *(subst)* = на бочку́ = бочко́м
(2.) досча́тый = доща́тый
3. чубу́к — stem (of a tobacco pipe)
4. отъе́здить *(pf, coll)* — to spend some time riding
5. как ни в чём не быва́ло — as if nothing had happened
6. на (+ *prep*) — made w or fr (of food)
7. юра́га *(dial)* — buttermilk; whey
8. сбор — preparation
9. задребезжа́ть *(pf)* — to start twanging
10. "Ба́рыня" — [R folk song and dance. Music can be found in *Русские народные песни Поволжья,* выпуск первый, М-Л, Академия Наук СССР, 1959, стр. 117-118.]
11. перебо́р — rapid sequence of musical sounds; agile plucking of strings (done w right hand)
12. перехва́т — sudden virtuoso changes of the fretting position (done w left hand)
13. коле́но — figure or part (of a piece of music)
14. не то — not right
15. рассыпа́ть/ рассы́пать — to disseminate the sound all around; to break into shorter notes; to liven up the tempo
16. отде́лывать/ отде́лать пе́сню — to perform a song
17. в раз or враз — in time
18. расходи́ться/ разойти́сь *(coll)* — to gather speed
19. весельча́к — merry-maker; jolly fellow
20. муженёк fr муж
21. как со ве́чера поро́ша/ выпада́ла хороша́ — [В. А. Лазаревский, ("В Ясной Поляне," *Международный альманах* "О Толстом," М. 1909 г.) writes that LNT's daughters, Mariia and Alexandra, used to sing this hunter's song on LNT's estate at Iasnaia Poliana. My thanks to the Soviet scholars, Aleksandr Anikst and Evelina Zaidenshnur, for this note and some others.]
22. склад *(coll)* — smoothness; gracefulness
23. лады́ — [physical traits of build, etc., characterizing any breed of dogs]

Two, IV, 8

1. Ди́ммлер — Dimmler [Maude says Dimmler is not fictitious]

Two, IV, 9

1. 20 гра́дусов моро́за — [i.e. by Réaumur; = minus 13 degrees F., or minus 25 degrees C.]
2. бу́дет игра́ть-то — enough playing
3. пету́х . . . овёс — [Maude writes that feeding grain to a fowl at Christmastime was a way of telling fortunes. Telling fortunes w grain and chicken is also mentioned in first stanza of "Светла́на" (1811) by Васи́лий Андре́евич Жуко́вский (1783-1852). "Светла́на" is mentioned in the fortune-telling passage in Chapter 5 of *Евге́ний Оне́гин* (1823-1831), by Алекса́ндр Серге́евич Пу́шкин (1799-1837).]
4. уж э́та ба́рышня *(mock anger)* — what can I do about that young lady
5. надува́ться/ наду́ться *(coll)* — to pout
6. куцаве́йка *(dial)* = кацаве́йка
7. "Бу́ря" — "Storm." [According to Grove's *Dictionary,* the "Storm Rondo" fr the Concerto No. 3 in E Minor (1797) was "enormously popular" in Europe at this time. Steibelt (1765-1823), a G pianist and composer who had been prominent in London and Paris, was invited to St P in 1808, and was named director of F opera in St P in 1810. His music is now all but forgotten.]
8. "Водоно́с" or "Водово́з" — "Water Carrier" [Cherubini's opera *Les Deux Journées* (1800) was called this in R and G]

Two, IV, 10

1. болва́нчик fr болва́н — manikin; doll
2. ты под капу́стою родила́сь — the stork brought you *(fig)*
3. Фильд — Field [John F. (1782-1837). Irish pianist and composer, especially of nocturnes, who lived in St.P. fr 1804 to 1831. Influenced Chopin.]
4. довспомина́ть *(pf)* — to remember sth to a certain point
5. метампсико́за *(obs)* = метемпсихо́з — transmigration of souls;

metempsychosis
6. пая́с *(obs)* = пая́ц
7. подре́з — runner *(of a sleigh)*
8. разго́нный *(obs)* — for everyday use
9. орло́вский — fr Orël province *(about 250 mi S of M)*
10. в корню́ = как коренни́к
11. прима́сливать/ прима́слить — to smooth down
12. иссе́ченный fr иссека́ть/ иссе́чь — to cut in different places
13. шип — nail *(on horseshoe)*
14. разлюбе́зный *(obs)* — darling; dearest
15. сбива́ть/ сбить — to slacken; to lower
16. разъе́женный fr разъе́здить *(pf)* — to make a road smoother by frequent use
17. Никола́й стал забира́ть вперёд — Nikolai began to draw ahead

Two, IV, 11

1. распашно́й — loose; unbuttoned
2. я ви́деть не могу́ — I can't stand looking [at them]
3. каза́нский тата́рин — [Kazan', on the Volga due E of M, was the capital of an independent, Moslem, Tatar kingdom in the 15th cent; Ivan IV conquered it in 1552. It is about 260 mi E (downstream) fr Nizhnii-Novgorod (now called Gor'kii), and is capital of the Tatar Autonomous SSR.]
4. ту́рка = ту́рок
5. э́то их зако́ном не запрещено́ — [Moslems are not supposed to drink alcohol]
6. Сашине́т fr Са́ша fr Алекса́ндра — Sachinette [A pseudo-F construct, derived by analogy w Annette fr Anna, Ninette fr Nina, etc. It may be termed, "смесь французского с нижегородским."]
7. прибо́р — place-setting
8. до петухо́в — until sunrise; until cock-crow
9. скры́пнуть *(obs)* = скри́пнуть *(pf)*

Two, IV, 12

1. перегоня́ться *(impf, obs, coll)* — to race in competition
2. отво́д — wing *(one of two bent beams going fr front of carriage as projecting sidepieces)*

Two, IV, 13

1. усо́вещивать/ усо́вестить — to appeal to smb's conscience or sense of shame
2. захли́пать *(pf)* — to start sobbing
3. брульо́н — rough draft *(obs) (F brouillon)*

Two, V, 1

1. Иверская часо́вня = Часо́вня Иверской бо́жией ма́тери — Chapel of the Iberian Virgin [Chapel nr Red Sq and Alexander Garden in heart of M. Built in 1669, the chapel housed an allegedly wonder-working icon of the Virgin so revered that the tsar paid his respects to it first, even before entering the Kremlin, when he visited M fr St. P. Removed after 1917.]
2. неза́езженный — unspoiled by too much riding
3. Си́вцев Вражо́к — [Street in M slums, S of Arbat]
4. Марго́ — Margaux [a type of F red wine]
5. импера́тор Франц . . . в незако́нные супру́ги — [N had married the widow Josephine de Beauharnais (1763-1814) in 1796, but had the marriage annulled in 1809. He was now casting about for a royal wife and, after considering the tsar's sister, among others, married Marie Louise (1791-1847), daughter of Franz I of Austria, in 1810. Pierre considers the annulment illegal.]
6. воссыла́ть *(impf, obs)* — to send up
7. 14 ию́ня — [Pierre may have in mind the battle of Talavera on July 15-16/27-28, 1809, in which the Duke of Wellington, w a British-Spanish-Portuguese army, defeated the F, altho F apparently thought otherwise. LNT has already confused "June" and "July" at One, I, 1 and One, I, 9 (in Jubilee Ed) or One, I, 7 in 1961-1963 ed.)]
8. Астре́я — Astraea [masonic lodge in St P]
9. Ищущие ма́нны — Manna-seekers [masonic lodge in St P]
10. Шотла́ндский ковёр — [Maude explains that such a carpet had masonic symbols on it and was highly desired by masons]
11. акт — document [Maude explains that acts were the rules of the masonic order]

Two, V, 2

[Traditionally, the prototype of old Bolkonskii's M house is that of LNT's grandfather, Gen N.S. Volkonskii, at what is now 9 ulitsa Kalinina.]

1. шу́бка — *(here)* a short, light jacket
2. выводи́ть/ вы́вести [его́] из себя́ — to drive smb mad
3. класть покло́ны *(impf)* — to bow *(in prayer)*
4. косты́ль *(m)* — *(here)* walking-stick *(obs)*
5. распоряже́ние — [A landowner, such as the old prince, decided which of his serfs to send to the army for the government's endless demands. He could use this power to punish serfs who displeased him.]
6. отда́ча — sending away
7. засту́па (*obs* or *pop*) — intercession
8. не вида́л ли кто — did anyone see

Two, V, 3

1. Нико́лин день — [St Nicholas' Day, is Dec. 6, the alleged death-day of the 4th cent Bishop of Myra in Asia Minor. A favorite saint in R.]
2. Лопу́хин — [Perhaps Ива́н Влади́мирович Л. (1756-1816). Mason, mystic, and senator, who lived in M, but was not a prince.]
3. что он — how is he
4. ге́рцог Ольденбу́ргский — [Oldenburg was a duchy in NW Germany on the N Sea. Through his father's mother, Alexander I was related to the House of Oldenburg. Furthermore, Alexander's sister, Ekaterina, had married Peter-Friedrich-Georg von O. (1783-1812), heir to the duchy (who, in 1812, would be генера́л-от-кавале́рии in R army, commanding means of communications). Her father-in-law, Duke Peter-Friedrich Ludwig, had also served in R army and the territorial integrity of his duchy had been guranteed by N at Tilsit. However, on Jan. 22, 1811, N.S. N annexed the Duchy of O. Duke Ludwig's wife was the sister of Alexander's mother. Alexander protested the annexation. F offered to give the Duke a residence in Erfurt.]
5. де́ло дохо́дит до па́пы — [In May, 1809, N had annexed the pope's lands to France. A few weeks later, F took Rome and took

the pope (Pius VII) prisoner to France, where he was made to sign a new concordat w the F.]

6. заме́сто *(pop)* = вме́сто
7. прое́зд — riding through
8. волю́м *(obs)* — volume *(F volume)*
9. где нам воева́ть — how can we fight
10. в за́шеи or вза́шей, or взаше́и *(pop)* — by the neck
11. три католи́чки — [The Roman Catholic Church was actively, but on a small scale, seeking converts among R gentry in high positions at this time]
12. Пётр Вели́кий — Peter the Great [(1672-1725). R tsar. Seized power in 1689 and ruled until his death. Founded St P.]
13. кунстка́мера *(obs)* — museum of rarities
14. гу́сли, всегда́ заслу́шаюсь его́ — I always listen w delight [to his psaltery-like words]

Two, V, 4: none

Two, V, 5

1. большо́е о́бщество — large gathering
2. буриме́ — *bouts rimés (F)* [a stylish game, giving smb words or syllables to rhyme verses w]
3. "Бе́дная Ли́за" — "Poor Liza" [Tale written by Никола́й Миха́йлович Карамзи́н (1766-1826) in 1792, which is outstanding example of K's "sentimentalism." K was also a devotee of melancholy, as in his poem by that name.]
4. пе́нзенский — [Penza province was about 500 mi SE of M, W of Volga hills]
5. нижегоро́дский — [Nizhnii-Novgorod province on upper Volga about 300 mi E of M]
6. чего́ с ним никогда́ ни в чём не быва́ло — which had never happened to him before w anything

Two, V, 6

1. ста́рая Коню́шенная [у́лица] — [Street off the Arbat in M]
2. вы́езд — going out (visiting or to a performance)
3. самова́р, что́бы согре́ть! — heat up the samovar!

4. перецеловать (ся) *(pf)* — to kiss many or all; to kiss several in turn
5. чтоль or что ль = что ли — or what?
6. Обер-Шельма — [Pun on Шальме, a fashionable M seamstress of time and о́бер, "senior," plus ше́льма. Acc to *Istoriia Moskvy* (III, 26) she was a spy for N.]
7. с меня́ не бери́те — don't look at me for a model
8. что день—но́вая мо́да — everyday there's a new style
9. всё вдруг подошло́ — everything happened at once
10. Ма́ринское — [N suburb of M]
11. нра́вный *(pop)* — w stern habits; wilful
12. оно́ *(intensifier)* — it is true that
13. колото́вка — quarrelsome woman

Two, V, 7

1. Вздви́женка = Воздви́женка [у́лица] — [Runs fr Alexander Garden W of Kremlin to Boulevard Ring just N of Arbat Sq]
2. Соба́чья Площа́дка — [In middle of triangle in M formed by Smolensk, Kudrinskaia, and Arbat Squares, W of Kremlin, betw Boulevard and Garden rings]
3. что он не е́дет? — why doesn't he come?

Two, V, 8

1. отку́да он взя́лся — where did he come from
2. ша́хов *(poss adj)* fr шах
3. да и — indeed; really
4. Семёнова — Semēnova [Нимфодо́ра Семёновна С. (1787-1876). R opera singer (1809-1831). More renowned for her acting than for her singing. Her much more famous sister, Екатери́на Семёновна (1786-1849), did not do opera at all.]

Two, V, 9

1. эксельба́нт = аксельба́нт

Two, V, 10

1. карусе́ль *(f)* — [horseback competitive games which replaced knightly jousting in 17th & 18th cents *(obs)*]
2. пока́ не — until

Two, V, 11

1. заём — a loan
2. перепива́ть/ перепи́ть — to outdrink; to drink a lot
3. магдали́на — sinner (*Gk* Magdalene)

Two, V, 12

1. прихо́д Успе́нья на могильца́х — [18th cent church in old Мёртвый переу́лок. Near Arbat, W of Kremlin, between Blvd. Ring and Garden Ring. So called because plague victims were buried in graveyard there in 1791.]
2. на живу́ю ни́тку — stitched together for a fitting
3. Тверь — Tver' [City on upper Volga, about 100 mi W by NW of M, on way to St P., now called Kalinin]
4. быть в си́лах — to be strong enough to; to be able to

Two, V, 13

1. во́льность *(f)* — departure fr gen norms
2. престу́пная любо́вь к сы́ну — [Perhaps *Phèdre* (1677) by Jean Racine (1639-1699), in which Phaedra, wife of Theseus, loves her stepson Hippolytus]
3. я не нахожу́ [, что она хороша́]
4. грос-фа́тер *(obs)* — *Grossvater (G)* — [G dance which starts w couples walking in a row and ends w a waltz. "Щелку́нчик" ballet (1890) by Пётр Ильи́ч Чайко́вский (1840-1893) contains a *Grossvater* dance in Act I.]

Two, V, 14

1. вы́петь *(pf, pop)* — to give it [to him] straight; to let [him] have it point-blank
2. ну, а [е́сли он] не хо́чет, [э́то] его́ де́ло

Two, V, 15

1. покупщи́к *(obs)* = покупа́тель

Two, V, 16

1. Ка́менка — Kamenka [Village in Volokolamsk District, M Province, about 40 mi W of M.]
2. тро́ечный fr тро́йка
3. перемори́ть *(pf)* — to be the death of; to exhaust
4. обезлоша́деть *(pf)* — to be deprived of one's horses
5. заре́зать *(pf)* — to overdrive horses
6. разобью́ *(pf, ft)* fr разбива́ть/ разби́ть
7. дух захва́тывало — it would take your breath away
8. запрёг *(m, pf, obs, past)* = запря́г fr запряга́ть/ запря́чь

Two, V, 17

(1.) на бекре́нь = набекре́нь
2. сесть на́до *(pf)* — [A R superstition is to sit down before a long trip so as to bring good luck]
3. ни жив ни мёртв — more dead than alive
4. гульба́ *(pop)* — carousing; spree
5. Стёшка — [Well-known M gypsy songstress of the time]
6. Ники́тский бульва́р — [part of inner ring of streets in downtown M]
7. тпру! — whoa!
8. Арба́тская пло́щадь — [Sq which unites inner ring w Arbat St]
9. дав два конца́ — having made a round trip

Two, V, 18

1. са́мый после́дний — worst
2. я бы с тобо́й-то сде́лала — I would really do sth to you
3. вски́дываться/ вски́нуться — to jerk
4. ли́повый цвет — lime-blossom tea or linden tea; tilleul *(used in medicine as sudorific)*

Two, V, 19

1. голова́шки (*pl; pop* and *dial*) — front part of a sleigh
2. час о́т часу не ле́гче — one bad thing after another; things keep getting worse
3. сам по себе́ — by himself; in his own right

Two, V, 20

1. ме́жду — in the middle of
2. возде́рживать/ воздержа́ть *(obs)* — to restrain
3. раз — first of all; that's one thing
4. быть в своём пра́ве — to have the right
5. по ме́ре того́, как — as

Two, V, 21

1. веселе́е обыкнове́нного = веселе́е чем обыкнове́нно
2. Meще́рский — Meshcherskii [Perhaps князь Пётр Серге́евич М. (1779-1856), senator at the time]
3. ссы́лка — [Speranskii was suddenly dismissed and exiled to Nizhnii-Novgorod on March 17, 1812, O.S. Although he was not anti-N, and most of the St P and M aristocrats were, it may have been more basic, as Florinsky suggests (p. 700), that his logic conflicted w "the tsar's faltering, emotional liberalism." There were obscure rumors when Speranskii was dismissed that he had been guilty of some kind of treason.]
4. крова́ть была́ разби́та — a bed was set up

Two, V, 22

1. ду́ху не хвата́ет [у меня́] — [I] don't have the heart to
2. я не сто́ю э́того — I am not worth it
3. де́сять гра́дусов моро́за — [Réaumur thermometer. About 10 degrees F., -12 degrees C.]
4. Пречи́стенский бульва́р — [Part of inner ring of M streets]
5. коме́та — [A bright comet appeared in 1812]
6. влепля́ться/ влепи́ться — to stick; to fasten itself

THREE, I , 1

ТОМ ТРЕТИЙ, ЧАСТЬ ПЕРВАЯ, ГЛАВА ПЕРВАЯ

1. континента́льная систе́ма — Continental System [On Nov. 21, 1806, N.S., N's Berlin decree declared Britain to be under a blockade and forbade British ships to trade w that part of Europe which the F dominated. On Dec. 17, 1807, N.S., N's Milan decree declared every ship bound to or fr Britain to be subject to seizure. Britain's control of the seas made enforcement impossible. R did not long adhere to this system, which worsened her relations with F.]
2. Меттерних — Metternich [Clemens, Prince von M. (1773-1859). Austrian foreign minister fr 1809 to 1848. He negotiated N's marriage to the Austrian princess, Marie-Louise, in 1810, and, after N's fall, was a leading figure in Holy Alliance.]
3. Таллейран or Талейран — Talleyrand [Charles-Maurice de T. (1754-1838). F bishop, excommunicated and turned diplomat. N's foreign minister (1799-1807). His skill in 1814, when he represented Louis XVIII, helped bring the Bourbons back to F and win F mild peace terms.]
4. св. Еле́на — St. Helena [Island in Atlantic, 1200 mi off Africa, where N was exiled after Waterloo in 1815 until his death in 1821]
5. сою́з Росси́и с Австрией в 1809 году́ — [In 1809, R was officially allied w F against Austria, but R moved very slowly to aid F, which defeated Austria without R help]
6. memorandum за No. 178 — [Apparently a real memorandum from Jean-Baptiste Champagny, Duc de Cadore (1756-1834), N's Foreign Minister, written in 1809 and made known to Alexander I in 1810. Alliance with R, the memorandum argued, would not be to F interest because R was so influential in northern and eastern Europe. Evelina Zaidenshnur, who furnished the essence of this note, says it is mentioned, but without the number, in LNT's source, *История Отечественной войны 1812 года* by M. Богданович, Санкт-Петербург, 1859, том 1, глава 2. She adds that LNT must have learned the number of the memorandum from archive materials.] (See Appendix Seven.)
7. Смоле́нская губе́рния — Smolensk Province [Smolensk is

about 250 mi W of M on headwaters of Dnieper. On Aug 5-6/17-18, 1812, a battle was fought to possess it, which F won. Retreating fr M, N spent 4 days here fr Oct 28/Nov 9, trying to reorganize what was left of his army.]

8. отка́з Наполео́на отвести́ свои́ войска́ за Ви́слу — [The Wisła (Vistula) is main rv of P flowing N fr Carpathians past Cracow, Warsaw, and Torun into Baltic nr Gdansk (Danzig). In 1811 and 1812, N poured troops into P and Prussia thus violating the Tilsit agreement. On April 27, 1812, N.S., Prince Kurakin, the R envoy in Paris, requested withdrawal of F troops fr Prussia. N reacted angrily. F did not comply.]
9. роево́й fr рой — [insect] hive
10. в руце́ *(OCS)* = в руке́ — [A quotation fr Proverbs 21:1 "The King's heart is in the hand of the Lord. . ."]
11. Дре́зден — [In May of 1812, N spent a month in Dresden being feted by Emperor Franz, the Kings of Saxony and Prussia, etc.]
12. име́ть *(impf)* — to have to

Three, I, 2

1. 29-го ма́я [N.S.]
2. Мари́я Луи́за — Marie-Louise [(1791-1847) N's second wife, whom he married in 1809. Daughter of Emperor Franz of Austria, and mother of N's son.]
3. Позен-Торн-Данциг — Posen, Thorn, Danzig [Towns then in Prussia and now in P called now Poznań, Torun, and Gdansk]
4. Кёнигсберг — Koenigsberg [Baltic port. Historical capital of E Prussia. Since 1945 in USSR. Now called Kaliningrad.]
5. переме́нный *(obs)* — relay (horses, changed at every post stage)
6. шестерня́ — team of six horses
7. Вильковиский *(adj)* — Vil'kovishki or Wiłkowyszki [Polish town, then in Duchy of Warsaw. In LNT's day, it was in R Empire, about 10 mi fr Prussian frontier, on Berlin-St P rr.]
8. Не́ман — Niemen Rv [then the frontier betw Duchy of Warsaw and R]
9. Ски́фский — Scythian [Scythians lived on Don Rv in what is now Ukr; Alexander the Great campaigned against them in 3rd cent B.C.]
10. Алекса́ндр Македо́нский — Alexander the Great [356 B.C.—

323 B.C. King of Macedon fr 336 B.C. to his death and greatest conqueror produced by ancient Europe]

11. зри́тельная труба́ — spyglass; telescope
12. Кашми́р — Kashmir [rich province now divided betw India and Pakistan and separating S Afghanistan fr SW China]
13. Ко́вно — Kovno [now called Kaunas, in central Lithuanian SSR, on Niemen Rv]
14. Ви́лия́ — Viliia [Rv Right tributary of Niemen Rv. Vilna is on Viliia Rv.]
15. вива́т — *vivat! (L)* = may he live long; long live [a traditional P cheer]
16. Бертье́ — Berthier [Louis Alexandre B, Prince de Neuchâtel (1753-1815). F marshall. N's chief of staff fr 1794 to 1814. Later joined Bourbons and was killed, perhaps by himself, when N escaped fr his first exile in Elba.]
17. Моско́вия — Muscovy

(18.) обмо́кнуть *(pf, pop)* — to get soaked

[19] обшлёпнуться — to stick; to get stuck *(because of wetness)*

Three, I, 3

1. Ви́льно (adj: Ви́ленский) — Vilnius; Vilna, [City now in Lithuanian SSR, where Vileika Rv falls into Viliia. In LNT's day, on rr fr Berlin to St P, about 64 mi past Kovno.]
2. в трёх [ру́сских] а́рмиях — [Barclay de Tolly commanded the First army, in the N. Bagration commanded a Second army, to the S of Barclay's. Count Aleksandr Petrovich Tormásov (1752-1819), commanded the Third army, in reserve, defending S Russia.]
3. Закре́т — [Bennigsen's estate 2 or 3 mi E of Vilna]
4. Балашёв — Balashev or Balashov [Алекса́ндр Дми́триевич Б. (1770-1837). R mil man, former mil gov of St P (1809-1810). Member of Council of State (1810-1834). Minister of Police (1810-1816).]
5. Пото́цкий — Potocki [Famous Polish aristocratic family]
6. Шишко́в — Shishkov [Алекса́ндр Семёнович Ш. (1754-1841). State Secretary who succeeded Speranskii. Vice-Admiral, Author of Manifesto declaring war in 1812. Amateur writer.

Made President of R Academy in 1813. Opposed Karamzin's reforms of R language. Mentioned in Pushkin's *Евгений Онегин,* Chapter Eight.]

7. Салтыко́в — Saltykov [князь Никола́й Ива́нович С. (1736-1816) Field Marshal. In 1812, he was chairman of state council and of committee of ministers.]
8. Лористон — Lauriston [Alexandre-Jacques Bernard Law, Marquis de L. (1768-1828). N's friend fr artillery school. Made N's adjutant in 1800. Succeeded Caulaincourt as F envoy to St P in 1811. Made marshall in 1823.]
9. Кура́кин — Kurakin [князь Алекса́ндр Бори́сович К. (1752-1818). R diplomat. Ambassador to Vienna (1806-1808) and then Paris (1808-1812). At N's birthday reception at the Tuileries in Paris on August 15, 1811, N.S., N harangued K. for forty minutes and threatened war.]
10. Бассано — Bassano [Marie-Hugues-Bernard Maret, (1763-1839). N's secretary in 1799. Made Count in 1807 and Duke of Bassano in 1809. Minister for Foreign Affairs, 1811-1813. In Vilna during R campaign as link betw N and Europe.]

Three, I, 4

1. Рыко́нты — Rykonty [Village on R side of Niemen, about 25 mi W of Vilna]
2. вспы́рскивать *(impf)* = вспа́рхивать *(impf)* — to fly up easily and rapidly
3. чувы́канье = чуфы́канье — hooting; the onomotopoetic sound чуф-чуф made by certain birds such as black grouse or larks
4. отдава́ть/ отда́ть честь *(mil)* — to salute
5. назначе́ние — appointment; assignment; goal
6. шу́рин — [Murat was married to N's sister Caroline]
7. разъе́вшийся *(pf)* fr разъеда́ться/ разъе́сться — to grow a bit fat fr overeating
8. Даву — Davout [Louis-Nicolas D. (1770-1823) Duke of Auerstedt. Prince of Eckmühl. F marshall. One of N's ablest officers.]

Three, I, 5

1. Аракче́ев не трус — an Arakcheev who was not a coward
2. заключа́ть/ заключи́ть — to contain
3. де Кастре — de Castries [Perhaps Edmond-Eugène Philippe Hercule, Marquis de C. (1787-1866)]
4. Monsieur de Turenne — [N's gentleman of chamber; Count]
5. Рустан — Roustan [(1780-1845). N's man-servant whom he acquired in Egypt in 1799 and who accompanied him everywhere until 1814.]

Three, I, 6

1. Дюрок — Duroc [Giraud Christophe-Michel D., (1772-1813). Duke of Friuli, F marshall, Grand Marshal of N's palace. Accompanied N on all campaigns fr 1805 to 1813.]
2. хол
   жить в хо́ле — to live in clover
3. осьмна́дцать *(obs)* = восемна́дцать
4. Одер — Oder [Rv in E G. It rises in Moravia (now in Czechoslovakia) and flows N past Wrocław (Breslau) and Frankfurt-an-der-Oder and into Baltic at Stettin. Its N part now is frontier betw E G and P.]
5. знать за собо́й *(impf)* — to be aware of
6. Молда́вия — Moldavia [Province now partly in USSR and partly in E Rumania, then in Ottoman Empire. Capital: Jassy. Chief port: Galati on Danube. Left in Ottoman Empire under Treaty of Bucharest a few weeks earlier.]
7. Валла́хия — Wallachia, Walachia [Lower Danube-plain area of what is now Rumania, including Bucharest. Left in Ottoman Empire under Treaty of Bucharest a few weeks earlier.]
8. тяну́ть/ потяну́ть но́сом — to sniff
9. Штейн — Stein [Karl, Freiherr vom und zum S. (1757-1831) Prussian premier (1807-1808) dismissed under pressure fr N. He then went to R where he served in 1812 war. He helped form R-Prussian alliance of 1813.]
10. Армфельд — Armfeldt [Count Gustav-Moritz A. (1757-1814) Swedish gen who fled to R after being accused of treason. In R svc fr 1811 on. Chairman of R Committee on Finnish Affairs and member of State Council.]

11. Бенигсен . . . ужа́сные воспомина́ния — [N's victory over Bennigsen at Friedland in 1807 had led to the Treaty of Tilsit]
12. Барклай — Barklai or Barclay [Михаи́л Богда́нович Б.-де-Толли (1761-1818). R gen, later field marshal, of Scottish ancestry. Commanded successful Finnish campaign of 1809. War Minister in 1810. Overall mil commander at first in 1812 campaign. After Kutuzov replaced him, Barclay took charge of 1st W army.]
13. Пфуль — Pful', Phull or Pfuel [Baron Carl Ludwig August P (1757-1826). Prussian gen and theoretician. Entered R service in 1806 as major gen. Drew up first R defense plan against F attack. His plan to make a stand against F at Drissa on Dvina was not adopted and he went via St P to England.]
14. ро́пщет fr ропта́ть *(impf)*
15. Шве́ды . . . сумасше́дшими короля́ми — [Gustav IV Adolph (1778-1837) was mentally unstable King of Sweden, who was forced to abdicate in 1809. His successor and uncle, Charles XIII (1748-1818) reigned fr 1809 to his death and adopted N's marshall, Bernadotte, as his successor in 1810.]
16. Бернадо́т — Bernadotte [Jean-Baptiste Jules B. (1763-1844). Actual ruler of Sweden fr 1810, when Charles XIII adopted B. as his successor. Bernadotte became Charles XIV on death of his predecessor in 1818. After N seized Swedish Pomerania, B, despite his F origins became hostile to N, which is what aroused N's resentment. Tarlé reports (p. 43) that at B's death, a tattoo was discovered on his arm reading, "Death to Kings."]
17. деру́тся *(pr)* fr дра́ться *(impf)*
18. сотру́ *(pf)* fr стира́ть/ стере́ть
19. Двина́ [За́падная] — [Western] Dvina [Rv rising in Valdai Hills in NW European R, and flowing through Belorussia and Latvia into Gulf of Riga]
20. Дне́пр — Dnieper [Rv rising in Valdai Hills in NW European R that flows S past Smolensk and Kiev into Black Sea near Kherson]

Three, I, 7

1. Бессьер — Bessières [Jean Baptiste (1768-1813) F marshall and Duke of Istria. Commanded F cavalry guards at Austerlitz. Commanded F cavalry corps and guards in 1812.]
2. Полта́ва — Poltava [Town on Vorskla Rv in

Ukr nr which Peter I of R defeated Charles XII of Sweden in 1709 and ended Sweden's importance as a great power]

3. потро́гивать *(obs)* = потра́гивать *(impf)* — to touch lightly
4. се́врский — Sèvres
5. Виртембе́ргский, Ба́денский, Веймарский — [Paul's widow and Alexander's mother, the Empress Maria Fedorovna, had been born Princess Sophie Dorothea of Württemberg. Alexander's wife Elizaveta Alekseevna, was by birth Princess Louise of Baden. Alexander's sister Mariia had married the Crown Prince of Saxe-Weimar in 1804.]

Three, I, 8

1. Молда́вская а́рмия — [The R army in Moldavia, nr what was then Turkish frontier. Kutuzov was named supreme commander on this front in 1811, and the war w Turkey ended w Treaty of Bucharest (May 28, 1812, N.S.) a few weeks before F invasion began.]
2. Туре́цкая а́рмия — [The R army on the Turkish front]
3. ухва́тываться *(impf)* fr ухвати́ться
4. вала́шка — Wallachian woman
5. Дри́сский ла́герь — [See Pful' in Three, I, 6 above]
6. переви́деть *(pf)* — to see a good deal of sth
7. разрумя́ниться *(pf)* — to become very rosy
8. Каме́нский — Kamenskii [граф Никола́й Миха́йлович К. (1778-1811), генера́л-от-инфанте́рии. Commander of R army on Moldavian front and victor at Batin.]
9. как поду́маешь кто и что — to think that such people
10. на съеде́ние [кому́] — at the mercy [of]

Three, I, 9

1. Тормáсов — Tormasov [граф Алекса́ндр Петро́вич Т. (1752-1819). R gen. In 1812, he commanded Third Army, defending S R.]
2. Паулучи — Pauluchi or Paulucci [Marquis Фили́пп Осипович П. (1779-1849) R Adj. Gen. After serving in F army, he spent 22 yrs in R army starting in 1807, and was known in R by names given above. In 1812, he was at first chief of staff of First Army, but was shortly thereafter named governor of Livonia

and Courland.]

3. Вольцоген — [Vol'zogen or Wolzogen, Freiherr Ludwig W. (1774-1845). Prussian gen and mil theoretician in R service fr 1807 to 1815. In 1812, W. was on Barclay's staff and then Kutuzov's. Later returned to Prussia as a gen.]
4. обли́ческое движе́ние — oblique movement [Frederick the Great of Prussia (1712-1786, reigned fr 1740) was a partisan of attacking a flank slantwise in this way rather than through parallel movements]
5. Ермо́лов — Ermolov [Алексе́й Петро́вич E. (1772-1861). A veteran of 1805 and 1807, in 1812 he was chief of staff of first army. Later on, from 1816 to 1827, he was commanding gen in Caucasus.]
6. произво́дство в не́мцы — promotion to [rank of a] G *(ironic)*
7. де́ятель *(m)* — doer
8. Ви́тебск — Vitebsk [Province capital on W Dvina Rv a few hundred miles W of M. F took it July 16/28.]
9. в Финля́ндии — [Barclay, in March 1809, had led a R corps across the ice of the Gulf of Bothnia to invade Sweden itself and to help force the peace whereby Sweden ceded Finland to R]
10. так не мо́жет итти́ — it can't go on like this
11. трутнево́й fr тру́тень *(m)*
12. оттруби́ть *(pf)* = протруби́ть

Three, I, 10

1. Мишо́ — Misho, or Michaud [граф Алекса́ндр Фра́нцевич М. де Боретур (1771-1841) colonel of engineers who entered R service fr Sardinian. Later, Kutuzov sent him to tsar with news that M had been abandoned.]
2. Че́рнышев — Chernyshev [светле́йший князь Алекса́ндр Ива́нович Ч. (1786-1857) gen, statesman, veteran of 1805 and 1807 campaigns. Later commanded partisans in 1812. War minister, 1827-1852. Chairman of State Council fr 1848 on.]
3. *s'wird was gescheites d'raus werden (G; ironic)* — sth clever will come of this

Three, I, 11

1. присове́товать *(pf, obs, coll)* = посове́товать *(pf)*

Three, I, 12

1. прилечу́ *(pf)* fr прилета́ть/ прилете́ть
2. Малоро́ссия *(obs)* — Little Russia [i.e. the Ukr]
3. отбыва́ть/ отбы́ть — to perform a duty *(here)*
4. Свенця́ны — Sventsiany [District town in Vilna Province, about 35 mi NE of Vilna]
5. сгоро́женный fr сгороди́ть *(pf, pop)* — to build sth any which way; to knock together (a building)
6. Рае́вский — Raevskii [Никола́й Никола́евич Р., Sr. (1771-1829) Commanding gen of 7th inf corps in Bagration's army. Later commanded famous Raevskii Redoubt at Borodino.]
7. Салта́новское сраже́ние — [At Saltanovka, near Mogilev, on June 11/23, 1812, there was a clash betw F under Davout and R under Raevskii]
8. пожима́ться/ пожа́ться — to huddle up
9. Фермопи́лы — Thermopylae [where a small band of Spartans under Leonidas, held up Persian army until destroyed in 480 B.C.]
10. сыновья́ Рае́вского — [Алекса́ндр (1795-1868) and Никола́й (1801-1843). The older was a пра́порщик in the 5th chasseurs in 1812; the younger in 1812 held the same rank in the Orël Inf. Regt. and then became a подпору́чик in his brother's regt. Several years later, Pushkin traveled S w R family on his way to his first exile. Pushkin's "Кавказский пленник" is dedicated to the younger Nikolai R. The older Nikolai R. denied to his adjutant, Batiushkov, on May 3, 1817, that he had sent his sons into battle. See *Сочинения К. Н. Батюшкова,* СПБ, 1887 г., стр. 388.]

Three, I, 13

1. хороши́! — fine fellows!
2. короли́ *(pl only)* — [a card game in which the "king" is the one who takes most tricks]
3. составля́ть па́ртию — to get up a game; to get the necessary no. of players together for a game

4. прохво́ст — booby prize
[5.] вспу́танный = спу́танный

Three, I, 14

1. Остро́вна — Ostrovna [Town in Mogilev Province, about 18 mi fr Vitebsk. A battle was to be fought here on July 13/25, 1812. w each side losing over 1,000 casualties, and the F continuing their advance. R troops included 4th corps, under Count A. I. Osterman–Tolstoi, of 1st army.]
2. заседа́ть/ засе́сть — to grow; to take root *(here)*
3. игре́невый — skewbald; red, w white mane and tail
4. взмы́ливаться/ взмы́литься — to froth at the mouth
5. дивизионе́р — commander of cavalry дивизио́н
6. перещёлкиваться/ перещёлкаться — to chop up one another with a clicking sound; to bang away at one another
7. трап-та-та-та — zing; rat-ta-tat [Onomatopoetic sound of bullets flying]
(8.) ра́нжевый *(obs)* = ора́нжевый — [The uhlans wore uniforms partly this color]

Three, I, 15

1. сомнём *(ft)* fr смять *(pf)*
2. заво́дная ло́шадь — reserve horse
3. бо́льше на́шего = бо́льше нас

Three, I, 16

1. второ́й план — background; position of secondary importance
2. бобо́ (R *children's language*) — sore; hurt place
3. котле́та — [dish gen made of ground or pounded meat]
4. Мудро́в — Mudrov [Матве́й Яковлевич M. (1772-1831). Physician and M Univ professor.]

Three, I, 17

1. Петро́вский пост — [The day of SS Peter and Paul was June 29. This fast began after Easter and went on to June 29. It could last 8 days to 6 weeks, depending on when Easter was.]
2. [свято́й] уго́дник — saint
3. отслу́шать *(pf, obs)* — to hear all of a rel service
4. [приобщи́ться *(pf)* has rel meaning whereas сообщи́ться *(pf)* does not]
5. зарезви́ться *(pf, coll)* — to start romping about, frolicking
6. поплева́ть *(pf)* — [Maude explains, R spit for good luck, as we touch wood]

Three, I, 18

Note: I am indebted to Dr. Christopher Wertz for his cogent explanations of the complexities in the following Church Slavic prayer. Students should remember 1) the infinitive in OCS tended to end in -ти rather than the modern R -ть 2) the acc in OCS is not like the gen, even when the word is animate.

1. Смоле́нск — [Smolensk would not fall until after the battle of August 5-6/17-18]
2. манифе́ст и воззва́ние — [On July 6, 1812, O.S., in Polotsk, Alexander issued a manifesto declaring war and appealed for a home guard]
3. домо́вый = дома́шний *(obs)*
4. перекивну́ться *(pf)* — to nod to one another
5. служи́ть *(impf)* — to officiate (at a rel svc); to serve
6. ца́рские две́ри = ца́рские врата́ — [In Orthodox churches, the central doors of iconostasis]
7. стиха́рь *(m)* — surplice; alb
8. ми́ром — in peace; w unity [Natasha understands it to mean "all together."]
9. свы́шний *(OCS)* — fr above
10. сино́д — Synod [R govt board overseeing R Orthodox Church and enjoying equal rights w Senate. Founded by Peter I in 1721 and consisting of high clergy appointed by tsar under chairmanship of Metropolitan of St P.]
11. ектенья́ — ectene [prayer said by deacon or priest fr pulpit to which worshippers respond. Prayer may be suppliant,

for the dead, or particular.]

12. ора́рь *(m)* — stole (of a deacon); a long ribbon worn by deacon over left shoulder during rel service
13. предава́ть/ преда́ть — to hand over; to give up
14. коленопреклонённый *(obs and high style)* — kneeling
15. Тро́ицын день — 50th day after Easter; Whitsunday (not Trinity Sunday!)
16. Бо́же *(old vocative case)* — oh, God
17. призре́ть *(OCS, pf, book)* — surround w care
18. на смиренные люди Твоя *(OCS)* = на смире́нных люде́й Твои́х
19. се = вот
20. смущаяй *(OCS)* = смуща́я
21. хотяй *(OCS)* = жела́я
22. положити вселенную всю пусту *(OCS)* = опустоши́ть всю вселе́нную
23. восста *(OCS)* = восста́л
24. ны *(OCS)* = нас
25. людие *(OCS)* = лю́ди
26. собрашася *(OCS)* = собрали́сь
27. еже *(OCS)* = что́бы
28. раскопати *(OCS)* — to tear up; to dig up
29. поругатися *(OCS)* = оскверни́ть *(pf)*
30. грешницы *(OCS)* = гре́шники
31. доколе употребити имать законопреступный власть? = как до́лго бу́дет у них престу́пная власть?
32. воздаждь *(OCS impv)* = возда́й [подаждь = пода́й also follows pattern of даждь = дай.]
33. бла́гость *(f; obs, book)* — kindness; mercy
34. Амалик or Амалек — Amalekites (cf. Exodus 17:8-17)
35. Гедеон на Мадиама — Gideon over the Midianites (cf. Numbers 31:9)
36. Давид на Голиафу — David over Goliath (cf. I Samuel 17:1-51)
37. медян *(OCS)* = ме́дный
38. препояши *(OCS, impv)* = опоя́сать *(pf)*
39. приими *(OCS, impv)* = прими́
40. мыслящии нам злая *(OCS)* = мы́слящие нам зло́е
41. да бу́дут = and let [them] be
42. лицем *(OCS)* = лицо́м
43. Ти *(OCS)* = Тебе́
44. яко *(OCS)* = как (*later:*= что́бы)

45. и Ангел Твой сильный да будет оскорбляяй и погоняй их — let Thine Angel be strong in hurting them and in driving them away.
46. приидет *(ft)* = придёт
47. юже = кото́рую [сеть]
48. сведают = зна́ют
49. их ловитва, юже сокрыша, да обымет их — let their trap, which they have concealed, catch them
50. ловитва = ло́вля
51. сокрыша = скры́ли
52. обымет = обни́мет fr обнима́ть/ обня́ть
53. попра́ние — complete destruction
54. вой (*OCS* or *obs*) — warriors; army
55. у Тебе *(OCS)* = у Тебя́
56. не изнеможет у Тебе спасати во многих и в малых — may thy salvation not be exhausted in the many and in the few (i.e. save both the many and the few) *(OCS)*
57. Ты еси Бог *(OCS)* — Thou art God
58. противовозможет *(OCS)* = противостои́т
59. противу *(OCS)* = про́тив
60. оте́ц *(OCS, gen pl)* = отцо́в
61. яже *(OCS)* = кото́рые
62. отвержи *(OCS, impv)* fr отверга́ть/ отве́ргнуть
63. ниже *(OCS)* — neither [shouldst Thou]
64. возгнушайся *(OCS, impv)* = гнуша́йся
65. велицей *(OCS)* = вели́кой
66. презри = пренебрега́ть/ пренебре́чь
67. грехи наша *(OCS)* = гре́хи на́ши
68. созижди *(OCS, impv)* = созда́й
69. утро́ба — life *(obs)*
70. Тя *(OCS)* = Тебя́
71. одержание *(OCS)* = власть; владе́ние
72. еже дал еси нам и отцем нашим = кото́рую Ты дал нам и отца́м на́шим
73. да не вознесется жезл нечестивых — may the sceptre of the unrighteous ones not rise up
74. жребие *(OCS)* = жре́бий
75. Твоея *(OCS)* = Твое́й
76. знаме́ние во благо — a favorable omen; a good omen
77. ненавидящии *(OCS)* = ненави́дящие
78. уведят *(OCS)* = узна́ют
79. возвесели́ть *(pf, obs, book)* — to make sth or smb merry
80. бо *(OCS)* = и́бо

81. еси *(OCS)* — art (fr быть, *pr, 2nd person sing*)
82. заступле́ние — intercession; defence
83. воссылаем *(OCS)* — we send up
84. присно *(OCS, obs, book)* — always
85. во ве́ки веко́в — forever more

Three, I, 19

1. Зде мудрость есть . . . *(OCS)* — "Here is wisdom. Let him that hath understanding count the number of the beast; for it is the number of a man; and his number is six hundred threescore and six." [Revelation 13:18.]
2. и даны быша ему уста . . . *(OCS)* — "And there was given unto him a mouth speaking great things and blasphemies; and power was given unto him to continue forty and two months." [Revelation 13:5]
3. *L'Empereur Napoléon* — [According to my addition, this totals 661. This could easily be corrected by changing the phrase to *le empereur Napoléon* or *L'Empereur Napoleone.*]
4. глаголати *(OCS)* — to speak
5. хульный *(OCS)* — blasphemous

Three, I, 20

1. сольфе́джи *(obs, pl)* = сольфе́джио *(indeclinable now)*
2. Оболе́нский — [R princely family]
3. в гуса́ры — [to join] the hussars
4. по де́сяти с ты́сячи — ten men per thousand
5. охло́пывать *(impf)* — to hit; to slap
6. шампиньо́н — mushroom [of type commonly sold in U.S.; apparently used here as malapropism for шпио́н]
7. ста́рый гриб — (*dial* or *pop; ironic* or *mocking*) — a puny old man
8. первопресто́льный *(obs)* — original; older [used only of M when govt was centered in St P]
9. уме́длить *(pf; coll)* — to slow up sth
10. у́ксусная соль — ammonium acetate [$C_2H_3O_2NH_4$. This has a sharp smell of both ammonia and acetic acid, and was then used as smelling salts to revive smb who had fainted]

Three, I, 21

1. Тро́ицкие воро́та — Troitskii or Trinity Gate [leads to Kremlin fr Alexander Garden]
2. лезть *(impf)* — to intrude; to get in the way
3. зати́скать *(pf, coll)* — to press; to squeeze
4. непрезента́бельный — unpresentable
5. Успе́нский собо́р — Uspenskii or Assumption Cathedral [About 250 or 300 yards fr Trinity Gate, and across fr stone palace built by Rastrelli for Elizaveta Petrovna in 1755. N later occupied it, and it burned down. The Great Kremlin Palace (built 1838-1849) stands on this spot now. R rulers were crowned there.]
6. царь пу́шка — Tsar Cannon [Still a Kremlin landmark, this was cast in 1586 and has a 40 inch bore. It is about 150 yards fr Trinity Gate at about a 45 degree angle fr way to Cathedral of the Assumption.]
7. серде́чный *(used as n)* — poor dear
8. собо́рне *(adv)* — church service performed by many priests w or without the bishop
9. бискви́т — sponge cake *(sometimes made w jam)* (*not* "biscuit"!) [Recipe is given in Molokhovets, p. 247, for бискви́т с вани́лью. The incident of the tsar and the sponge cake is fictitious.]
10. так и вы́шло — that's how it worked out

Three, I, 22

1. Слободско́й дворе́ц — [Building in Lefortovo District in E M. In Soviet times, a higher technical school.]

[2.] пристро́иваться *(impf, obs)* = пристра́иваться

3. у́зкий — tight *(of clothes)*
4. *états généraux (F)* — States General or Estates General [Traditionally, the F national assembly, composed of three estates: clergy, nobility, and commons. Louis XVI convoked the States-General of 1789 to solve his financial crisis; the commons took it over, defied the King and the F Revolution was underway.]
5. воево́да *(obs)* — [head of a town or small district in R fr 16th to end of 18th cent]
6. чеаёк *(phonetic)* = чаёк fr чай
7. смоля́нин — man fr Smolensk
8. госуда́ю — госуда́рю *(pronounced w back-*

of-throat "r")

9. буаро́дное = благоро́дное *(pronounced w back-of throat "r")*
10. гуса́й = госуда́рь *(pronounced w back-of-throat "r")*
11. мой многоуважа́емый . . . [Phrase from F parliamentary debate, alien to R tradition]
12. комюники́ровать *(pf)* — to communicate
13. ско́лько у нас во́йска . . . — [In real life, Pierre's question was asked by S.N. Glinka (*Istoriia Moskvy,* III, 82), who is mentioned here]
14. поруга́ть *(pf)* — to desecrate *(obs, book)*
15. сыны́ *(book)* = сыновья́
16. вот так, так! — to be sure!
17. Гли́нка — [Glinka. Серге́й Никола́евич Г. (1776-1847), writer and editor of M, anti-F monthly "Ру́сский ве́стник", which stood for official-style R patriotism, and was published fr 1808 to 1820 and again in 1824]
18. всё ни по чём [or нипочём] — we can face anything; we can take it

Three, I, 23

1. выставля́ть/ вы́ставить — to furnish
2. зашелести́ть *(pf, obs)* = зашелесте́ть *(pf)*
3. откупщи́к — [one who leases a govt. monopoly, such as of vodka, for a given area]
4. конституцио́нный — [and therefore possibly subversive of R autocracy]
5. Мамо́нов -- Mamonov [граф Матве́й Алекса́ндрович Дми́триев-М. (1790-1863). Son of a favorite of Catherine II, he outfitted at his own expense a cavalry regt, which fought well at Tarútino and at Maloiaroslávets.]
6. покря́хтывать *(impf)* — to grunt softly or fr time to time

Three, II, 1

1. отума́ниться *(pf)* — to lose one's common sense
2. тщесла́виться *(impf, obs)* — to boast; to show vanity
3. противу- *(obs)* = противо- *(first part of compound)*
4. предводи́ть *(impf, obs)* = предводи́тельствовать *(impf)*
5. военонача́льник — commander
6. Барклай . . . не́мец — [Any ethnic N European was termed a не́мец, not just a G]
7. утроя́ть *(impf, obs)* = утра́ивать *(impf)*
8. госуда́рев *(poss)* fr госуда́рь *(m)*
9. Любоми́рский — Liubomirskii or Lubomirski [князь Константин Ксавье́рович Л. (1786-1870). Aide-de-camp to tsar in 1812.]
10. Брани́цкий — Branitskii or Branicki [perhaps Владисла́в Ксавье́рович Б. (1782-1843). Aide-de-camp to tsar in 1812.]
11. Вло́цкий — Vlotskii or Włocki [Adjutant-Gen to tsar in 1812]
12. и тому́ подо́бные — [These three names just given are Polish]
13. во́ля госуда́ря — as the sovereign likes
14. не могу́ [рабо́тать] —
15. Неве́ровский — Neverovskii [Дми́трий Петро́вич Н. (1771-1813). R gen. He fell back fr Krasnoe NW to Smolensk w his 27th Div before superior F forces under Ney. Neverovskii fought well but lost most of his command in the actions of August 1-4/13-16.]

Three, II, 2

1. тебе́ то́лько и ну́жно бы́ло — that's all you needed *(ironic)*
2. я не могу́ слы́шать говори́ть — [Julie's letter has F turns of speech which sound odd in R, such as this one]
3. жидо́вский — Jewish *(obs); (used now only in pej)*
4. на войне́ как на войне́ — *(Gallicism) à la guerre, comme à la guerre (F)* — war has its own rules
5. ко́рпия — lint (used as bandaging material)
6. ро́степель *(f; dial or pop)* — thaw
7. должно́ [быть] — it must be

Three, II, 3

1. зо́лото-обре́зный — gilt-edged
2. е́жели что ну́жно — if sth is needed
3. споко́й *(pop)* = покой
4. виту́шка *(dim)* — sth w a twisted shape

(5.) росписно́й *(obs)* = расписно́й — w a design on it

6. Зу́бов — Zubov — [граф Плато́н Алекса́ндрович З. (1767- 1822) , a favorite of Catherine II]

Three, II, 4

1. закла́дывать/заложи́ть[бума́гой] — to stuff [papers] into sleigh bells so as to deaden their sound
2. сбо́ры — preparations *(for a journey)*
3. двои́ть *(impf)* — to plow a second time
4. зажина́ть *(impf, dial)* — to start reaping
5. покорми́в [лошаде́й]
6. креста́ на них нет *(obs, pop)* — they're no Christians; they've no conscience
7. э́то не шу́тки шути́ть *(impf)* — this is no joke
8. переве́шать *(pf)* — to hang all or many
9. да ну — not really; come on now [expresses surprise]
10. Аш — Ash or Asz or Asch [баро́н Казими́р Ива́нович А., governor of Smolensk fr 1807 to 1822]
11. запоте́лый — sweaty; perspiring
12. встрепыха́ться *(pf, pop)* — to rouse oneself; to shake one's wings
13. зача́ть *(pf, pop)* = нача́ть *(pf)*
14. сочтём *(pf)* fr счита́ть/ счесть
15. Дорогобу́ж — Dorogobuzh [Town on Dnieper, about 70 or 75 mi fr Smolensk on way to M]
16. куль *(m, obs)* — [9 poods or about 325 lbs.]
17. должно́ [быть] на́ша [а́рмия] взяла́ [верх]
18. наме́сь = на днях
19. Марина = Мере́йка — Mereika [Rv, right tributary of Dnieper in Smolensk Province]
20. чудотво́рная ико́на — [In the Успе́нский собо́р in Smolensk was a wonder-working icon of Mary attributed to St. Luke. It had come fr the Byzantine Gks.]

21. реши́ться *(pf, pop)* — to cease existing
22. Рассе́я *(subst)* = Росси́я
23. фризово́й or фри́зовый *(obs)* fr фриз *(obs)* — frieze *(cloth)*
24. Усвяж or Усвят — Usviazh or Usviat [Village in Velizh Uezd, nr W Dvina Rv, Smolensk Province]
25. пошла́ драть — the fighting has started

Three, II, 5

1. курча́вый — fleecy *(of clouds)*
2. на корню́ — on the stalk; unharvested
3. встолченный *(past, pass, prich)* fr встолочи́ть *(pf)* — to shake up; to fluff up; to cause dust to rise; to pulverize
4. валёк — a wooden bat used for beating clothes
5. англи́йский парк — E-style park [where trees etc. grow more or less in natural shapes rather than in the formal, geometric patterns of a F-style park]
6. вы́ставка — [open place where bees and hives are placed in summer, to catch the sunlight, along w (sometimes) hothouse plants]
7. обдёргать *(pf; pop)* — to pull off
8. си́живать *(impf, many-x)* fr сиде́ть *(impf)*
9. лы́чко fr лы́ко
10. житие́ — saint's life; hagiography
11. с се́рдцем — with annoyance
12. че́тверть *(f)* — [about 223 U.S. quarts or 210 litres (a pre-metric measure of volume used for grain); about 7 inches, or one-fourth of an *arshin [obs]*)
13. в ряза́нскую [дере́вню]
14. пища́ *(pr deep) fr* пища́ть *(impf)*
15. гик *(coll)* = ги́канье
16. у́ханье — saying "ookh"
17. Миха́йловка — Mikhailovka [Posting station in 1812 betw Smolensk and Dorogobuzh]
(18.) по напра́сну = понапра́сну
19. соглаша́ть/ согласи́ть (*obs* or *pop*) — to convince
20. но и того́ нет — but not even that
21. как быть — what is to be done
22. поста́вить *(pf)* — to consider; to suppose

Three, II, 6

1. разде́лывать/ разде́лать *(pf, pop)* — to commit violence against
2. распуска́ть/ распусти́ть слух — to start a rumor
3. Плута́рх — Plutarch [(ca. 46-120 A.D.). Gk biographer and essayist, whose *Parallel Lives* paired 46 Gk and Roman biographies]

(4.) он оста́нется не при чём — he will remain w nothing

5. Букаре́шт — Bucharest [Kutuzov had been one of Russia's main negotiators in the Treaty of Bucharest ending the war w Turkey on May 22, 1812 N.S.] (Now spelled Бухаре́ст.)
6. Лопу́хин — Lopukhin [князь Пётр Васи́льевич Л. (1744-1827). Under Catherine II, governor-gen. of Iaroslávl and Vólogda. Under Alexander, fr 1803 to 1810, minister of justice, chairman of state council and of committee of ministers.]
7. разнонача́лие — a split command; disunity in commanding
8. Жоко́нда — "La Joconde" [A supposedly improper tale by Jean de La Fontaine (1621-1695), F fable writer]

Three, II, 7

1. возвра́тность *(f)* — going back
2. Вя́зьма — Viaz'ma [Town on Viaz'ma Rv in Smolensk Province, about 110 mi fr Smolensk and 150 mi fr M]
3. Царёво-Займище — Tsarevo-Zaimishche [Village in Viaz'ma District, Smolensk Province, about 27 mi fr Viaz'ma on way to M, on Rivers Sezh and Liubigost'. This was where Barclay wanted to give battle, and where Kutuzov took command of the army.]
4. Бородино́ — Borodino [Village about 75 mi W of M where the great battle of the R campaign took place on Aug. 26/Sept. 7, 1812. F won a pyrrhic victory by capturing the battlefield, but suffering great losses while failing to destroy the R army. F call it the battle "de la Moskowa".]
5. Дон — Don [R rv, rising S of Tula, and flowing past Voronezh and Rostov-on-Don into Sea of Azov. Home of Don Cossacks.]
6. Янково — [Located at start of Three, II, 13 below as 15 versts fr fictitious Bogucharovo]

Three, II, 8

1. опу́щенность *(f)* — idleness; sloppiness; inertness; depression
2. попада́ться/ попа́сться ему́ на глаза́ — to let him catch sight of her; [for her] to set foot before him
3. три неде́ли — [Maude points out that LNT has slipped up here because the old Prince was well on Aug 5/17 (when Smolensk was bombarded) and died on Aug 15/27]
4. доро́гой fr доро́га
5. чему́ же быть? = что мо́жет быть? — what can happen?
6. же́нщины обмы́ли — [As was true elsewhere, in R too women prepared the corpse for burial in this way]
7. печа́тная моли́тва — [printed prayer to accompany corpse to grave at burial]

Three, II, 9

1. сно́сливость *(f)* — endurance; patience
2. подсобля́ть *(impf)* fr подсоби́ть *(pf)*
3. листы́ *(pl)* — edict
4. Пётр Фёдорович — Pētr Fēdorovich [Peter III (1728-1762). He became tsar on death of aunt, Elizaveta Petrovna, in 1762, and was deposed in favor of his wife, Catherine II, in 1762. Although he was murdered almost immediately, rumors persisted that he was still alive. His son and heir became Paul I only in 1796.]
5. казённый — belonging to the crown or state
6. обро́чные поме́щичьи [сёла] — villages belonging to private landowners whose serfs paid *obrók* (quit rent)
7. выкупа́ться/ вы́купиться — to buy [a serf's] freedom
8. мир — peasant commune
9. входи́ть/ войти́ в года́ *(obs)* — to grow old
10. бурми́стр *(obs)* — serf entrusted w management of an estate
11. ужи́н *(dial)* — amount of grain cut fr the fields
12. беско́рмщина = беско́рмица
13. княжни́н *(poss adj)* fr княжна́
14. взбуро́вить *(pf)* — to agitate; to work up

Three, II, 10

1. сафья́нный = сафья́новый — Morocco leather
2. плерéзы *(pl, obs)* — weepers; white strips worn on black clothing as a sign of mourning. *(F—pleureuses)*
3. Рамó — [According to Georges Six's book, the only F gen bearing a name similar to this who took part in R campaign was Gabriel-Pierre, vicomte de Rambourgt (1773-1848), who commanded 13th light cavalry brigade in Prince Eugène's IV Corps. But the name may be fictitious.]
4. чтóбы князь Андрéй знал — just let Prince Andrew know *(a wish)*
5. что бы они́ сказа́ли = что они́ сказа́ли бы
6. опа́вший fr опа́сть *(pf)*
7. пря́ники — [Viaz'ma was famous for its high-quality gingerbread]
8. каки́е лóшади бы́ли — what horses there were
9. как бы [нам] сами́м

(10.) в конéц = вконéц

11. бра́тнин *(poss adj)* fr брат — [Bogucharovo had been given to Andrew earlier]

Three, II, 11

1. мéсячина *(obs)* — [a month's pay given in kind and clothes by landowner to landless peasants working his fields]

Three, II, 12

1. дéвичьей *(dat)* fr дéвичья

Three, II, 13

1. перегоня́ться *(impf, obs, coll)* — to race one another
2. перегóнка — racing
3. и́зволок *(dial)* — elevation; gently sloping hillock; long incline
4. брать/ взять вперёд — to win (a game)
5. одина́кий (*obs* or *pop*) = одина́ковый

6. развесе . . . оо . . . ооо . . . лая = развесёлая
7. бе . . . се = бесéда — group *(obs or dial)*
8. чур — hands off
9. не отбивáть *(impf; pop)* — to interfere; to deprive smb of his wish; to take away
10. вы́прягут *(pf)* fr выпрягáть/ вы́прячь

Three, II, 14

1. шкýру спускáть/ спусти́ть *(pop)* — to give smb a bad beating; to beat the tar out of
2. *áли (obs, dial)* = и́ли
3. ни синь пóроха *(obs)* — nothing; not a trace
4. вот онá и вся *(subst)* = вот и всё
5. гладýх *(subst)* fr глáдкий — sleek; fat; plump [Dal' gives *f* only and calls it SW regionalism]
6. забри́ть *(pf)* — [to shave the beard of a peasant being sent by a landowner to the army]
7. откáзчик — refuser; denier
8. блюдём fr блюсти́ *(impf)*
9. знáчит *(coll)* — so; well *(a stalling word)*
10. рундýк *(dial)* — store-room
11. потрётся *(pf)* fr терéться/ потерéться
12. сенцó fr сéно
13. цепля́ть *(impf)* = цепля́ться *(impf)*
14. здорóвый — big
15. и нáдо бы́ло егó сестрé отказáть кня́зю Андрéю — [The incest prohibition of R orthodox church forbids a brother and sister of one family to marry a sister and brother of another family]

Three, II, 15

1. светлéйший *(obs)* — [title given to a князь of highest degree. Kutuzov had just been so named.]
2. усмехáться в усы́ — to laugh to himself
3. колбáсник — *lit*: sausage-maker; *fig*: a Kraut, G *(pej slang)* [There were many G on R staff]
4. отдувáться *(impf)* свои́ми бокáми — to pay for someone else's error; to be the fall guy
5. партизáнский — [A word which, ironically,

entered R fr F. In real life, one of those who started partisan warfare in R against F was Denis Davydov.]

6. сам — himself *(in the Irish sense);* the chief
7. расплыва́ться/ расплы́ться *(coll)* — to grow very fat or corpulent
8. фю-фю — [onomatopoetic sound representing smb whistling]
9. представи́тельство — making a good impression *(obs)*
10. ныря́ть *(impf)* — to move across an uneven surface
11. что оте́ц — what is new w your father
12. ца́рство ему́ небе́сное — God rest his soul; may he rest in peace
13. обер-интенда́нт — senior supply officer
14. Коновни́цын — Konovnitsyn [граф Пётр Петро́вич К. (1764-1822) In 1812, he commanded a division and then the R rear-guard during R retreat. At Borodino, he replaced the mortally wounded Bagration briefly, and was replaced by Dokhturov. After Borodino, he was a senior assistant of Kutuzov's. War Minister, 1815-1819.]
15. кана́т — combed yarn, used for ears instead of cotton *(obs)*

Three, II, 16

1. заложи́ть *(pf)* ножо́м — to use a knife as a bookmark
2. свёртывать/ сверну́ть — *lit*: to fold; *fig*: to close
3. "Les Chevaliers du Cygne" — [Novel from 1795]
4. дай срок — just wait
5. был слаб на слёзы — had a weakness for crying or tears
6. иди́ с Бо́гом! — go, and God be with you!
7. Рущук — Rushchuk [Turkish fortress in what is now Bulgaria. N. Kamenskii's attempt to storm it on July 22, 1810, O.S. failed, with 20,000 R casualties.]
8. захли́пать *(pf)* — to start sobbing

Three, II, 17

1. Растóпчинские афи́шки — [As governor-gen of M, R published various things both in "Московские ведомости" and separately. His aim was to arouse patriotism by giving the news in the best light. LNT cites *afishka* fr July 1, 1812, O.S. Karniushka Chikhirin was the hero of these things.]
2. целовáльник *(obs)* — innkeeper; keeper of shop where food and drink are sold
3. крючóк — a drink of vodka *(obs, pop)*
4. тычóк *(Siberian dial)* — tavern
5. Васи́лий Львóвич Пу́шкин — V.L. Pushkin [(1770-1830). Minor poet and uncle of Aleksandr Pushkin. Wrote patriotic verse in 1812, e.g. "К жителям Нижнего Новгорода".]
6. раздýются *(pf, ft)* fr раздувáться/ раздýться
7. перелóпаться *(pf)* — to burst *(of many or all)*
8. Харóн — Charon [Gk mythology. Ferried souls of dead across Styx Rv to Hades.]
9. ничегó не бýдет брáть — will not charge anything
10. когдá говоря́т о сóлнце—ви́дят егó лучи́ — speak of the devil! *(said when person being talked about unexpectedly turns up).*
11. Иоáнна д'Арк = Жáнна д'Арк — Joan of Arc [(1412-1431). She started to force the E out of F and is the most famous female soldier in history.]
12. Бéлая Цéрковь *(f)* — [Town in what is now Ukr, 60 mi SW of Kiev, and thus, far S of F invasion route]

Three, II, 18

1. Виттгенштейн — Vittgenshtein or Wittgenstein [граф Пётр Христиáнович В. (1768-1842), генерáл-фельдмáршал. In 1812, he commanded I corps of 25,000 men protecting the road to St P. At Kliastitsy, on July 30, 1812, N.S. his subordinate, A.P. Kul'nev (in charge of R rearguard), attacked and defeated Marshal Oudinot. Kul'nev himself was killed the next day, when F won.]
2. конфýзно — uncomfortably; awkwardly
3. какóй бы там [он] ни был
4. съéзжая *(obs)* — detention room in police station
5. долюбéзничаться *(obs)* — to be the consequence of compliments
6. сходи́ться/ сойти́сь *(pop)* — to work out; to come out

7. Воронцóво — Vorontsóvo [Village about 4 mi past Kaluga Gate of M]
8. Леппих — Leppich [Franz Leppich, also known as Smit, was a Dutchman in M who assured Rostopchin that he could build a balloon to take him over N's forces and destroy them. When he had offered the balloon to N in 1811, N ordered him deported. The balloon leaked too much gas ever to fly, and Leppich disappeared.]
9. Болóтная плóщадь — [On S shore of island in M Rv just S of SW corner of Kremlin]
10. кобы́ла — stocks *(used for punishment) (obs)*
11. Лóбное мéсто — [Stone, round, small elevation on Red Sq in M fr which important official announcements were made in pre-Petrine M and where Peter I executed *strel'tsy* in a group]
12. мусьó *(subst)* — monseer [fr *monsieur.* Used for F]
13. ки́сел fr ки́слый
14. Лубя́нка — [Sq about half a mile NE of Red Sq in M. Also st off that sq.]
15. Можáйск — Mozhaisk [Town about 70 mi W of M where Mozhaika Rv and Shelkovka Rv fall into M Rv]
16. Перхýшково — Perkhushkovo [Village in Zvenigorod District, M Province, about 20 mi fr M, which had a posting station]
17. Шевáрдино — Shevardino — [Village within walking distance of Borodinó. Two days before Battle of Borodinó, F stormed R redoubt there.]

Three, II, 19

1. Ути́ца — Utitsa [Village on what was then Smolensk—M Road, about 3 mi fr Borodino, and half that distance fr Shevardino. Other villages on LNT's map will not be identified here. Nor will rivers.]
2. Гри́днево — Gridnevo [Village in Mozhaisk District, M Province, nr Borodino]
3. Понятóвский — Poniatowski [Prince Józef P. (1763-1813). Nephew of Stanisław Augustus, last King of P. Himself a P gen, he commanded P Corps in N's army]

Three, II, 20

1. собо́р — [Cathedral of St. Nicholas, dating fr 16th cent, dominated Mozhaisk]
[2.] пе́сельник (*obs* or *dial*) = пе́сенник
3. гря́дка — edge of chassis of a wagon
4. что́бы они́ держа́ли к одно́й [стороне́ доро́ги]
5. скопа́ть *(pf)* — to dig out; to shovel away
6. шине́ный fr шини́ть *(obs)* — to put a tire on
7. вбра́ться/ взя́ться за [что] — to touch [sth]
8. запропа́сть *(pf, pop)* — to be doomed
9. Ах, запропа́ла да ежо́ва голова́ — [fr song "Загуляла тут ежова голова". Cf. Б. и Ю. Соколовы, *Сказки и песни Белозерского края,* М. 1915 г., с. 494 ("Юмористические песни", № 659) .]
10. часть *(f.)* — specialty
11. косо́й во́рот — a standing collar, buttoned on the side

Three, II, 21

1. Коло́цкий монасты́рь *(m)* — [Monastery on Kolocha Rv]
2. низо́чек fr низ
3. спра́ва от Москвы́ [реки́]
4. досчита́ться *(pf)* — [to find smb present at roll-call]
5. я так — I'm just looking (talking, passing by, etc)
6. Иверская [Часо́вня]
7. тур — gabion
8. зажгли́ *(past)* fr заже́чь *(pf)*
9. спаси от бед рабы твоя, Богородице — *(OCS)* — Oh, Mother of God, save your slaves fr misfortunes [A troparion or short hymn of R Orthodox Church]
10. яко вси по Бозе к Тебе прибегаем, яко нерушимой стене и предстательству *(OCS)* — For, after God, we all resort to Thee as to an indestructible wall, and protection
11. топча́сь *(pf, deep)* fr топта́ться *(impf)*

Three, II, 22

1. Ка́йсаров — Kaisarov [Паи́сий Серге́евич К. (1783-1844). R gen. In 1812 was on Kutuzov's staff, and later commanded forward troops. Later, commanded an infantry corps.]
2. неоцене́нный *(obs)* = неоцени́мый
3. меня́ не убу́дет *(pop)* — it won't hurt me any
(4.) съу́живаться = су́живаться
5. прива́л — halting place; quarters
6. к ва́шим услу́гам — at your service
7. Ка́йсаров — Kaisarov [Андре́й Серге́евич К. (1782-1813) Professor of R at Dorpat (Tartu) University. Writer. Brother of gen. Killed at Hanau in G.]
8. Ма́рин — Marin [Серге́й Ники́форович М. (1775-1813). Aide-de-camp to tsar. Known for satiric verses and parodies. One parody was "На Геракова".]
9. Гераков — Gerakov [Гаврии́л Васи́льевич Г. (1775-1838) teacher and writer of Gk descent. Taught history in First Cadet Corps in St P. Wrote untalented but very patriotic pieces.]

Three, II, 23

1. ко́лча *(dial)* — small pile of congealed mud
2. флеш or флешь — flèche [an arrow-shaped fortification built on open field w sides making an obtuse angle]
3. Тучко́в — Tuchkov [Никола́й Андре́евич Т. (1761-1812). R gen, veteran of 1799, 1807 and 1808 campaigns. Fatally wounded at Borodino, where he commanded III infantry corps.]
4. усумни́ться *(pf, obs)* = усомни́ться *(pf)*

Three, II, 24

1. су́чья *(nom pl)* fr сук
2. как не́жный голубо́к ба́сни — [Andrei may have had in mind any of the following: 1) "Les deux pigeons," Book IX, Fable 2 fr the *Fables* (1678) of Jean de La Fontaine (1621-1695); of course, Andrei knew F; 2) "Два го́лубя" (1809), Book I, Fable 18, by Ива́н Андре́евич Крыло́в (1769-1844), a tr of the F fable; 3) "Два го́лубя" (1795), an earlier tr of F fable by Ива́н Ива́нович Дми́триев (1760-

1837), or 4) "Сто́нет си́зый голубо́чек" (1792), a poem on the same theme by the same Dmitriev. Perhaps the best version in E is "The Two Doves," in *The Fables of La Fontaine,* tr by Marianne Moore, N.Y., 1954, pp. 208-211.]

3. что́бы меня́ уби́ли *(a wish)* — let them kill me

Three, II, 25

(1.) т.е. = то есть — that is; i.e.

2. не смей [,нам сказа́ли]
3. Кла́узевиц — Clausewitz [Karl von C. (1780-1831). Prussian gen, then in R service, which he entered as Phull's adjutant. In 1818, he was appointed head of Prussian War School. His book, *Von Kriege* (published posthumously, 1832-1837; E tr *On War,* 1873), set forth doctrine of total war against enemy civilians and territory as well as army and became very influential in mil theory. His memoirs of R campaign in 1812 were published separately in E as *The Campaign of 1812 in R,* London, 1843; this tr was reprinted in Hattiesburg, Mississippi, in 1970.]
4. парламентёрство fr парламентёр
5. вестфа́лец — Westphalian [Region around Münster. N created Kingdom of Westphalia for brother Jérome. Today, part of N Rhine-Westphalia state in W Germany. Much of N's army invading R was composed of non-F (especially G) soldiers.]
6. ге́ссенец — Hessian [Hessia is region on Main and Rhine rivers. Part of it was given by N to brother Jérome for Kingdom of Westphalia. Today it is in W G, divided betw states of Hessia and Rhineland-Palatinate.]
7. война́ так война́ — war is war
8. дре́во позна́ния — tree of knowledge [Genesis 3]
9. пче́льник — beekeeper

(10.) обжо́г = обжёг *(past, pf, m)* fr обжига́ть/ обже́чь

Three, II, 26

1. Beausset or Bossuet — [Louis-François-Joseph de B. (1770-1835). Prefect of N's palace fr 1805. Later, B. wrote, *Mémoires anecdotiques sur l'intérieur du Palais et sur quelques événemens de l'Empire depuis 1805 jusq'au l-er mai 1814 pour servir à l'histoire de Napoléon* (Anecdotal Memoirs on the Inside of the Palace and on some

Events of the Empire from 1805 to May 1, 1814, to use in the History of Napoleon) (Paris, 1827-1829, 4 vols.). LNT used this work in *W&P*.]

2. Fabvier — [F colonel who, acc to Thiers, reported to N that day about Battle of Salamanca in Spain]
3. пожима́ться *(impf)* — to twitch
4. го́рба́титься *(impf, coll)* = го́рбиться *(impf)*
5. Салама́нка — [At Salamanca, on July 22, 1812, N.S., Wellington's Anglo-Spanish-Portuguese army won a limited victory over the F under Marshal Marmont. Thiers states that this began the ruin of F affairs in Spain. The F, acc. to Tarlé, (p. 185) had twice as many troops in Spain as at Borodino.]
6. подра́ть *(pf, coll)* — to tweak
7. Жера́р — Gérard [François-Pascal Simon, Baron G. (1770-1837) F portrait painter. Pupil of Jacques Louis David (1748-1825).]
8. Сиксти́нская мадо́нна — Sistine Madonna [Famous portrait of Mary and baby Jesus painted by Raphael in 1518 and in gallery at Dresden, E G]
9. коро́ль Ри́мский — The King of Rome [(1811-1832). Title given by N to his son, the grandson of Emperor Franz of Austria. Later called Duke of Reichstadt.]
10. бильбоке́ *(indecl)* — cup and ball *(toy)*; bilboquet

(11.) ци́почка = цы́почка

Three, II, 27

1. Компан — Compans [Count Jean-Dominic C. (1769-1845). F gen. Commanded div. under Davout at Borodino, where he was wounded and therefore replaced.]
2. Ней — Ney [Michel N. (1762-1815). F marshall. Commanded first a corps then F rearguard in R. Made Duke of Elchingen in 1808 and Prince "de la Moskowa" after Borodino. Went over to Louis XVIII in 1814 but returned to N in time to lead last charge of Old Guard at Waterloo. Sentenced to death and executed after return of Louis XVIII.]
3. за́втрему fr за́втрие *(obs)* = за́втра
4. Пернетти — Pernety [Joseph-Marie, Viscount de P. (1766-1856). Commanded F I Corps artillery in R.]
5. Дессе — Dessaix [Joseph-Marie, Count D. (1764-1834). F gen. Commanded div on right under Davout at Borodino.]

6. Фриан — Friant [Count Louis F. (1758-1829). F gen. Veteran of 1805, 1806, 1807, and 1809 campaigns. Served under Davout at Borodino, where he was carried off the field, wounded.]
7. фуше — Foucher [Count Louis-François F. de Careil (1762-1835) F gen. Commanded III Corps artillery of Marshall Ney at Borodino.]
8. Сорбье — Sorbier [Jean-Barthélemy S. (1762-1827). F gen. Commanded Guards artillery at Borodino.]
9. Моран — Morand [Count Charles-Alexis-Louis-Antoine M. (1771-1835). F gen. Commanded division in center at Borodino, where he was badly wounded.]
10. вице-коро́ль — Viceroy [Eugène de Beauharnais (1781-1824). F gen and N's stepson by first marriage. Made Viceroy of Italy by N in 1805.]
11. Жерар — Gérard [Count Etienne-Maurice G. (1773-1852). F gen. At Borodino. Commanded a brigade and then a division. Named marshall in 1830.]
12. вы́равняться *(pf, obs)* fr выра́вниваться/ вы́ровняться
13. всего́ — in all; totaling
14. по-пусто́му = по́пусту
15. диви́зии же — but the divisions

Three, II, 28

1. на́сморк — [Thiers states that N's cold did *not* paralyze his intellect at Borodino]
2. Варфоломе́евская ночь — [St. Bartholomew's Day massacre took place on night before August 24, 1572. Catherine de' Medici, mother of King Charles IX and former regent, plotted to assassinate Protestants visiting Paris then to attend wedding of their champion, Henry of Navarre. Many Protestants were murdered and the Fourth Religious War ensued.]
3. Карл IX — Charles IX [(1550-1574). King of F. Persuaded by mother to sanction St. Bartholomew Day's massacre. (Reigned fr 1560 to death.)]

Three, II, 29

1. Рапп — Rapp [Count Jean R. (1772-

1821). F gen. N's adjutant (1800-1814). Warded off attempted assassination of N by G student, Friedrich Staps, in 1809. Wounded five times and put out of action at Borodino after replacing Gen Compans. Replaced by Gen Dessaix as temporary commander of Compans's division.]

2. пасти́лька — lozenge
3. принюхиваться *(impf)* = принюхаться *(pf)*
4. Корвизар — Corvisart [Baron Jean-Nicolas C. des Marets (1755-1821). Famous F physician and medical author. Chief physician to N.]
5. слы́шный — perceptible (*not* just "audible")

Three, II, 30

1. повыходи́ть/ повы́йти — to go out *(used of all or many)*
2. прорыси́ть *(pf)* — to trot past
3. вы́сеченный *(pf, past, pass, prich)* fr высека́ть/ вы́сечь
4. Во́йна — Voina [Rv]
5. расплыва́ться/ расплы́ться — to spread; to be diffused
6. гуртово́й fr гурт

(7.) разростя́сь *(pf, obs, pr, deep)* fr разраста́ться/ разрасти́сь

8. посмирне́е *(comp)* fr сми́рный

Three, II, 31

1. то́пчущий *(impf; pr, deep)* fr топта́ть *(impf)*

[2.] посерёд *(subst)* = посреди́

3. вле́во возьми́ — go left; bear left
4. жарня́ *(obs)* — a hot fight
5. бреду́щий *(pf deep)* fr брести́ *(impf)*
6. несо́мый *(pr, pass, deep)* fr нести́
7. подвёртывать/ подверну́ть — to twist
8. курга́н Рае́вского — [Raevskii's mound battery in center of line became one of focal points of fighting at Borodino. The F finally took it w great cost in life on both sides and beat off a R counter-attack.]
9. присва́ивать/ присво́ить — to accept [him] as one of their own
10. красноро́жий fr кра́сная ро́жа
11. как же? — didn't you know that?

[Anticipating answer "коне́чно!".]

12. шмя́кать/ шмя́кнуть — to squish; to thud
13. так кишки́ вон — and your guts spill out
14. на́ше де́ло солда́тское — we're soldiers, and that's our job
15. вот так ба́рин! — what a brave gentleman! *(expresses pleasure and encouragement)*
16. фо́рменность *(f, obs, coll)* — official behavior; formality
17. чине́нка — a live shell; a bomb stuffed w sth
18. дружне́е fr дру́жный
19. по-бурла́цки — in бурлак style [i.e. all together; as a team]
20. заколя́ниться *(pf, obs)* — to lag behind [cf. *Словарь русского языка,* 2-й том, выпуск 4-й, СПБ., Имп. Акад. Наук, 1900, col. 1228.]
21. тое кое — such-and-such *(swearing)*
22. неу́бранный — not picked up; not taken away
23. обожжённый *(pf, past, pass, prich)* fr обжига́ть/ обже́чь

Three, II, 32 — none

Three, II, 33

1. флéши Багратио́на — [Bagration's flèches were on the R left nr Semēnovskoe]
2. в полови́не дня — at midday
3. столкнове́ние Понято́вского с Тучко́вым — [Poniatowski seized the heights of Utítsa fr Tuchkóv, who had been killed, and temporarily opened the R left to the F, but news of Uvarov's raid precluded the F fr following up this advantage]

Three, II, 34

1. стро́йный — evenly lined up; in good order
2. Клапаред — Claparède [Michel C. (1774-1841), F gen. Commanded division at Borodino.]
3. забра́ние fr забира́ть/ забра́ть
4. Лоди — Lodi [Town in N Italy on Adda Rv where N defeated Austrians on May 10, 1796, N.S. during Italian

campaign of 1796-1797, for his first great battlefield victory]

5. Маренго — Marengo [Village in NW Italy where N won a brilliant victory over Austrians under Melas on June 14, 1800, N.S.]
6. Ваграм — Wagram [Town in Austria NE of Vienna where N defeated Austrians on July 5-6, 1809, N.S.]

Three, II, 35

1. принц Виртемберский — Duke of Württemberg [Alexander-Friedrich, Duke of W (1771-1833) brother of tsar Alexander's mother, had entered R service in 1800]
2. Щерби́нин — Shcherbínin [R family of old gentry]
3. избежа́ние fr избега́ть — избежа́ть/ избе́гнуть

Three, II, 36

1. ста́птывать/ стопта́ть *(coll)* — to trample
2. бубу́хать *(impf)* fr бу́хать *(impf)*
3. распоро́шить = распору́шать/ распору́шить *(obs)* — to demolish; to crumble
4. размина́ть/ разма́ть — to soften sth by rubbing it
5. калмы́жка — clump of dirt
6. плетёночка — a woven basket
7. заступи́ть *(pf)* — to press sth down w one's foot
8. шарша́вить *(obs)* = шерша́вить *(impf, coll)* — to make sth rough
9. ошмуры́гивать — to take off [the flowers in one motion]
10. береги́сь *(impv)* fr бере́чься *(impf)*
11. срони́ть *(pf; coll)* — to drop

[12.] всхра́пывать *(impf, coll)* — to snort fr time to time

13. мужичьё *(obs, pop, w a shade pej)* = мужики́
14. подла́живать/ подла́дить — to be or to act in harmony w others
15. Хвёдор *(N dial)* = Фёдор
16. хребту́г *(dial)* — feed-bag attached to shaft for harnessed horse
17. оттéда *(subst)* = отту́да
18. долбану́ть *(pf)* — to give a strong blow; to hit hard

19. побраса́ть *(phonetic spelling)* = поброса́ть *(pf)*
20. лезе́рвы *(subst)* = резе́рвы
21. бра́тец ты мой — old pal; my dear friend
22. зва́ния не оста́лось — not a trace remains; there is nothing left [of him]

Three, II, 37

1. тот свет — the other world
2. рва́ться *(impf)* — to strain to get loose

Three, II, 38

1. расслу́шать *(pf, coll)* — to listen properly; to hear sth properly
2. ходи́ть/ идти́ на приво́де — to walk a treadmill
3. ско́лько прихо́дится ру́сских на одного́ францу́за — how many R each F cost
4. распростране́ние — aggrandizement
5. рассева́ть *(impf)* = рассе́ивать *(impf)*
6. виртембу́ргец — Württemberger [Württemberg is a former state in SW Germany, w Stuttgart its capital. Now part of Baden-Württemberg in W Germany.]
7. мекленбу́ргец — Mecklenburger [Mecklenburg was a Grand Duchy on Baltic Sea N of Berlin, including cities of Rostock and Stralsund. Now in E Germany.]
8. пьемо́нец — Piedmontese [Piedmont is in NW Italy along F and Swiss borders, w Turin its capital. Fr 1798 to 1814, it was annexed to France.]
9. тоска́нец — Tuscan [Tuscany is in central Italy along Tyrrhenian Sea, and includes Florence, Leghorn, etc.]
10. жи́тели 32-й вое́нной диви́зии — [Mainly Hamburg and Bremen on the N Sea in NW G]
11. Калиш — Kalisz or Kalisch [Provincial capital in W Poland on way from Wrocław (Breslau) to Warsaw. On Prosna Rv. In N's time, last town in R empire before Prussia.]

Three, II, 39

1. Давы́довы — [See Давы́дов, Four, III, 3 below]
2. казённый крестья́нин — peasant belonging to the state [rather than to a landowner]
3. куда́ попа́ло — in any direction
4. расплю́скивать = расплю́щивать/ расплю́щить — to flatten, to crush
5. вде́сятеро-ме́ньше — one tenth as many

Three, III, 1

1. како́й бы то ни был — whatever; any kind
2. восстановля́ться *(impf)* = восстана́вливаться *(impf)*

Three, III, 2

1. двуна́десят = двана́десять языко́в *(obs, set phrase)* — the twelve nations which invaded R under N in 1812.

(2.) нароста́ть *(impf, obs)* = нараста́ть *(impf)*

3. Калу́жская доро́га — [The road fr M to Kaluga, on the Oká, S by SW of M]
4. Ма́ло-Яросла́вец or Малояросла́вец — Maloiaroslavets [Town about 75 mi fr M on way to Kiev. On Oct. 11/12, 1812, O.S., N was stopped here and forced to leave R by the road he had devastated in his invasion.]
5. Березина́ — Berezina [Left tributary of Dnieper Rv, about one third of a mile wide at Studēnka (8 mi NW of Borisov) where F retreat crossed it on Nov 14-17/26-29. R under Wittgenstein and Chichagov attacked stragglers on Nov 16/28. Kutuzov arrived a few days later. Battle there, in freezing weather, is often considered final one of N's R campaign.]
6. Фили́ *(pl)* — Fili [Village about 1.5 miles fr old Dorogomílovskaia Zastáva (in M) on road W to Mozhaisk. Here on September 1/13, 1812, R decided to evacuate M.]
7. сбива́ть/ сбить — to knock away

Three, III, 3

1. Поклóнная горá — [Hill 4 miles SW of M past Dorogomílovskaia Zastáva (in M) on way W to Mozhaisk]
2. Сарагóсса — Saragossa [City in NE Spain on Ebro Rv. It withstood first F siege (1808) but, after losing 50,000 men, surrendered to second F siege on Feb. 20, 1809, N.S. F still had to take it by force.]

Three, III, 4

1. лýчший — very good *(comp used as emph posit)*
2. крáсный ýгол *(obs)* — [corner of a room beneath the icons where the table was and where honored guests were seated]
3. егó ломáло *(impf only)* fr ломáть *(impf)* — he was in pain
4. откачнýться *(pf; coll)* — to slouch back
5. в ночи́ *(obs)* = нóчью
6. длиннопóлый — having a coat w long tails; long-coated

(7.) палáти *(f pl)* = полáти

8. тóлько бы — if only *(a wish)*

Three, III, 5

1. бóлее важнéйший = бóлее вáжный
2. Иверская [богорóдица]
3. Три Гóры = Тригóрная застáва — [Place in what was then outskirts of M, on S. On Sept. 1, O.S. Rostopchin called for people to meet there to "destroy" F.]
4. шути́ха *(f)* fr шут
5. сарáтовский fr Сарáтов — Saratov [Town and province on W bank of lower Volga]
6. Августин — Avgustin or Augustin [Алексéй Васи́льевич Виногрáдский (1766-1819), called A. in rel. Preacher and rel writer. *De facto* head of M eparchy because of age of Metropolitan Platón Levshin (1737-1812). A. was then Bishop of Dmitrovo, and became Archbishop of M & Kolomna in 1818.]
7. Ключарёв — Kliucharev [Фёдор Петрóвич К. (1754-ca. 1825) Mystic writer and mason, friend of N.I. Novikov

in youth. Became director of M post-office in 1799. Aroused Rostopchin's wrath by trying to intercede for Vereshchagin. (See Three, III, 10 below.) Rostopchin removed K fr post-office on suspicion of Martinism. Later, in 1815, tsar named K a Senator.]

Three, III, 6

1. Общество Иису́сово — Society of Jesus (Jesuits) [The Jesuit gen fr 1805 to 1820, was Tadeusz Brzozowski, a Pole]
2. Ка́менный Остров — [Island in Neva Delta, where St P rich had summer places a couple of miles fr Winter Palace]
3. короткопо́лый Иезуи́т or иезуи́т в коро́тком пла́тье — *à robe courte* [Jesuits were not expelled fr St P and M until 1813 and fr R until 1820. Jesuits *à robe courte* were lay members of the Order who wore ordinary civilian clothes.]

(4.) долгопо́лый = длиннопо́лый *(i.e. in priestly cassock)*

5. па́па — the pope
6. Колу́мбово яйцо́ — Columbus's egg [The phrase means to solve a complicated question boldly and resourcefully, and is also used in F and G. Acc to tradition, Columbus stood an egg up on a table after smb else was not able to do so.]

Three, III, 7

1. вы́йти за́муж от живо́го му́жа — to take a husband while her husband was alive
2. упережа́ть/ упереди́ть — to leave behind; to outstrip
3. разво́дный — divorced
4. сде́рживать/ сдержа́ть сло́во — to keep one's word

Three, III, 8

1. кавардачо́к fr кавардá́к — a soupy mixture of meat or fish, plus flour, etc.
2. куды́ *(subst)* = куда́
3. ты, ста́ло [быть], ба́рин
4. на полови́не горы́ — halfway up the hill
5. прощава́й *(subst)* = проща́й
6. кажи́сь (*pop* or *dial*) = ка́жется

Three, III, 9

1. изна́нка — the hidden side
(2.) на яву́ = наяву́
3. сопряга́ть *(impf, book)* — to tie together

Three, III, 10

1. Васи́льчиков — Vasil'chikov [Perhaps князь Илларио́н Васи́льевич В. (1777-1847). R Adjutant-Gen. Wounded at Borodino. Was in rear guard of Second Army. Later commanded IV cavalry corps. Still later was chairman of State Council and of Committee of Ministers.]
2. разберёмся *(pf ft)* fr
разбира́ться/ разобра́ться с (+ *instr*) — to handle; to deal w; to cope w
3. ви́лы-тройча́тки *(pl)* — pitchfork w three equal parts
4. Екатери́нинская го́шпиталь — [On site of present-day Страстно́й бульва́р, № 15/29]
5. чу́йка *(obs)* — [man's cloth overcoat which reached knees, it was worn up to early 20th century]
6. Вереща́гин — Vereshchagin [Михаи́л Никола́евич В. (1790-1812) Merchant's son. In 1812, he supposedly tr fr *Hamburg Gazette* N's letter to King of Prussia and alleged speech to princes of the Confederation of the Rhine, for which Rostopchin accused him of treason. V was jailed on July 17, O.S., and sentenced to exile forever in Nerchinsk, E Siberia. On August 19, O.S., Senate added 25 lashes to this. On September 2, O.S., Rostopchin ordered two non-coms to kill V. for alleged treason. This was done. Tarlé thinks V. wrote the alleged tr himself and may have been insane.]
7. я́ма — prison *(obs)*
(8.) недоучёный = недоу́ченный — half-learned; insufficiently learned
9. ку́пчик *(coll)* — young merchant
10. ста́чка *(pop)* — collusion
11. стать на э́том *(pf)* — to refuse to budge
12. ему́ чорт не брат — he is as cocky as hell; he doesn't give a damn for anything
13. Ка́менный мост — [Bridge across M Rv just SW of Kremlin, built in 17th cent and replaced by iron bridge in 1859]
14. Вседержи́тель or вседержи́тель *(m)* — Almighty

Three, III, 11

[1.] достосла́вный — glorious; famous
2. подъём — going; traveling
3. гро́мче пре́жнего = гро́мче чем пре́жнее

Three, III, 12

1. де́йствующий полк — regiment at front
2. пушо́к fr пух
3. повы́ехать *(pf, coll)* — to go out *(of all or many)*
4. разне́жничаться *(pf, coll)* — to become too aff
5. передава́ться/ переда́ться — to be transmitted
6. мазь *(f)* — grease

Three, III, 13

1. перекли́киваться (*impf, obs* or *pop*) = перекликáться *(impf)*
2. киби́точка *(dim)* fr киби́тка — hood of a carriage *(obs)*
3. вот бы хоть к нам — you might even come to our place
4. мамзе́ль *(f, obs, pop)* — mamzel; miss *(F mademoiselle)*
5. переходи́ть/ перейти́ — to move fr one place to another
6. холосто́й — uninhabited *(building)*
7. го́фманские ка́пли — Hoffman's drops [Much used in R as a tranquilizer. They contained 1 part by weight of purified sulfur ether and 2 or 3 parts of ethyl alcohol. They were named for Dr. Friedrich Hoffmann (1660-1742).]
8. досиде́ться *(pf)* — to stay too long and thereby incur unpleasant consequences

Three, III, 14

1. Мясни́цкая у́лица — [A main st of M going NE fr Lubianskaia Sq]
2. *gobelin (F)* — Gobelin tapestries [made by F state in Paris since 1662]
3. ки́евские таре́лки — [Perhaps fr Межегорьевский porcelain factory in Kiev]
4. саксо́нские блю́да — [Perhaps fr Meissen in Saxony; this fine china is called "Dresden" in E]

5. распуска́ться/ распусти́ться — to get loose
6. ча́ем fr ча́ять *(impf)*
7. Иису́се Христе́! — oh, Jesus Christ! *(old vocative case)*

Three, III, 15

1. бла́говестить/ отбла́говестить — to ring bells for church
(2.) и́з полу = и́сполу — charging half the value of the thing itself; going fifty-fifty w owner as payment
3. ба́рышнин *(poss adj)* fr ба́рышня
4. [дать . . . подво́ды] под ра́неных — for the wounded
5. о чём вы это [говори́те]

Three, III, 16

1. Анна на ше́е — [Order of St Anne, Second Class, was worn around the neck. (For Order itself, see Two, IV, 1 above.) It was often given for distinguished mil or civil service. Chekhov has a great story by this title.]
2. Юсу́пов дом — [On Харито́ньевский переу́лок and Мясни́цкая у́лица in M]
3. а́глицкий *(obs)* = англи́йский
4. секре́т — secret compartment or mechanism
5. запе́рхать *(pf, pop)* — to begin coughing fr a tickling in the throat
6. бе́гивать *(many-x impf)* fr бе́гать *(impf)*
7. повы́ползти *(pf)* — to crawl out *(of all or many)*
8. сложи́ть то и то *(pf)* — to unload this and that
9. запя́тка or запя́тки *(pl)* — [footboard for servants behind old-style carriage]

Three, III, 17

1. при́ смерти — dying; at death's door
2. что ты? — what's wrong w you? *(expresses surprise or fright)*
3. трепа́ть/ потрепа́ть — to pat

4. образна́я [ко́мната] *(obs)* — icon-room *(used for praying)*
5. гайду́к *(obs)* — footman
6. влёг fr влечь *(pf)* — to wedge oneself; to jut out
7. Кудрино — [Area in W M, where Пова́рская у́лица intersects w Кудри́нская Садо́вая, or Garden Ring]
8. Ники́тская — [A main st of M which ran fr Kremlin to Кудри́нская пло́щадь]
9. Пре́сня — [Section of M just N of Кудри́нская пло́щадь. Outside of Garden Ring, the continuation of Ники́тская was called Пре́сненская.]
10. Садо́вая — Garden St. [The outer ring of M in 1812, lying N of M Rv]
11. Су́харева ба́шня — [Tower erected by Peter I in 1689 to honor Sukharev Regiment. 185 ft. high. Near where Garden Ring crosses Lubianka St.]
12. Меща́нская — [St that enters Garden Ring fr N near Sukharev Tower, N of center of town]

Three, III, 18

1. Патриа́ршие пруды́ — [In M, just inside Garden Ring and less than half a mi N of where Povárskaia joins Kudrinskaia Ploshchad']
2. Торжко́вский or торжко́вский fr Торжо́к

Three, III, 19

1. на Ряза́нскую доро́гу — [i.e. to SE]
2. Дорогоми́ловский мост — [Bridge across Moscow Rv carrying the road fr Smolensk (and Borodino) to M, where Borodino Bridge now is, betw Dorogomilovskaia St. and Smolenskaia]
3. запружа́ть *(impf)* = запру́живать *(impf)*
4. обвози́ть/ обвезти́ *(coll)* = to drive around sth
5. Дорогоми́ловское предме́стье — [On S side of M Rv, just N of where Kiev Station now stands]
6. кре́пнет fr кре́пнуть *(impf)*
7. Тучко́в — Tuchkóv [Па́вел Алексе́евич Т. (b. 1776) R gen. Wounded and captured at Smolensk, and sent back to France. Brother of gen commanding R III corps at Borodino, and of Aleksandr (1777-1812), who was killed at Borodino in charge of his

brigade.]

8. боя́рин — boyar [N is unaware that boyars had been abolished as such by Peter I about a century earlier]
9. бурну́с — burnoose
10. Тверска́я заста́ва — [Gate in NW M, out Tverskaia St on road to St P. Where Belorussian Station is now.]
11. Калу́жская заста́ва — [Gate on S side of Moscow R in SW M where Leninskii Prospekt now is]
12. Ка́мер-Колле́жский вал — [M st running N to Moscow Rv fr Dorogomilovskaia zastava]

Three, III, 20

Acc to "Энциклопедический словарь", XIX, 932 (СПБ., 1896), M had 8771 private buildings and 387 public and state buildings in 1812. The fire destroyed 6341 private buildings and 191 public and state buildings. Of all buildings, 6591 were wooden and 2567 stone before the invasion. The population of M in 1812 is given (*Ibid.*, p. 936) as 251,131.]

1. домира́ть *(impf)* — to die out
2. обезма́точеть *(pf)* — to become queenless *(of a beehive)*
3. поджима́ть/ поджа́ть — to draw in
4. не несёт отту́да тепло́м полноты́ — the warmth of fullness is not wafted over fr there
5. коло́дезня *(obs)* — cover of beehive
(6.) шо́пот = шёпот
7. сметённый *(pf, past, pass, prich)* fr смета́ть/ смести́ — to sweep up
8. детва́ *(collec)* — larvae and young bees
9. укра́дистый — stealthy
10. коро́ткий — friendly
11. блюду́щий *(pf deep)* fr блюсти́
12. коло́дка — log w middle hollowed out [Maude explains that R beehives were generally made fr hollowed-out tree trunks]

Three, III, 21

1. Москворе́цкий мост — [Crosses M Rv just SE of Krem-

lin. It was wooden in 1812.]

2. Яузский мост — [Crosses Iauza Rv in M a few hundred yards N of where Iauza falls into M Rv, E of Kremlin]
3. спёрлись *(pf)* fr спира́ться/ спере́ться (*obs* or *pop*) — to squeeze; to press
4. прошны́ривать *(impf)* — to dart
5. Васи́лий Блаже́нный — [Church started by Ivan the Terrible on Red Square in 1554. Often mistranslated as "St. Basil's." Васи́лий (1489-1552) was M rel юро́дивый reburied in its lower wall.]
6. Борови́цкие воро́та — [Kremlin gate on SW, near M Rv, which N used to enter Kremlin]
7. Гости́ный двор — [A collection of stands and stores on E side of Red Square opposite Kremlin, where GUM now stands]
8. гостинодво́рец — storekeeper or employee of Gostinyi dvor]
9. сиде́лец *(obs)* — store clerk; salesman
10. сбор *(mil)* — fall-in; assembly
11. лю́ди в се́рых кафта́нах и с бри́тыми голова́ми — [Maude identifies these as released prisoners]
12. Ильи́нка — [M St going fr Red Sq past the shops and to NE]
13. нам не расчёт пустя́к како́й ни на есть *(subst)* — them little things don't bother us none (*implying*: just protect us!)
14. мы [даём] с на́шим удово́льствием — we give w pleasure

(15.) по́ пусту = по́пусту

16. бери́, что кому́ лю́бо — let any of you take what he likes
17. бо́жью власть не рука́ми скласть — [human] hands cannot prevail against God's power

Three, III, 22

1. диву́ясь *(impf, deep) fr* дивова́ться (*pop* or *dial*) = диви́ться *(impf)*
2. на э́то вас взять! — is that your job! is that what you are hired for!
3. сби́ться с ног *(pf; coll)* — to bc bushed, beat, dead tired
4. дай срок! — hold it! wait a minute!
5. полего́ньку *(coll)* — gently; carefully
6. пострелёнок fr постре́л

7. Рого́жская — [District of M E of M Rv and S of Iauza, fr which the Riazan' road (along which Kutuzov retreated) began]
8. тепе́реча = тепе́рича *(pop)* = тепе́рь

Three, III, 23

1. Варва́рка — [M st running fr Васи́лий Блаже́нный E, thru trading rows and on for a few blocks, 1 block S of Il'inka]
2. чтож ты челове́ка уби́л = почему́ же ты челове́ка уби́л
3. как же связа́л одного́ тако́го-то — just try and tie up smb like me
4. ча́стный [при́став] — captain of a police station *(obs)*
5. но́нче (*obs* or *dial*) = ны́нче
6. Маросе́йка — [St on N side of Ильи́нская пло́щадь, this continues what had been called Ильи́нка]
7. разочти́ *(pf)* fr рассчи́тывать/ расче́сть — to pay off
8. он наро́д разочти́ — he should have paid people off
9. квит = кви́ты
10. на́ша не взяла́ [верх] си́ла
11. он покажи́ поря́док *(subst)* = пусть он [нам] пока́жет поря́док *(wish)*
12. а то гра́бить-то ма́ло ли их — or else there are plenty of them to do plundering
13. на́ смех — for a joke; in fun
14. так его́ [францу́за] и пусти́ли
15. ба́ет *(pr)* fr ба́ять (*impf, obs, dial* or *pop*) = говори́ть *(impf)*
16. Кита́й-го́род — the old walled city of M [Sometimes mistranslated "Chinatown". Part of inner city lying NE of Kremlin w Il'inka as its main street. So called because of its wall. Tatar "Kitai" means first "wall", and then (because of the wall) a "fortress". This is where R word for "China" comes fr (*cf E* "Cathay".)]
17. ста́нем и мы из них дух . . . — [unfinished phrase; искореня́ть continues it a few lines later]
18. диста́нция — position *(obs)* [Anticipating Chekhov and Zoshchenko, character uses fancy word meaningless in context.]
(19.) мо́лнии *(misprint)* = молча́нии
20. э́то сам и есть — that's him there
21. как же успроси́л *(subst)* — combines упроси́л and спроси́л = how were you able to question him

22. пущáй *(subst)* = пускáй

Three, III, 24

1. канапé *(obs)* — small couch with raised head
2. ёрнический *(obs, pop)* — rakish; libertine
3. потеклó *(past)* fr потéчь *(pf)*
4. я держáл Москвý вот как — I had M under control; I had M in palm of my hand
5. вóтчинный департáмент — [Registry office, existing in M fr 1756 to 1852, and dealing w ancestral estates. Attached to Госудáрственный архúв прéжних вóтчинных дел, which was renamed Архúв вóтчинного департáмента.]
6. консистóрия — [office under eparchial bishop w administrative and judicial functions]
7. викáрный — suffragan bishop [assistant to main bishop]
8. Владúмир — [City on Kliaz'ma River about 120 mi E of M]
9. колóдник *(obs)* — prisoner; prisoner in stocks
10. Мешкóв — Meshkov [Пётр Алексéевич М. (1780-after 1815). Not in civil service in 1812. Copied and helped circulate Vereshchagin's supposed trs of N's statements. Arrested for this and sentenced to loss of gentry status and to joining the army as a private. Pardoned by tsar in 1815.]

Three, III, 25

1. подвéдомственный — subordinate
2. усех *(dial, southern)* = всех
3. зарóсший — w some hair grown back
4. поскóнный — hemp
5. брянчáть *(impf, obs)* = бренчáть *(impf)*
6. горя́чечный — feverish
7. измéнщик (*obs* or *pop*) = измéнник
(8.) по делóм = поделóм
9. нарóд-то что зверь = народ как зверь
10. подворáчиваться/ подворотúться — to turn awkwardly on [its] side
11. ля́жет fr лечь *(impf)*

Three, III, 26

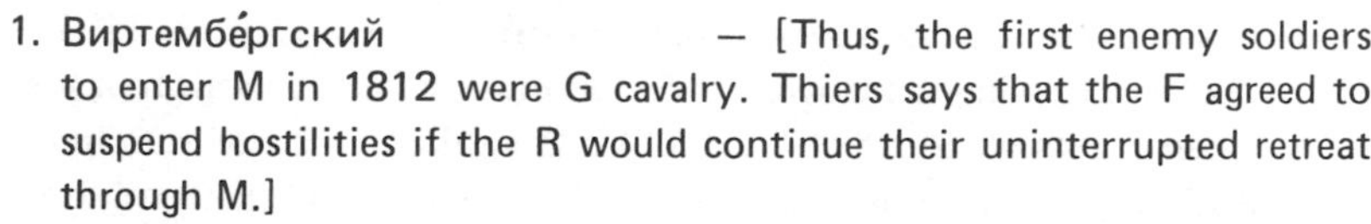

1. Виртембе́ргский — [Thus, the first enemy soldiers to enter M in 1812 were G cavalry. Thiers says that the F agreed to suspend hostilities if the R would continue their uninterrupted retreat through M.]
2. Арба́т — [A main st of M leading fr Smolensk Sq on outer Garden ring NE to Arbat Sq on inner, boulevard, ring, fr which the Vozdvizhenka (Vzdvizhenka) leads on to the Troitskii Gate of the Kremlin. The Arbat ''начисто выгорел'' in 1812. (See Сытин, стр. 283.)]
3. Нико́ла Явле́нный — [M church on Arbat, very close to Успе́нье на могильца́х]
4. явле́нный *(rel)* — miraculously appearing *(of an icon)*
5. ничево́ *(subst)* = ничего́ — not bad
6. Кута́фьевские воро́та or Кута́фья ба́шня — [A small round tower w gates which stood before the bridge that linked Vozdvizhenka St and Troitskii Gate of Kremlin by crossing the Neglinnaia Rv, which then flowed there on its way to M Rv, and which has since been put underground]
7. Мохова́я — [St in downtown M parallel to and a few hundred yards fr W wall of Kremlin. M University was located here.]
8. па́льник — linstock [a wooden staff w iron pincers at end used for igniting shells to be fired by cannon]
9. крыл *(obs, gen, pl)* = кры́льев fr крыло́
10. Зна́менка — [St. running fr Arbat Sq to Borovitskii Gate at SW corner of Kremlin]
11. Сена́тская пло́щадь — [Inside the Kremlin nr its N corner. The Senate Bldg lay just E of it, also fronting on Red Sq.]
12. Покро́вка — [St E by NE of Kremlin continuing Marose̕ika St up to Garden Ring]
13. Нико́льская — [St that runs fr N tip of Kremlin and Red Sq to Lubianskaia Sq]
14. что-то сре́днее — sth in between
15. вса́чиваться *(impf)* — to penetrate gradually into sth *(of liquids);* to be slowly absorbed
16. Каре́тный Ряд — [St N of Kremlin continuing Petrovka and so called because of carriage works located there]
17. влага́ть *(impf)* fr вкла́дывать *(impf)*

Three, III, 27

1. покуше́ние студе́нта на жизнь Наполео́на — [On Oct 12, 1809, N.S., N was reviewing his Guards at Schönbrunn Palace, in captured Vienna, when Friedrich Staps (1792-1809) a G student, tried to stab him, and was caught before he could do so. The student was executed five days later.]
2. неpереме́нное бельё — unchanged underwear
3. бра́ться *(impf)* — to grab
4. входно́й fr вход

Three, III, 28

1. распуска́ть/ распусти́ть — to relax; to allow to part

Three, III, 29

1. де́ло 7-го сентября́ — [Capt. Ramballe uses F, N.S. calendar for the battle *"de la Moskowa."* For R, it was Aug. 26, O.S., and the battle of Borodinó.]
2. квас — [a very mild sour drink fermented fr rye bread and malt]
3. ба! — is that right! *(expresses surprise)*

(4.) отма́чивать/ отмочи́ть *(coll)* — to make a wisecrack

5. би́ться/ поби́ться об закла́д *(obs)* — to bet
6. Тальма — Talma [François-Joseph T. (1763-1826) F actor who excelled in tragedy and reformed both costuming and technique.]
7. Дюшенуа — Duchesnois [Catherine-Joseph Rafuin, called D (1777-1835). F tragic actress and rival of Mlle George. A close friend of Talma's.]
8. Потье́ — Potier [Charles P. (1773-1838). F comic actor who, from 1809 to 1812 and beyond, was a constant favorite of the public at the Variétés theater in Paris.]
9. la Sorbonne — [the University of Paris, founded about 1257, by Robert de Sorbon, chaplain to Louis IX (St. Louis)]

(10.) под ряд = подря́д

11. покру́чивание — twirling

[12.] вишь ты! — well!

13. Петро́вка — Petrovka [St in downtown M

running NW fr Theater Sq past Boulevard Ring to Karetnyi Riad]

Three, III, 30

1. Мыти́щи больши́е — Mytishchi bol'shie [Village 12 mi N of M]
2. Мыти́щи ма́лые — Mytishchi malye [Village 8 mi N of M]
3. Суще́вская — Sushchevskaia — [A district of M lying NW of Kremlin and outside Garden Ring]
4. шала́ва *(coarse, pop)* — madman; nut; unbalanced man
5. белок[а́менная] — [a traditional adj for M]

Three, III, 31

1. Тро́ица — Troitsa [Тро́ице-Се́ргиева Ла́вра at Се́ргиево (now called Заго́рск), a famous monastery about 44 mi NE of M on road towards Iarosla̍vl'. The monastery, founded by St. Sergii in 1340, was one of the great holy sites of R, and still is.]
2. связь *(f)* — group of buildings sharing same roof (*obs* or *dial*)
3. подвёртывать/ подверну́ть но́ги — to tuck in one's legs; to place one's legs beneath one (while sitting)
4. на переко́ске = на́искось — cater-cornered; diagonally across *(the street corner)*
5. ско́бка — knob; latch

Three, III, 32

1. что же ча́ю? — how about tea?
2. проявле́ние — manifestation
3. облегчи́тельный — alleviating; giving relief
4. предположе́ние — plan; project; consideration

Three, III, 33

1. ло́же *(obs)* = ло́жа — pistol-handle
2. Замоскворе́чье — [The S side of M, across M Rv

fr the Kremlin]

3. несвойственность *(f)* — sth unsuitable
4. сады́ до́ма кня́зя Грузи́нского — [Betw Ма́лая and Больша́я Грузи́нская у́лица in Пре́сненская District NW of Kremlin, and just outside Garden Ring. Area is still called Грузи́ны. Nr Кудри́нская пло́щадь.]
5. вицмунди́р *(obs)* — uniform tunic
6. леле́[яла]
7. должно́ [быть], сестри́ца унесла́ [её]
8. а то бо́льше где же быть — or else where can [she] be
9. истука́н — statue; idol; *(here)* heartless man or monster *(popularly used as a swearword)*
10. броса́ть/ бро́сить — to move quickly
11. хвать дете́й *(subst)* = я хвати́лась дете́й
12. ди́тятко *(aff, pop)* — my baby
13. фате́ра *(subst)* = кварти́ра
14. снопови́дный — sheaf-like
15. круг — circular area

Three, III, 34

1. кры́тый [тулу́п] — cloth-trimmed; cloth-covered
2. не зна́ет ли кто её — doesn't anyone know her

[3.] Никола́вна *(dial)* = Никола́евна

4. ти = ты — [The F interpreter's accent is given phonetically]
5. ти должно отвечать начальство *(F accent; ungrammatical)* = ты до́лжен отвеча́ть нача́льству
6. объе́зд — mounted patrol *(obs)*
7. де́ну *(pf)* fr дева́ть/ деть
8. Дюронел — Durosnel — [Antoine-Jean Auguste Count D. (1771-1849). F gen named by N commander of fortress and city of M.]
9. Зу́бовский вал — [Zubovskii Blvd., running fr Zubovskaia Sq (on Garden Ring SW of Kremlin] to M River and Ostozhenko Street]

FOUR, I, 1

ТОМ ЧЕТВЕРТЫЙ, ЧАСТЬ ПЕРВАЯ, ГЛАВА ПЕРВАЯ

1. трубе́ние fr труби́ть *(impf)*
2. столь (*pop;* or *dial*) — such
3. уго́дник Се́ргий — St. Sergii [of Radonezh (1314-1392). He blessed Dmitrii Donskoi, Prince of M, before the Battle of Kulikovo in 1380 and foretold Dmitrii's victory over Tatars there. Sergii also founded the Troitse-Sergievo monastery in what is now Zagorsk, 44 mi NE of M. He came to be regarded as patron saint of R.]
4. Австри́йские знамена́ — [Maude says these banners were captured at Kliastitsy on June 18-19, O.S., and adds that the point of the comment, w its reference to II Peter 2:15, "lies in its allusion to the recent alliance of R w Austria, whose troops were now fighting on N's side."]
5. Петро́поль — Petropolis [poetic name for St P]
6. обраще́ние — turning smb's attention to sth
7. всеми́лостивейший *(obs, book)* — most gracious; most merciful [epithet used for God and tsars]
8. прие́млет *(obs, book)* — принима́ет
9. твоея *(OCS)* = твое́й
10. оса́нна — hosanna
11. гря́дый — one who comes [This echoes Psalms 118:26 in Jewish and W Christian traditions, "Blessed be he that cometh in the name of the Lord." Bible in R, N.Y. Отъедин. Библ. Общества, no date, gives this as Psalms 117:26. It is echoed in Matthew 21:9 and 23:39, Mark 11:9 and Luke 13:35 in both R and W Christian Bibles. Used in a liturgical hymn by R Orthodox Church.]
12. кровожа́ждущий *(OCS)* = кровожа́дный
13. боле́зную fr боле́зновать *(impf, obs)* — to regret
14. лицезре́ние *(obs, book)* — seeing smb close-up

Four, I, 2

[Note: Maude notes several historical inaccuracies in this chapter, such as that August 30 was the tsar's name-day rather than his birthday, and certain anachronisms.]

1. Тата́ринова or Тата́риново — [Village nr Borodino]
2. Кута́йсов — Kutaisov [граф Алекса́ндр Ива́нович К. (1784-1812), генера́л-майо́р. Commanded R artillery at Borodino, where he was killed]
3. уступле́ние fr уступа́ть *(impf)*
4. Яросла́вль *(m)* — Iaroslavl' [city on right bank of upper Volga, about 175 mi NE of M]

Four, I, 3

1. на полови́ну груди́ — to the middle of his chest

Four, I, 4

1. на почто́вы́х *(obs)* — post-chaise [pulled by govt. horses belonging to posting service and running regularly over given routes]
2. пасу́щийся fr пасти́сь *(impf)*

(3.) чи́сто на чисто = чи́сто на́чисто — clean as could be

4. ста́тский or шта́тский генера́л — [a tsarist civil servant whose rank was equivalent to that of a gen according to the table of ranks (See Appendix Four.)]
5. [ко́нный] заво́д — stud farm
6. по четверга́м у нас собира́ются — [As in the W at that time, R were "at home" to guests who chose to drop in at a set time of the week]
7. перекладна́я *(obs)* — carriages and/or horses changed at posting stations
8. ковёрная [ко́мната] — a carpeted room
9. венге́рское [вино́]
10. ка́зовый коне́ц — the best part
11. разма́шистость *(f)* — sweep; lack of constraint
12. трын-трава́ — all the same; it doesn't matter
13. возде́ржность *(f, obs)* = возде́ржанность *(f)* — restraint
14. захлопота́ть *(pf)* — to start bustling about

Four, I, 5

1. прищу́риваться/ прищу́риться — to narrow one's eyes
2. пойдёт [за́муж]

Four, I, 6

1. приме́ривать *(impf)* = примеря́ть

Four, I, 7

1. в полови́не — halfway through; in the middle of
2. ужа́[сно]
3. кулье́р *(subst)* — курье́р

Four, I, 8

(1.) выроста́ть *(impf, obs)* = выраста́ть *(impf)*
2. вкла́дчик — contributor
3. подойти́ под благослове́нье *(pf)* — to ask a blessing
4. то́лько бы он был жив *(a wish)* — if only he lives

Four, I, 9

1. поджига́тельство — arson
2. превыша́ть/ превы́сить — to surmount
3. принима́ть/ приня́ть *(coll)* — to take sth away
4. идти́ к чему́ — to befit sth; to suit sth
5. Кры́мский брод — [At site of Кры́мский мост across M Rv about 1.5 mi SW of Kremlin]
6. сожжённый *(pf; past, pass, prich)* fr сжига́ть/ сжечь

Four, I, 10

1. Де́вичье по́ле — [Field in Khamovniki section of M about 1.5 mi SW of Kremlin and just outside Garden Ring. So called because, during the Tatar occupation, the R girls who formed part of

the annual tribute, were assembled there. For Khamovniki, see Four, II, 13 below.]

2. ни́зом *(coll)* — along the bottom
3. Ива́н Вели́кий — [Bell-tower in Kremlin completed under Boris Godunov in 1600. For centuries this was tallest structure in R.]
4. Новоде́вичий монасты́рь *(m)* — [Convent about 1 mi SW of Де́вичье по́ле. Founded in 1524 by Васи́лий Ива́нович, Grand Duke of M.]
5. Щерба́тов — Shcherbatov [князь Дми́трий Михайлович Щ. (1760-1839). Reserve colonel, marshall of nobility of Serpukhov District, M Province. His house later belonged to M. P. Pogodin and, in Soviet times, is located on corner of Пого́динская у́лица and Са́винский переу́лок nr Де́вичье поле.]
6. Экмю́льский — [i.e. Marshall Davout, Prince of Eckmühl]
7. по одному́ — one at a time
8. отупле́ние fr отупе́ть *(impf)*

Four, I, 11

1. остро́жный *(obs)* — prisoner; convict
2. подбива́ть/ подби́ть — to shoot; to wound; to injure
3. то́ ли — whether it was that
4. лопа́тина — shovelful
5. примыка́ть/ примкну́ть — to move close

Four, I, 12

1. зага́женный *(pf; past, pass, prich)* fr зага́живать/ зага́дить
2. прощён *(pf; past, pass, prich)* fr проща́ть/ прости́ть

[3.] ко́лышек fr кол — post, stake *(wood)*

4. что-то . . . кру́глое — sth . . . well-rounded; sth . . . plump
5. бу́де *(subst)* = бу́дет — [Platon sometimes drops -т ending in 3rd pers sing pr]
6. важне́ющий *(subst)* — real good; very fine
7. дожёвывать *(impf)* — to finish chewing
8. гло́же *(subst)* = гло́жет fr глода́ть *(impf)*
9. сове́т — harmony or friendship (*obs* or

pop)

10. сумá — beggar's bag
11. случи́сь *(subst)* = случи́лось
12. ан *(dial)* — but in fact
13. солдáтство — soldiering; mil service
14. живóт — farmyard animal *(usually a horse)* (*obs* or *dial*)
15. зáработки *(pl)* fr зáработок — working for pay; hired labor
16. Никóла угóдник — St. Nicholas
17. Фрóла и Лáвра *(subst)* = Флор и Лавр — Florus and Laurus [Two brothers, second-century stonemasons who built a pagan temple, dedicated it to God, and were martyred as a result by being buried alive in a dry well. Their day is Aug 18. They are supposed to protect animals.]
18. кáмушек fr кáмень
19. положи́ [меня́] кáмушком, подними́ [меня́] калáчиком
20. ась? *(pop)* — hmm? what?
21. угрéться *(pf, pop)* = согревáться/ согрéться

Four, I, 13

1. кáрий — brown (*not* hazel!)
2. снóсливость *(f)* — endurance; patience
3. спóрость — quickness
4. стóило емý — he only had to; all he had to do was

(5.) точáть = тачáть/ стачáть

6. расходи́ться *(impf)* — to get used to walking after walking a while; to get one's second wind
7. портки́ *(pop)* — pants; trousers
8. солдáт в отпускý — рубáха из портóк — a soldier on leave has an easy life [Soldiers had to tuck their shirts into their pants; peasants wore their shirts outside their pants. A soldier on furlough was not under immediate mil discipline and could get sloppy.]
9. тошнéнько мне = мне тóшно

Four, I, 14

1. Ли́пецк — Lipetsk [District town then in Tambov province some 70 mi N of Voronezh where Lipovka Rv and

Voronezh Rv join. The Voronezh is left tributary of Don.]

2. Шýя — Shuia — [District town then in Vladimir Province on Tēza Rv, which flows into Kliaz'ma, and eventually into Volga. Town is about 19 mi SE of Ivanovo, which is about 145 mi NE of M. Nowhere does Masha's route come within 100 miles of M.]
3. недалéче (*obs* or *pop*) = недалекó
4. над сáмой над Вóлгой — [Repeating the prep gives speech a folklore touch]
5. пошлй *(pf, impv)* fr посылáть/ послáть
6. нагноéние — suppuration; festering

Four, I, 15

1. отрóсший *(pf, past pass, prich)* fr отрастáть/ отрастй
2. Еван[гéлие]
3. птйцы небéсные . . . — "the fowls of the air sow not, neither do they reap, yet your Father feedeth them" (Matthew 6:26)

Four, I, 16

1. тем лýчше — so much the better
2. закрáлась *(past pf)* fr закрáдываться/ закрáсться
3. любóвь есть Бог — [Inversion of "God is love," I John 4:8]
4. ухвáтываться *(impf)* fr ухватйться *(pf)*
5. исповéдывать *(impf, obs)* = исповéдовать *(impf and pf)*

Four, II, 1

1. утверждённость *(f)* — fixity
2. движéние рýсской áрмии . . . к Тарýтинскому лáгерю — [Kutuzov left M on road SE to Riazan' via Bronnitsy, Kolomna and Zaraisk. However, on Sept. 4, O.S., he turned sharply W at M Rv w most of army and moved along Pakhra Rv to Podol'sk and on past Krasnaia Pakhra to Tarutino. Both these last villages were on the M-Kaluga Road. At Tarutino, on Nara Rv in Kaluga Province about 20 mi fr Kaluga, the R army made camp fr Sept. 20, O.S. to Oct. 6, O.S. In

camp, they rested and again built up their numbers to 120,000 after this flank march.]

3. при том — along w this
4. е́сли бы Мюра́т не потеря́л из ви́ду ру́сских — [When Kutuzov turned W, he left two regts. of Cossacks to continue towards Riazan', followed by Murat. When Murat realized what had happened, contact had already been lost w main R army, whose whereabouts the F did not learn again until Sept. 14, O.S.]
5. Нижегоро́дская доро́га — [The road E fr M via Vladimir and Murom to Nizhnii Novgorod]
6. Ланско́й — Lanskoi [Васи́лий Серге́евич Л. (1754-1831). Senator. In 1812, he supervised supplies. Later, Minister of Internal Affairs, 1825-1828.]
7. Ока́ — Oka [Right tributary of Volga. Rises nr Kursk, bends thru Orel, Kaluga, Tula, M, Vladimir, provinces and joins Volga at Gor'kii. Navigable most of its 912-mi length.]
8. первози́мье *(dial)* — start of winter (when there is thin ice on rivers)
9. Ту́льский [руже́йный] заво́д — [Peter I set up a small arms factory in Tula in early 18th cent. For a long time it was the sole source of small arms for R army. Tula is about 120 mi S of M on Upá Rv, which falls into Oka.]
10. Подо́льск — Podolsk [District town, about 25 mi S of M on road to Tula. Also, see Note 2 to this chapter.]
11. диференциа́льный *(obs)* = дифференциа́льный — varying

Four, II, 2

1. присы́лка Лористо́на — [Lauriston appeared at R outposts on evening of Oct. 5, N.S.]
2. заси́м *(obs)* — w which; wherewith

Four, II, 3

1. Тару́тинское сраже́ние — [Fought on Oct. 6, 1812, O.S., this battle betw Murat and Bennigsen resulted in F being driven off w losses. Next day, F began to leave M.]
2. Се́рпухов — Serpukhov [town about 60 mi S of M in M province on way to Orēl]
3. Дми́тров — Dmitrov [District capital in M

province on Iakhroma Rv about 45 mi N of M]

4. Ру́за — Ruza [District capital in M province on Ruza Rv about 60 mi W of M and 15 mi NNE of Mozhaisk]
5. забрёл fr забрести́ *(pf)*
6. хору́нжий *(obs; used only for Cossacks)* = подпору́чик
7. предполага́емое им [Куту́зовым]

Four, II, 4

1. Ки́кин — [Пётр Андре́евич К.(1772-1834), дежу́рный генера́л. Later, статс-секрета́рь to Alexander I.]
2. во-олузях *(subst)* = во луга́х [R folk song]
3. торба́н — [A stringed instrument without frets played by plucking it. It went out of style after 1850 or so.]
4. ай да — good for [Nikolai Ivanovich]; bravo
5. подкати́ть *(pf)* — to scheme against [Konovnitsyn, as дежу́рный генера́л of R army after Borodino, would most likely be blamed if Kutuzov's orders were not carried out]

Four, II, 5

1. Леташе́вка — Letashevka [Village in Borov District, NE Kaluga Province, site of Kutuzov's hq in early October, O.S. Borov District touches M Province.]
2. с дрова́ми в подшта́нниках — and w firewood in [their] underwear pants
3. Эйхен — Eikhen or Eichen [Perhaps Фёдор Яковлевич Э. (died 1847), a colonel in 1812. Tarlé says Eichen resigned from army after this scolding, but Brodin stayed on.]
4. поднима́ть/ подня́ть на́ смех — to make fun of someone; to hold smb up to ridicule
5. надсмея́ться *(pf, pop)* = насмея́ться *(pf)*

Four, II, 6

1. улегли́сь fr уле́чься *(pf)*
2. Орло́в-Дени́сов — Orlov-Denisov [граф Васи́лий

Васи́льевич О.-Д. (1775-1843). R gen. Commanded Life-Guard Cossack Regt. At Tarutino, his Cossacks attacked F flank by surprise, but lost initiative when they stopped to loot.]

3. Стромилова — Stromilova [Village nr Tarutino]
4. Дмитровское — Dmitrovskoe [Village 3 mi fr Tarutino]
5. Гре́ков — Grekov [Perhaps Тимофе́й Дми́триевич Г. (born 1780). Генера́л-майо́р Во́йска Донско́го, i.e. of Don Cossacks.]
6. черво́нец — [3-ruble gold coin minted in R in 18th and 19th centuries]
7. Гре́ковым *(inst)* — [Grekov's forces]
8. пожима́ться/ пожа́ться — to huddle up; to shrink up
9. с дро́тиками на переве́с — w lances at "trail arms" [i.e. pointing forward and slightly down]
10. спросо́нков *(coll)* = спросо́нок
11. опомина́ться *(impf, obs)* fr опо́мниться *(pf)*
12. Багговут — Baggovut [Карл Фёдорович Б. (1761-1812), Estonian gen in R svc who attacked F flank at Tarutino and was killed there.]

Four, II, 7

1. знак [отли́чия] — medal
2. по поря́дку — in order; in succession

Four, II, 8

(1.) восме́тный = несме́тный

2. Еги́пет — [N campaigned in Egypt fr 1798 to 1801 to threaten E communications w India. He defeated Mamelukes in July 1798 but lost his fleet next month to Nelson on the Nile at Aboukir. Anglo-Turkish forces soon forced out F.]
3. 40 веко́в смотре́ли — [Echoes N's speech to his soldiers in Egypt before Battle of the Pyramids, on July 21, 1798, N.S.: "Soldiers, forty centuries look down on you fr the summit of the Pyramids."]

Four, II, 9

1. Себастиани — Sébastiani [Count Horace-François-Bastien S (1772-1851) [F marshall. In charge of N's vanguard. It was he who lost contact w Kutuzov's army after pursuing it SE to Bronnitsy on road to Riazan' fr M.]
2. Яковлев — Iakovlev [Ива́н Алексе́евич Я. (1767-1846). Retired captain in 1812. He did not get out of M in time and N allowed him to leave if he would agree to take a message to tsar in St P. The story is told in opening pages of Iakovlev's son's autobiography:
"Было́е и ду́мы" by Алекса́ндр Ива́нович Герцен (1812-1870).]
3. Тутолми́н — Tutolmin [Ива́н Васи́льевич Т. (1751-1815), генера́л-майо́р. In 1812, he was director of M Foundling Hospital and remained in M under F. He too was sent to tsar by N w a message.]
4. муниципалите́т — municipal administration; organ of local self-government
5. пещи́сь *(impf, obs)* = пе́чься *(impf)*
6. градско́й (*obs* or *poetic*) = городско́й
7. сле́дуемые несча́стию — adequate to the misfortune
8. кой *(obs)* = кото́рый
9. ослу́шиваться *(impf)* fr ослу́шаться *(pf)*
10. Охо́тный ряд — Okhotnyi riad [M sq. just N of Kremlin and Alexander Garden]
11. до́блесть *(f)* — virtue
12. венцено́сец *(obs, high style)* — sovereign; monarch

Four, II, 10

1. Тьер *que son génie* — [In Thiers (III, 174), these F words refer to a plan of N's to leave M by retreating obliquely to NW and possibly threatening St P in the spring of 1813. However, N withdrew the plan because his generals so opposed it.]
2. Фен — Fain [Baron Agathon-Jean-François F (1778-1837). N's secretary and, later, historian, who accompanied him on all campaigns until 1814. His *Manuscrit de 1812* was published in Paris in 1827. Thiers argues w him in a footnote (III, 174).]
3. подведе́ние fr подводи́ть/ подвести́
4. и то́лько, по слова́м Тьера, иску́сству и, ка́жется, то́же гениа́ль-

ности Мюра́та — [Thiers talks neither about Murat's art nor about his genius, but does praise Murat's *"instinct d'officier d'avant-garde "* (instinct of a vanguard officer, III, 172).]

5. посеще́ние мече́ти — [In Egypt in 1798-1799, N visited a mosque to show Arabs that he was not anti-Islam and thus help keep them quiet]
6. дом Позняко́ва — [On corner of Больша́я Ники́тская у́лица and Лео́нтьевский переу́лок, less than a mi W of Red Square in M]
7. ста́рая гва́рдия — [the crack troops of Napoleon's army]
8. обер-церемонийме́йстер — grand marshal (of N's palace)
9. ходи́ть на час *(impf, euphemism)* — to relieve oneself (i.e. to urinate)
10. перехва́ты обо́зов по Смоле́нской доро́ге — [This news, says Thiers, reached N in M on Sept. 21 or 22. Cossacks had forced the surrender near Smolensk of two F squadrons convoying ammunition wagons to F army in M.]

Four, II, 11

1. ви́слый — lop-ears; hanging down (*cf.* вислоу́хий)
2. пана́ш *(F — panache)* — tuft of feathers
3. курча́виться *(impf)* — to curl
4. подо́бранность *(f)* — being in good shape or condition
5. разъе́здиться *(pf, coll)* — to start riding a lot or frequently
6. по-дома́шнему — informally; as if at home
7. по ча́сту = поча́сту *(dial)* = ча́сто

[8.] кляну́сь святы́м Фомо́ю — [Mistranslation into R of F. Should be as in Jubilee Ed. St. Thomas is F man's name.]

9. знать толк *(impf)* — to know what one is talking about
10. сапо́жный това́р — shoemaker's materials
11. в са́мый раз — just the right size
12. струме́нт *(subst)* = инструме́нт
13. вша *(pop gen)* = вши fr вошь *(f)*
14. эхма́ *(pop)* = эх — *(expressing admiration and surprise)*
15. не́христь *(m, obs, pop)* — *lit*: un-Christian; *fig*: cruel person w no conscience

16. таровáтый *(obs)* = торовáтый

Four, II, 12

1. Россúи да лéту—союзу нéту *(subst)* — Russia and summer have nothing in common

Four, II, 13

1. ломáться *(impf)* — to be taken apart, dismantled
2. цúбик — goatskin [цы́ба is a folk term for a goat]
3. чешуя́ — strap of a soldier's shako
4. драм-да-да-дам — tum-ta-di-dum *(onomatopoetic sound of drums)*
5. казáнский халáт — many-colored, oriental-style man's robe, as worn in Kazan'
6. Никóла, Влас — [Church of St. Nicholas was built in Khamóvniki (see item 9 below) near Zubovo (see item 7 below) in XVII century and is still standing. Church of St. Vlas was not reconstructed after great fire of 1812; it was next to Никóла Явлéнный, which LNT possibly had in mind here.]
7. Зу́бово — [Area nr Zubovskaia Sq. on inner boulevard ring nr M Rv, a mile or so SW of Kremlin, and nr Zubovskii Blvd. leading fr that sq to M Rv as part of inner ring]
8. половúны нет [бóльше]
9. Хамóвники — [M section lying outside Garden Ring and on N bank of M Rv about 2 or 3 mi SW of Kremlin. The house there at which LNT would later winter w his family, at No. 21 Khamóvnicheskii pereúlok, is now an LNT museum.]

Four, II, 14

1. Калу́жская — [M st on S bank of M Rv running SW fr Kalúzhskaia Sq. to Kalúzhskaia Zastava and on to Kaluga]
2. Неску́чное — [Garden lying on S bank of M Rv, betw Rv and Kaluzhskaia. Name comes fr name of estate of Count A.G. Orlov, to whom the land had once belonged.]
3. Большáя Орды́нка — [St beginning just SE of Kremlin

on S bank of M Rv and continuing S to Serpukhovskaia Sq]

4. кото́рые отделя́ют мост от Калу́жской — [A wooden Кры́мский мост had been built at Кры́мский брод in 1786]
5. до пло́щади, где схо́дятся — [Presumably Калу́жская пло́щадь]
6. стерве́ц *(coarse, pop, swearing)* — rat; swine; rogue
7. вон те на! = вот тебе́ на! *(pop)* — well, I never! well, I'll be darned! *(expresses surprise)*
8. так его́ по мо́рде — hit him in the kisser
9. разря́женный *(pf, past, pass, prich)* fr разряжа́ть/ разряди́ть
10. па́луба — *(here)* hooded carriage
11. втесни́ться *(pf)* — вти́скиваться/ вти́снуться
12. замина́ть/ замя́ть разгово́р — to change the subject of conversation
13. отпряжённый *(pf, past, pass, prich)* fr отпряга́ть/ отпря́чь

Four, II, 15

1. озна́чить *(pf)* — to mark or designate *(obs)*
2. До́рохов — Dorokhov [Ива́н Семёнович Д. (1762- 1815) . R gen who had served under Suvorov, Commanded cavalry brigade at Borodino. Made lieutenant gen there. Later, commanded partisans on Mozhaisk Road. On Sept. 29, O.S., his partisans captured Vereia (on N's escape route betw Maloiaroslávets and Viáz'ma) and destroyed its fortifications. Wounded severely at Maloiaroslávets.]
3. Фоми́нское — Fominskoe [Village in Borov District, NE Kaluga Province, near Tarútino. District is about 40 mi SW of M.]
4. Брусье — Broussier [Count Jean-Baptiste B. (1766-1814). F divisional gen, then corps commander]
5. Малахо́вские or Молохо́вские воро́та — [Gate in S part of Smolensk Kremlin]
6. Фигнер — Figner or Fiegner [Алекса́ндр Само́йлович Ф. (1787-1813), штабс-капита́н in artillery at start of 1812, colonel at end. Disguised as a peasant, he entered occupied M to gather intelligence on F. He then returned to R lines and organized a partisan unit; he became an outstanding partisan commander. Killed while crossing Elbe River in Germany. A partial prototype for LNT'S Dolokhov.]
7. Сесла́вин — Seslavin [Алекса́ндр Ники́тич

С. (1780-1858), генера́л-лейтена́нт. Veteran of 1805, 1807 and 1810 campaigns. Began 1812 as capt of guards artillery. First to learn that F had left M and moved on to Kaluga road. Distinguished partisan leader who harrassed F retreat very effectively.]

8. Боро́вск — Borovsk [District town in NE Kaluga Province about 60 mi SW of M]
9. Болхови́тинов — Bolkhovitinov [Real name: Болого́вский, Дми́трий Никола́евич (1780-1852). In 1812, a major and staff-officer under Dokhturov.]

Four, II, 16

1. Алексе́й Петро́вич [Ермо́лов]
2. больнёшенек *(aff dim)* fr бо́лен *(implies speaker is sorry for him)*
3. мо́жет [быть, про́сто] так
4. руби́ть *(impf)* ого́нь *(m)* — to strike a light *(w flint on steel)* [Maude explains that the sparks fr this fell on tinder, which smoldered. Then, a splinter dipped in sulphur was put into the tinder to get the desired light.]
5. се́рник (*obs* or *dial*) — wooden splinter dipped in sulphur
6. быть на ножа́х с кем-то — to be at daggers drawn w smb

Four, II, 17

1. сыпа́ть *(impf, obs)* = спать *(impf)*
2. Бертелеми — Barthemy [F colonel. On Oct. 20, 1812, N.S., he was sent w a letter fr Marshall Berthier, (Napoleon's chief of staff) to Kutuzov, hinting at peace. Kutuzov's answer was non-committal.]
3. не добьёшься то́лку — you can't make any sense out of it
4. Меды́нь — Medyn' [District town in NE Kaluga Province, about 140 mi SW of M and about 35 mi SW of Borovsk]
5. mme Staël — [Germaine de Staël (1766-1817). F writer. Author of novels *Delphine* (1802) and *Corinne* (1807). Her major work, *De l'Allemagne* (On Germany, 1811) hailed G romanticism. In her Paris salon, she opposed N, and was therefore banished. She spent years in exile in Switzerland, G, E, and (in 1812)

St P. She described this in *Dix Ans d'exil (Ten Years of Exile)* published posthumously in 1821.]

6. сщу́риться *(pf)* = сощу́риться *(pf)*
7. и он запла́кал — [The и give this sentence a Biblical flavor]

Four, II, 18

1. До́хтуров идёт к Малояросла́вцу — [On October 10/22, Kutuzov sent Dokhturov to Fominskoe to attack a F detachment there. However, it turned out that in and near Fominskoe was the whole F army, moving towards Kaluga. The R moved to Maloiaroslavets to block the way S and a fierce battle ensued there on October 11/23 w the city changing hands 8 times (see Four, II, 8 above for battle).]
2. Муто́н — Mouton [Baron Régis-Barthélemy M. — Duvernet (1779-1816) F gen. At F council of war held at Maloiaroslávets on Oct. 13/25, he advised leaving R as quickly as possibly by the shortest and best known route. Later executed for Bonapartism in Restoration France.]
3. импера́торское ура́ — [Maude explains that ура́ was the traditional yell given by R troops in the assault. The assault mentioned almost captured N.]

Four, II, 19

1. полони́ть (*impf* and *pf*) — to take prisoner; to capture (doublet of плени́ть, *impf*)
2. побива́ть/ поби́ть — to kill *(all or many of);* to defeat

Four, III, 1

1. Вели́кая а́рмия — *Grande Armée (F)* [N's army in R]
2. переймка — interception; seizing
3. *en quarte (F) (fencing)* — [Position in thrusting or parrying w inside of hand turned up and weapon pointing at right part of

opponent's chest]

4. *en tierce (F) (fencing)* — [Position in parrying w wrist turned in, fingernails pointing down a bit, and point of weapon at eye-level and slightly to right]
5. *prime (F) (fencing)* — [First posture of defense, w weapon pointing somewhat up]
6. гвозди́ть *(impf, coll)* — to bash; to bang
7. не как францу́зы в 1813 году́ — [Виктор Шкловский, pp. 69-70, indicates that this statement is untrue, and LNT knew (or should have known) it fr his much-used source:
Илья Радожицкий [И.Р.] *Походные записки артиллериста с 1812 по 1816 г, М, 1835, 4 тома.*]
8. отсалютова́ть *(pf)* — to salute

Four, III, 2

1. гверилья́с — guerilla [Spanish irregular who fought against F occupation of Spain (1800-1814)]
2. мно́житель *(m)* — multiplier
3. подстановле́ние = подстано́вка
4. наивы́годнейший = вы́годный (+ *superl pref & suff*)
5. бьют без приказа́ния францу́зов = бьют францу́зов без приказа́ния

Four, III, 3

1. забе́глый — stray *(animal)*
2. Давы́дов — Davydov [Дени́с Васи́льевич Д. (1784-1839). R poet, hussar, and hero of partisan warfare in 1812. A lt. col., he organized partisan warfare after Borodino (where his estate was) and ended up a lt. gen. LNT telescoped his names to get "Denisov" in *W&P* Davydov published an essay on partisan warfare and three essays (including his diary) on 1812. A friend of Pushkin's.]
3. Васили́са [Кожина] — [Wife of ста́роста in Sychev District, Smolensk Province who killed several F w a pitchfork]
4. Мику́лина or Мику́лино — Mikulino [Village in Borov District, NE Kaluga Province, nr Tarutino]
5. Ша́мшево or Ша́мшева — Shamshevo [Village W of Mikulino in NE Kaluga Province]

Four, III, 4

1. подтя́нутый — sunken; hollow
2. коси́ть *(impf)* — to twist; to incline
3. поджима́ть/ поджа́ть у́ши — to press one's ears against one's head
4. эсау́л *(obs)* = есау́л *(hist)*
5. раски́снуть *(pf)* — to grow soft fr moisture; to become sodden, miry
6. смо́кнуть *(pf)* — to be drenched, soaked
7. склизкий *(dial)* = ско́льзкий
8. подпряжённый *(pf, past, pass, prich)* fr подпряга́ть/ подпря́чь — to harness an animal alongside one already harnessed
9. взбива́ться/ взби́ться — to ride up *(of clothing);* to move up on the body in untidy fashion
10. рыси́ть *(impf)* — to trot
11. писто[ле́та]
12. карау́лка *(pop)* — watchman's hut
13. борода́ — you w a beard

Four, III, 5

1. выдира́ться/ вы́драться — to pull oneself out w difficulty
2. на полу́горе — halfway up the hill
3. э́ка! — my goodness! wow! *(expresses surprise)*
4. булды́хнуться = булты́хнуться *(pf)* — to plop into water
5. пласту́н *(obs)* — [dismounted Cossack used for sentry and intelligence work]
6. Гжать *(f)* — Gzhat' or Gzhatsk [Old name of Гжатск, a town on Гжать Rv in Smolensk Province, about 120 mi W of M, and about 40 mi NE of Viaz'ma]
7. они ничего́ знать не зна́ют, ве́дать не ве́дают — they don't know a blessed thing
8. забреда́ть/ забрести́ — to stray
9. миродёр *(subst)* = мародёр [миродёр is a Leskov-style false etymology of a foreign word, such as "chaise lounge" for *"chaise longue"* in E. The peasant commune was a мир; the same spelling (with an *"i"* in R) was used in LNT'S day for "world," or "universe." The verb драть is "to flay; to flog; to strip off." Thus,

миродёр would seem to mean, "he who flays or fleeces everyone alive."]

10. чёрная рабо́та — unskilled work
11. мушкето́н — musketoon; blunderbuss [old cavalry firearm w short, wide barrel]
12. переку́сывать *(impf)* fr перекуси́ть *(pf)*
13. выстра́гивать *(impf)* fr вы́строгать *(pf)*
14. мерени́на = ме́рин
15. побра́ть *(pf, pop)* — to take prisoner; to capture

Four, III, 6

1. каза́нская шля́пка — high felt hat
2. отви́сший = отви́слый
3. что ж не взял? — why didn't you take one prisoner?
4. взять-то взял — I did take one
5. не ла́ден — he's not a good one
6. поаккура́тнее — filling the bill a bit better
7. гожа́ющий *(subst)* = годя́щий fr годи́ться *(impf)*
8. представля́ть в ли́цах *(impf)* — to act sth out
9. наверни́сь *(subst)* = наверну́лся

[10.] сграбь = сгрёб fr сгреба́ть/ сгрести́ (pop) — to grab strongly or clumsily

11. как загалди́т — suddenly he'll start screeching
12. что вы [де́лаете]
13. стречо́к — [in expression зада́ть стречка́ or зада́ть стрекача́ — to turn tail and run]
14. неспра́вный *(pop)* — no good; low quality; incorrigible
15. одежо́нка fr одёжа = оде́жда *(plus pej suff)*
16. одна́ назва́ния = одно́ назва́ние — [soldiers] in name only *(ungrammatical, i.e. mistake of one particular person)*
17. со́тню горя́чих [уда́ров]
18. серча́ть *(impf, pop)* = серди́ться *(impf)*
19. позатемня́ть *(pf)* — to grow a little dark
20. табе́ *(subst)* = тебе́

Four, III, 7

1. Вя́земское сра́жение — [Battle of Viaz'ma, Oct. 21-22/ Nov. 2-3. R attacked main F army in and nr Viaz'ma at night. F lost thousands of dead who could not be replaced. Next day, first snow fell.]
2. когда́ 21-го октября́ — [Apparently an anachronism, since this was day of Battle of Viaz'ma, in which Petia had taken part]
3. обива́ться/ оби́ться — to wear out
4. мальчёнок or мальчо́нок *(aff dim)* fr ма́льчик

Four, III, 8

1. чекме́нь *(m)* — [old-fashioned outer garment worn by Cossacks and peasants]
2. ва́точный *(obs)* = ва́тный
3. моло́дчик — rascal; rogue
4. помру́т *(pf ft)* fr помира́ть/ помере́ть
5. оси́нка fr оси́на
   на оси́нку — [string you and me up] on an aspen tree

(6.) на обу́м = наобу́м

7. наобу́м Ла́заря — any which way; any old way [Cf. Luke 16:19-31. Lazarus wanted crumbs fr rich man's table.]

Four, III, 9

1. кру́пною ры́сью — at a fast trot
2. кто идёт? *(mil)* — who goes there?
3. о́тзыв *(mil)* — countersign
4. с кра́ю — at the edge (of the fire)
5. *Il les fera marcher, les lapins (F)* — he will make those guys dance to his tune [Jubilee Ed. mistranslates and 1961-1963 ed. simplifies tr]

Four, III, 10

1. Караба́х — Karabakh [Maude explains that Karabakh is S Caucasian area famous for its horses]
2. затупи́[лась]

3. се́нцы fr се́ни
4. со стра́ху спи́тся — after his scare, he's really sleeping
5. ната́чивать *(impf)* fr наточи́ть *(pf)*
6. ожи́г, жиг [later: вжиг] — [onomatopoetic noises of a blade being sharpened]
7. валя́й *(coll)* — go on; go ahead
(8.) на́ двое = на́двое

Four, III, 11

1. кусну́ть *(lx pf)* fr куса́ть *(impf)*
2. переезд — ride, trip *(coll)*
3. сере́дь (*obs* or *pop*) = среди́
(4.) молодцова́тый *(obs)* = молодцева́тый
5. провизжа́ть *(pf)* — to whistle past; to fly by w a whistle
6. пуста́я пу́ля — spent bullet; hollow-sounding bullet
7. упира́ться/ упере́ться — to dig one's heels in
8. гото́в *(pop, short form only)* — dead; done for
9. брать не бу́дем — [i.e. kill all the prisoners on the spot]

Four, III, 12

1. Жюно — Junot [Andoche J. (1771-1813). F gen (not a marshall), Duke of Abrantès. Wounded at Borodino. Commanded 8th (Westphalian) Corps.]
2. депо́ *(indecl)* — storehouse *(obs);* collection point *(obs);* depository *(obs)*
3. мёрли fr мере́ть *(impf)* — to die *(wholesale) (pop)*
4. стёртый — rubbed sore
5. заструпе́лый — scabby
6. сели́тренный *(obs)* = сели́трный

Four, III, 13

1. вороньёв *(subst gen pl)* fr воронье

2. гла́же *(comp)* fr гла́дкий
3. Мака́рий = Мака́рьев — Makar'ev [Town on Volga about 60 mi E of Nizhnii-Novgorod where a great annual fair was held from 1641 until its buildings burned down in 1816. Fair was then moved to Nizhnii-Novgorod.]
4. как сле́довает *(subst)* = как сле́дует
5. собери́сь *(subst)* = собрали́сь
6. ночны́м де́лом = но́чью
7. акромя́ *(subst)* = кро́ме
8. оделя́ть/ одели́ть — to give sth to [smb]
9. под голова́ *(subst)* = под поду́шку
10. слезьми́ *(pop)* = слеза́ми
11. жа́льче *(coll)* = comp fr жа́лко
12. [Maude notes that this tale was one of LNT's favorites. LNT later retold it in, "Бог правду видит да не скоро скажет" (1872).]

Four, III, 14

1. прогреме́ть *(pf)* — to thunder past; to make a racket or din while passing

Four, III, 15

1. у́гольев *(pop)* = угле́й fr у́голь *(m)*

Four, III, 16

1. изжа́риваться *(impf)* = жа́рить *(impf)*
2. [Here are railroad distances given in Baedeker's *Russia* (Leipzig, 1914), which are not quite the same, but close:
   M—Viaz'ma — 150 mi
   Viaz'ma-Smolensk — 109 mi
   Smolensk-Bereziná-River — 164 mi]
3. спе́шенный — dismounted

Four, III, 17

1. [кому́] приходи́ться/ прийти́сь — to fall to the lot *(of smb)*

2. Кра́сный or Кра́сное — [Town in Smolensk Province, about 40 mi E of Orsha and 40 mi W of Smolensk. Here on November 3-6/15-18, R attacked retreating F. The battle was indecisive but the F could ill afford new casualties, esp since stragglers and badly wounded men were captured by R.]
3. Орша — Orsha [Town in Mogilev Province where Orzhitsa Rv falls into Dnieper, about 75 mi W of Smolensk by rail]
4. укра́дучись (*obs* or *pop*) = укра́дкой

Four, III, 18

1. бе́гство нача́льника от а́рмии — [N left the Grand Army at Smorgony for Vilna and Paris on December 5 or 6, N.S.]
2. Ней в Оршу — [Ney left Smolensk w F rear guard on Nov. 17, N.S., w 6,000 fighting men. He arrived at Orsha three days later w only 900, fighting superior R forces and bad weather on the way.]
3. от вели́чественного до смешно́го то́лько оди́н шаг — [more usually in R от вели́кого до смешно́го . . . . Михельсон (p. 297) traces similar expressions to Wieland, Tom Paine, Marmontel and even Longinus. N said words quoted in Warsaw after R campaign.]
4. ма́лость *(f)* — pettiness *(obs)*

Four, III, 19

1. Чича́гов — Chichagov [Па́вел Ва́сильевич Ч. (1765-1849). Admiral, naval minister and member of state council. In 1812, tsar entrusted him w army to cut off and trap N at Berezina, which Chichagov failed to do.]
2. одна́ со́тая всего́ во́йска — [Acc to Florinsky, pp 674 and 678, N had sent 575,000 men E across the Niemen, but only 30,000 F crossed the Berezina going W]
3. J. Maistre — [Count Joseph-Marie de Maistre (1754-1821). Sardinian ambassador to St P (1802-1817). For an interesting opinion of de Maistre's influence on LNT in *W&P,* see Isaiah Berlin, *The Hedgehog and the Fox: An Essay on Tolstoy's View of History* (various editions fr 1951 on), Chapters 5 through 8.]
4. Витгенштейн — [Commanded a slow-moving R corps at this time]

5. 15 гра́дусов моро́за — [Réaumur thermometer = minus 2 degrees F. = minus 19 degrees C.]

Four, IV, 1

1. перемина́ть *(impf)* — to rumple; to knead

Four, IV, 2

1. ручья́ми fr руче́й
2. что ты прие́хал — [The countess thinks she is talking to the young man]

Four, IV, 3

1. сто́ра *(obs)* = што́ра
2. что у ней на душе́? — what is in her heart?

Four, IV, 4

1. перере́зывать *(impf)* fr перере́зать *(pf)*

(2.) за одно́ = заодно́

3. Принц Евге́ний Виртембе́ргский — Prince Eugene of Wūrttemberg [Nephew of tsar's mother and генера́л-майо́р (later, генера́л-от-инфанте́рии) in R service. Saw action at Borodino. Later, commanded R IV corps.]
4. кто как мог да́льше — each as far as he could
5. *le chevalier sans peur et sans reproche (F)* — Knight without fear or blame [Traditionally said of Pierre du Terrail, seigneur de Bayard (ca. 1474-1524), F knight who fell in battle]
6. ма́ршальский жезл — [Davout's marshall's baton was captured at Krasnoe]
7. он [Куту́зов] ду́мает то́лько об удовлетворе́нии свои́х страсте́й — [The historical Kutuzov was a notorious woman-chaser]
8. Полотня́ные Заво́ды — Polotnianye Zavody [Village in Medyn District, just W of Bobrov District in NE Kaluga Province.

The Goncharovs (to which family Pushkin's wife belonged) had a hereditary estate there.]

9. подкýплен им — [Maude says the diary of Sir Robert Thomas Wilson (1774-1849), published in 1861, makes this charge. Wilson was British mil commissioner at R headquarters, 1812-1814.]

Four, IV, 5

1. в истóрии напи́санной недáвно — [М. Богданович, *История Отечественной войны 1812 года по достоверным источникам. Составлена по высочайшему повелению.* СПБ, 1859-1860, 3 тома.]
2. за минýту — a minute earlier
3. золотóй мост [стрóить] — to ease [their] way out of disaster [Михельсон cites examples of this idiom in F, G, Italian and L.]

Four, IV, 6

1. противу-приказáние — counter-order
2. Доброе — Dobroe [Village in Krasnenskii District, Smolensk Province, W of Krasnoe]
3. нагни́ *(impv)* fr нагнýть *(pf)*
4. послéдний — lowest, worst

(5.) по делóм = поделóм

6. м . . . и . . . в г . . . —
   мать их в гýзно — f— their mothers in the ass

Four, IV, 7

1. налегни́ *(impf)* fr налéчь *(pf)*
2. рочáг *(subst)* = рычáг
3. с нáкрика — move out at the shout
4. идёт — it's coming; it's giving
5. рéжа *(pr deep)* fr рéзать
6. чегó стал — what did you stop for
7. вы чегó [дéлаете]
8. госпóдá тут — there are [F] gentry here
9. матерши́нник *(coarse)* — one who uses the word

"mother" in cursing.

10. я вас *(threat)* — I'll give it to you
11. раскровянить *(pf)* = раскровенить *(pf, pop)* — to get sth all bloody
12. пригораживаться/ пригородиться — to be set up; to be enclosed
13. осьмой *(obs)* = восьмой
14. подпёрт *(pf, past, pass, prich)* fr подпирать/ подпереть
15. сошка — rifle-stand

(16.) до нага = донага — naked

Four, IV, 8

1. 18 градусов мороза — [Réaumur = –8 degrees F = –22 degrees C]
2. запропал *(m, past)* fr запропасть *(pf, pop)* — to disappear
3. ворона *(coll)* — lazybones; gawk
4. вострый (*pop* or *dial*) = острый
5. беремя *(nt, dial)* — a big armful; a bundle (*variant of* бремя)
6. надавливать/ надавить — to put sth down heavily
7. экой яд плясать — what a passion for dancing
8. зайтись *(pf)* — to lose one's sense of feeling; to grow numb
9. align зазнобить *(pf, dial)* — to start freezing
10. похудает *(subst)* = похудеет
11. а то всё одно отстанешь — or else you [i.e. the speaker] will lag behind all alone
12. поразуть *(pf)* fr разуть — to take the boots off smb
13. разворочать *(pf, pop)* = разворотить *(pf)*
14. лопочет fr лопотать *(impf)*
15. корона — state *(obs)*; government *(obs)*
16. отворотить *(pf)* — to turn aside (*obs* or *pop*)
17. должно [быть] от пищи
18. дён (*obs, dial* or *pop*) = дней fr день *(m)*
19. волков этих что = сколько этих волков
20. допущают *(subst)* = допускают fr допускать *(impf)*
21. Полион *(subst)* = Наполеон
22. слова не знает [по-русски]
23. возьмёт-возьмёт — he does capture him
24. на те = нате
25. прикинуться *(pf)* — to turn into [sth else, as in fairy tales]

26. положе́ние — [wrong word. He means sth like возмо́жность.]
27. посмотрю́ я на тебя́ — that's what I see when I look at you
28. излови́мши *(subst)* = излови́вши fr излови́ть *(pf)*
29. что наро́ду = ско́лько наро́ду
30. всё одно́ — just the same; anyhow
31. не бу́дет ходи́ть *(impf, many-x)* — he won't be walking [in R]
32. дрове́ц *(coll; aff, gen, pl; no nom)* fr дрова́
33. грохо́чут *(impf)* fr грохота́ть *(impf)*
34. то-то сме́ху — it's out-and-out laughing
35. кура́жный — swaggering
36. бяда́ *(subst)* = беда́

Four, IV, 9

1. отягчи́ть *(pf; book)* = отяготи́ть *(pf)*
2. хряск *(dial)* — crunch
3. су́чьев *(gen pl)* fr сук
4. ведме́дь *(subst)* = медве́дь *(m)*
5. подстели́ть *(pf, pop)* = подостла́ть *(pf)*
6. то-то мужи́к — a real muzhik
7. по-ба́бьи — like a peasant woman (ба́ба)
8. переймý *(ft pf)* fr перенима́ть/ переня́ть
9. *Vive Henri Quatre* — [Old F song. For words and music, see René Deloup, *Vieilles Chansons et Rondes Françaises,* Paris, Max Eschig, and London, Schott & Co., no date (copyright 1939), p. 90.]
10. *ce diable à quatre (F)* — that hell-raiser
11. виварика́! виф серувару́! сидябляка́ . . . кю . . . кю летриптала́, де бу де ба и детравагала [F words of song attempted phonetically by R who knows no F; кю, as a sound sequence, does not occur in native words, which is why speaker has a hard time saying it.]
12. к моро́зу — a sign of frost

Four, IV, 10

1. блестя́щий адмира́л [Чича́гов]
2. Куту́зов был в Ви́льне губерна́тором — [In 1799-1801 and 1809-1811]

3. опроки́дыватель *(m)* — one who overturns
4. строево́й рапо́рт — report *(mil)* [formal report to superior officer on troops present or accounted for]
5. Бори́сов — Borisov [District town on Berezina Rv in Minsk Province]
6. перека́чиваться *(impf)* — to waddle *(in walking)*
7. шля́па к фро́нту — [Maude explains this as a cocked hat w its peaks turned sideways. фронт *(F front)* — forehead. Hat was pushed forward onto forehead.]
8. в раз or враз — just in time
9. Гео́ргий I-й сте́пени — [A very high decoration, including a star and a ribbon. First Class was reserved for successful commanding generals. Kutuzov was the 8th man to be given this honor since it was first awarded in 1770.]

Four, IV, 11

1. заступа́ть/ заступи́ть — to replace (*obs* or *pop*)
2. и он у́мер — [Kutuzov died April 16/28, 1813, while campaigning w R army nr Bunzlau in Prussian Silesia. Again a Biblical turn of phrase.]

Four, IV, 12

1. Орёл — [Province capital about 240 mi by rail S of M, where Orlik Rv flows into Oká]
2. жёлчная горя́чка — fever of the bile; bilious fever
3. постро́йка — construct; structure
4. Еле́ц — [District town in Orël Province on left bank of Sosna Rv, 70 mi NW of Voronezh]

Four, IV, 13

1. простéть/ попростéть *(coll)* — to become simpler

Four, IV, 14

1. копышущихся (*obs* or *dial*) = копоша́сь fr копоши́ться *(impf)*

2. влеко́мый *(pr pass prich)* fr влечь *(impf)*
3. руби́ться *(impf)* — to be built of wood or logs
4. погоре́лый *(coll, obs)* — burned-out; fire-damaged
5. Грanови́тая пала́та — Hall of Facets [Building on Собо́рная пло́щадь in M Kremlin, built of stone by Italian architects, 1473-1491. Used in early days for rulers' banquets and receptions.]

Four, IV, 15

1. портре́тная *(obs)* — portrait-gallery *(room in rich houses)*

Four, IV, 16: none

Four, IV, 17

1. поко́йный — convenient *(obs);* comfortable *(obs)*
2. дурачо́к — simpleton
3. при слу́чае — upon occasion
4. у́мственное хозя́йство — mental equipment
5. что ты = что с тобо́й
6. осо́бенный — unlike; different

Four, IV, 18

1. за таки́ми господа́ми — under the protection of such masters
2. Колизе́й — Colosseum or Coliseum [in Rome]
3. коми́ссия — errand *(obs)*
4. я зае́ду за коми́ссиями — I'll drop by to see if there is sth I can do for you

Four, IV, 19: none

Four, IV, 20

1. она не мо́жет [де́лать] ина́че

EPILOGUE, I, 1

ЭПИЛОГ, ЧАСТЬ ПЕРВАЯ, ГЛАВА ПЕРВАЯ

1. Фо́тий — Fotii or Photius [Name in rel of Пётр Спа́ский (1792-1838). Archimandrite. Head of Monastery, and rel fanatic, who had visions of Satan. Fotii was encouraged by Arakcheev and intrigued against masons, Bible Society, etc.]
2. Шеллинг — Schelling [Friedrich Wilhelm Joseph von S. (1775-1834). G philosopher. He believed nature and mind to be inseparable, differing in degree only fr unity of mind and matter in Aristotle. Once sympathized w F Revolution.]
3. Фихте — Fichte [Johann Gottlieb F. (1762-1814). G philosopher and liberal nationalist]
4. Шатобриа́н — Chateaubriand [François René, Viscount de C. (1766-1848). F author and royalist foreign minister (1823-1824). Famous as imaginative stylist who greatly influenced F romanticism. Author of *Le Génie du Christianisme* (The Genius of Christianity, 1802) and *Mémoires d'outre-tombe* (Memoirs from Beyond the Tomb, published 1849-1850).]
5. дав конститу́цию По́льше — [Alexander signed P constitution on November 27, 1815, O.S. Poland was given autonomy, a bicameral legislature, etc. under the tsar. This constitution was suppressed in 1830 after P Insurrection.]
6. Свяще́нный Сою́з — Holy Alliance [Triple alliance betw R, Austria, and Prussia signed September 14/26, 1815]
7. раскаси́ровав Семёновский полк — [In Oct. 1820, this guards regt. mutinied against its commander, because of his cruelty. Regt. was disbanded and soldiers were punished.]
8. професси́ровать — to profess *(Gallicism)*

Epilogue, I, 2

1. разнесе́ние fr разноси́ть *(impf)*
2. денни́к *(dial)* — separate, covered, warm stall for animals
3. о́бли́тый — covered over

Epilogue, I, 3

1. италья́нская а́рмия — F army in Italy (1796-1797)
2. неми́лость *(f)* — [Gen N Bonaparte first won fame by capturing Toulon fr E for Robespierre's govt. in 1793. When Robespierre was deposed on July 27, 1794 (the Ninth of Thermidor), Bonaparte fell into disgrace and retired. He returned to service in August 1795 and, in October, "saved" the republic by putting down the Vendémaire insurrection in Paris w artillery.]
3. ру́сские войска́ — [N was in Egypt in 1798 and 1799 when Suvorov and his R defeated F in Italy and Switzerland in 1799]
4. Ма́льта — [The Knights Hospitalers surrendered Malta to Napoleon in 1798]
5. Ке́сарь *(m, obs)* = Це́зарь *(m)* — Caesar [See Записки Цезаря, One, I, 6 above]
6. середи́нные наро́ды — the nations in the middle [of Europe]
7. своди́ться/ свести́сь — to grow close to; to hobnob w
8. дочь Ке́сарей — [i.e., daughter of Holy Roman Emperors]
9. не име́ющих приме́ров — unexampled; unprecedented
10. о́стров в двух днях перее́зда от Фра́нции — [Elba. Island in Tyrrhenian Sea to W of Tuscany in Italy where N was exiled in 1814 until he escaped to lead the Hundred Days (which ended after Waterloo) in early 1815. He was then exiled to St. Helena.]

Epilogue, I, 4

1. о́тплеск — backwash
2. сурьма́ — kohl
3. противодвиже́ние — counter movement
4. не нам, не нам, а Имени Твоему́ — [Words on medal struck by tsar to commemorate F defeat of 1812. Issued Dec. 1813.]
5. цвето́чная пыль *(f)* = пыльца́
6. выведе́ние — hatching; raising

Epilogue, I, 5

1. зао́чно — in smb's absence

2. особо́роваться = собо́роваться (*impf* and *pf*) — to receive last rites of the church
3. безде́нежный — gratuitous *(obs)*; not costing anything *(obs)*
4. оборо́т — turn; way of action *(obs)*; money turnover
5. посажа́ть *(pf)* — *lit*: to plant; *fig*: to be jailed
6. [долгова́я] я́ма — [debtors'] prison *(obs)*
7. перенесе́ние — endurance

Epilogue, I, 6: none

Epilogue, I, 7

1. назём *(dial)* — manure
2. дели́ться *(impf)* — to receive one's portion and leave the common unit [such as the peasant commune]
3. одо́нье *(dial)* — small haystack
4. улыба́ться под уса́ми *(impf)* — to smile to oneself
5. горча́вка = гореча́вка — gentian
6. сангвини́ческий — joyful; responsive to outer stimuli, but not deep; sanguine
7. сраба́тывать/ срабо́тать — to work; to do
8. наперёд — first

Epilogue, I, 8

1. любе́зности *(f, pl)* — polite words
2. кама́ or каме́я or камэ́ — cameo
3. Лаоко́он — Laocoōn [Trojan priest who warned against Trojan horse and was killed w his sons by giant snakes. A famous ancient Gk statue of this event is in Vatican (cf. Virgil's *Aeneid,* Book II).]
4. всё то же — in the same business
5. "Иму́щему даётся, а у неиму́щего отни́мется" — "For he that hath, to him shall be given: and he that hath not, fr him shall be taken away even that which he hath." (Mark 4:25) [Cf also Matthew 13:12 and Luke 8:18 for same idea.]

Epilogue, I, 9

1. дворя́нские вы́боры — [The gentry of districts and provinces had periodic elections in connection w corporate self-government under Charter of 1785]
2. пришли́ благодари́ть ста́рую графи́ню — [Maude explains it was customary to thank hostess after dinner, and old lady was treated as hostess out of politeness]
3. тупо́й — broad
4. взойти́ *(pf, obs)* — to enter; to come in
5. по[ложе́нии] — [she is pregnant]
6. не по хорошу́ [хоро́шему] мил, а по милу́ хоро́ш *(saying)* — One is dear not because one is good-looking, but good-looking because one is dear
7. Malvina — [A recurrent character in Ossian as "tr" by James MacPherson (1736-1796). She was daughter of Toscar and beloved of Oscar. Although Samuel Johnson attacked Ossian as a forgery, these pieces were quite popular in 19th century Europe. *Malvina* (1801) was the title of a novel published anonymously by Mme. Marie (called Sophie) Cottin, née Risteau (1770-1807).]
8. я не так — I'm not like that

Epilogue, I, 10

1. ширéть/ поширéть = ши́рить/ поши́рить — to grow broader; to spread out

(2.) заму́жство *(obs)* = заму́жество

3. в де́вушках — as an unmarried girl
4. разро́сся *(past)* fr разрасти́сь *(pf)*
5. жёлтое [пятно́] . . . — tan [spot]
6. ему́ сто́ило *(+ inf.)* — he had only; all he had to do was

Epilogue, I, 11

1. тетёшкать *(impf; dial)* — to dandle
2. ви́дишь, [ребёнок] де́ржит [го́лову]
3. задо́к — backside; seat

Epilogue, I, 12

1. прора́нивать *(impf)* fr пророни́ть *(pf)*
2. сплóчивать *(impf, obs)* fr спла́чивать *(impf)*
3. добрóта — high-quality material
4. по рублю́ — a ruble *(per arshin)*
5. сби́ла [с тóлку]
6. купи́ть да купи́ть — I had to buy it
7. гран-пасья́нс — solitaire *(card game); grand patience (F)*
8. просморка́ться *(pf, coll)* — to blow one's nose

Epilogue, I, 13

1. недолóженный — incompletely laid out
2. благода́рствуй *(obs)* = благода́рствую *(obs)* = благодарю́
3. Семёновский полк — [See Epilogue, I, 1 above]
4. Библéйское óбщество — [The Bible Society was founded in St P in 1818 and soon had 300 branches in R for disseminating Bible. Its president was князь Алекса́ндр Никола́евич Голи́цын, and the tsar was a member. But Golitsyn was fired as Minister of Education in 1824 (under Fotii's influence) and the society fell out of favor. Tsar Nicholas I closed it in 1826.]
5. Госнер or Госснер — Gossner [Johan G (1773-1858). A renegade Roman Catholic priest fr Munich, invited by Bible Society to St P in 1820. A mystic, he wrote there *Geist des Lebens und der Lehre Jesus* (The Spirit of Jesus' Life and Teaching, St P, 1822-1824). The book was burned, and author deported to W.]
6. Тата́ринова — Tatarinova [Екатери́на Фили́повна Т., née Буксгевден (1753-1856). Baltic G widow of guards officer and convert to R Orthodoxy. In 1817, she founded mystic "Духóвный Сою́з" and considered she had a gift of prophecy. She influenced tsar briefly, but lost influence in 1822 and 1823. Her society was broken up by govt. in 1837, and she was sent to a nunnery.]
7. залива́ется [сме́хом]
8. довя́зывать/ довяза́ть — to finish knitting

Epilogue, I, 14

1. mme Крю́днер — Kriudner or Krüdener [Baroness Barbara-Juliane von K, née Vietinghoff (1764-1824). Another Baltic G widow, mystic, and self-professed prophetess, who influenced tsar through rel and flattery, especially in Paris during 1815. She moved to Livonia in 1818, and St P in 1821, but did not regain her influence over tsar. Later, ordered to leave St P, she died in the Crimea. Her novel, *Valérie ou Lettres de Gustave de Linar à Ernest de G* (1804) is mentioned in Pushkin's "Евгений Онегин", Chapter Three, Stanza IX. (For commentary, see Nabokov's notes in his commentary to Pushkin's *Eugene Onegin,* II, 343-344.)]
2. повы́бить *(pf, coll)* — to knock all out
3. Шварц — Shvarts or Schwarz [The cruel col. against whom Semënovskii Regt. mutinied in 1820]
4. [вое́нное] поселе́ние — [In 1816, Arakcheev started mil colonies again, in which soldiers farmed the land to raise own food. These colonies were associated w cruelty. By 1825, there were 375,000 soldiers living in them. Nicholas I acknowledged their failure, but they were not finally abolished until 1857.]
5. соревнова́ть *(impf, obs)* — to keep up w others; not to fall behind others
6. Пугачёв — Pugachëv or Pugachov [Емелья́н Ива́нович П. (1726-1775). Cossack leader of rebellion on Volga that bears his name (1773-1775). He tried to pass himself off as Peter III and killed many gentry in areas he captured.]
7. тугенбунд — *Tugenbund (G)* = League of Virtue [G society formed in 1808 to foster patriotism, but secretly seeking to get rid of N, who had it dissolved. It then went underground and continued as a focus of liberal opposition in G of 1820's and 1830's. The R govt., of course, opposed it.]
8. бунт — [Homonym of бунд. Final sound in both is unvoiced.]
9. вели́ мне Аракче́ев — if Arakcheev ordered me

Epilogue, I, 15

1. чуть де́ло до (+ *gen*) — once the question barely touches
2. а он [говори́л] своё
3. по душе́ — in [his] heart
4. всё не то, что — it's still not the same as

5. како́е де́ло мне до (+ *gen*) — what business is it of mine; what do I care
6. не о еди́ном хле́бе — "not by bread alone"; "not by bread only" [Deuteronomy 8:3. Quoted by Jesus in Matthew 4:4, and Luke 4:4.]
7. Тамбо́в — Tambov [Province about 300 mi SE of M on way to Saratov]

Epilogue, I, 16

1. Сисмонди — Sismondi [Jean-Charles Léonard Simonde de S. (1773-1842). Swiss historian who wrote *Histoire des républiques italiennes* (History of the Italian Republics in the Middle Ages, 16 vols. 1809-1818).]
2. вот ещё! — what next! really!
3. Му́ций Сцево́ла — Mucius Scaevola [Caius M.S. Roman hero fr 6th century B.C. M.S. went out to kill Etruscan King Lars Porsena, who was besieging Rome. M.S. was captured. Porsena ordered him burned at stake. M.S. thrust his hand into fire and kept it there to show his contempt for death. This so impressed Porsena that he freed M.S. and lifted the siege. Or so we are told.]

Epilogue, II, 1

1. Гибон or Гиббон — Gibbon [Edward G. (1737-1794). E historian most famous for *Decline and Fall of Roman Empire* (1776-1783).]
2. Бокль — Buckle [Henry Thomas B. (1821-1862). E historian very widely read in LNT's day by R intelligentsia. Wrote *History of Civilization in England* (1857-1861).]
3. Людови́к XIV — Louis XIV [(1638-1715). "Sun King" of F, who reigned fr 1643 to his death, and brought F monarchy to its zenith.]
4. Людови́к XVIII — Louis XVIII [(1755-1824). Brother of Louis XVI. Put on F throne after first fall of N in 1814 by victorious allies. Reigned until death.]
5. кре́сло — [On September 30, 1814, N.S., Metternich, in Vienna, invited Talleyrand to his home. This was before

the Congress of Vienna was to open. On entering the reception room, the F diplomat noticed an empty chair between Lord Castlereagh (who was representing Great Britain) and the host, which Talleyrand promptly "occupied" (his word). Talleyrand then began his successful campaign for "legitimism," and thus won for F the right to retain her pre-revolutionary frontiers. (See his letter to Louis XVIII of October 4, 1814, in *Mémoires complets et authentiques de Charles Maurice de Talleyrand,* Paris, Jean de Bonnot, 1967, II, 318 ff.) I would like to thank Mr. George Spater of Kingston near Lewes, Sussex, England, for putting me on the track to the above source.] (See Appendix Seven.)

Epilogue, II, 2

1. Lanfrey — [Pierre L. (1828-1877). F historian of anti-N and republican convictions. Author of *Histoire de Napoléon I-er* (History of N I, Vol I, 1867).]
2. Гервúнус — Gervinus [Georg-Gottfried G. (1805-1871). G historian and Shakespeare critic. Wrote *Geschichte des 19-ten Jahrhunderts* (History of the 19th Century) 8 vols, 1854-1860.]
3. Шлóссер — Schlosser [Friedrich-Christoph S. (1776-1861). G historian. Wrote *Weltgeschichte* (History of the World), 19 vols, 1843-1857.]
4. на половúне дорóги — at the halfway point; halfway
5. разлагáть/ разложúть — to break sth down into component parts

(6.) замледéлец *(misprint)* = земледéлец

Epilogue, II, 3

1. Лютер — Luther [Martin L. (1483-1546). G Reformation leader, tr of Bible into G, for whom Lutheranism is named.]
2. обращáющиеся [дéньги] — [money] circulating
3. ассигнáция — paper money [At the time of *W&P,* and at the time it was written, two currencies circulated in R. Gold and silver were worth face value, but paper bills of same denomination were worth much less. The exact value of paper in terms of gold and silver frequently changed.]
4. жетóн — token *(metal, used as coin)*

Epilogue, II, 4

1. Людови́к XI — Louis XI [(1423-1483), King of F (1461-1483). Strengthened central authority of F Kings.]
2. разме́нная ка́сса — a cashier's office at which gold and silver could be obtained for paper money; exchange bureau
3. Наполео́н III . . . в Було́не — [Louis N, or N III (1808-1873), nephew of N I and son of Louis Bonaparte, was arrested in Boulogne in 1840 for trying to seize power (his second effort to do so). However, he escaped fr prison, returned to F after 1848 Revolution, became President of F that year and proclaimed himself Emperor in 1852. He was on the throne when LNT wrote *W&P,* but was deposed in 1871, after losing Franco-Prussian War.]
4. Ре́йнский Сою́з — Confederation of the Rhine. [N set up this Confederation of G princes in 1806. It lasted 7 years.]
5. Конве́нт — [The National Convention in F was in power fr 1792 (when it abolished the monarchy) until, after the overthrow of Robespierre in 1794, it was replaced by the Directory in 1795]
6. Директо́рия — [The Directory. F govt fr 1795 to 1799, consisting of 5 Directors in executive branch. It was overthrown on November 9-10, 1799 (the 18 Brumaire *coup d'état*), by Gen. Bonaparte, who set up the Consulate w himself as First Consul.]
7. Импе́рия — [N I had himself declared Emperor of the F in 1805]
8. Иоа́нн IV *(obs)* = Ива́н IV — Ivan IV [Ива́н Гро́зный, or Ива́н Васи́льевич (1530-1584), First R tsar. Ruled fr 1547 to death.]
9. Карл I — Charles I [(1600-1649). King of England (1625-1649). Lost E Civil War. Tried, convicted of treason, and executed.]
10. Карл X — Charles X [(1757-1836). Succeeded brother, Louis XVIII, as King of F in 1824. Forced to abdicate by July Revolution of 1830.]
11. Людови́к-Фили́пп — Louis-Philippe [(1773-1850). Son of Louis-Philippe-Joseph, Duke of Orléans (1747-1793), who supported Jacobins in F Rev, changed his name to Philippe Egalité, and was guillotined. The younger Louis Philippe was chosen King of F under July monarchy in 1830, and affected bourgeois manners, but was forced to abdicate by Feb Revolution of 1848.]
12. республика́нское прави́тельство — F Second Republic lasted fr Feb 1848 until its President set himself up as N III, Emperor of the Second Empire, in 1852.]

13. Дидеро́т or Дидеро́ — Diderot [Denis D. (1713-1784). F Encyclopedist, playwright, novelist, critic, skeptic and leading figure of rationalist, liberal Enlightenment.]
14. Бомарше́ — Beaumarchais [Pierre-Augustin Caron de B. (1732-1799) F playwright and secret agent. Wrote *Le Barbier de Seville* (1775) and *Le Mariage de Figaro* (1784), on which Rossini and Mozart based famous operas.]
15. Ку́рбский — Kurbskii [князь Андре́й Миха́йлович К. (1528-1583). Friend and gen of Ivan IV until he went over to P enemy in war time. Fr P he may have conducted a famous correspondence w tsar; Edward L. Keenan's *Kurbskii-Groznyi Apocrypha* (Cambridge, MS. 1971) challenges its authenticity.] (See App. 7)
16. Готфрид — Godfrey [of Bouillon (ca. 1058-1100). Duke of Lower Lorraine. Leader of First Crusade, which captured Jerusalem. Called self "Protector of the Holy Sepulchre."]
17. Пётр Пусты́нник — Peter the Hermit [(ca. 1050-1115). F preacher who encouraged First Crusade and led one group of crusaders himself.]

Epilogue, II, 5

1. смотря́ по (+ *dat*) — depending on
2. познава́ние = позна́ние
3. Францу́зы иду́т в Ме́ксику — [The F sent an army to Mexico in 1864 to take advantage of U.S. Civil War and make Maximilian von Hapsburg (brother of Emperor Franz Joseph of Austria) Emperor of Mexico. F army was withdrawn after U.S. Civil War ended. Maximilian was captured by the Mexicans under Benito Juarez, and was shot.]
4. Бисмарк . . . в Боге́мию — [Prince Otto von Bismarck (1815-1898), the Prussian militarist and chancellor, ordered Prussian army to invade Bohemia. At Sadowa, in the summer of 1866, Prussia defeated Austria and thus ended victoriously the brief Austro-Prussian War, which he had provoked.]

Epilogue, II, 6

(1.) приходи́ться/ прийти́сь — to turn up, to be present
2. жжёт fr жечь *(impf)*

Epilogue, II, 7

1. неприложи́мый — inapplicable

Epilogue, II, 8

1. неразрешённость *(f)* — insolubility; inability to solve
2. неутверждённый — unreinforced; unstrengthened

Epilogue, II, 9

1. потопля́ть *(impf)* — to drown
2. Атти́ла — Attila [the Hun, "the Scourge of God," died 453 A.D. after reigning about 20 years. Extorted tribute fr Rome.]

Epilogue, II, 10

1. наидосту́пнейший = (досту́пный + *superlative prefix and suffix*)
2. Ньютон — Newton [Sir Isaac N. (1642-1727). E physicist, who derived law of gravitation and formulated laws of motion.]

Epilogue, II, 11

1. Ке́плер — Kepler [Johannes K. (1571-1636). G astronomer. Discovered laws of planetary motion. His third law was used by Newton in deriving law of gravitation.]
2. по́прище — field of activity *(obs)*
3. дробле́ние fr дроби́ть *(impf)*
4. суммова́ние = сумми́рование

Epilogue, II, 12

1. Копе́рник — Copernicus [Nicholas C. (1473-1543), P astronomer, described sun as center of solar system, w Earth as one of its satellites and thereby superseded Ptolemaic system of

astronomy, which centered on Earth as stationary center of universe. Claudius Ptolemaius, a Graeco-Egyptian astronomer of 2nd century B.C., had founded earlier system.]

2. птоломе́евый — Ptolemaic
3. призна́й они́ = е́сли бы они́ призна́ли
4. твердь *(f, Biblical)* — firmament
5. Иису́с Нави́н — Joshua, son of Nun [According to Bible, he caused sun to stand still in Aijalon so he could smite the Amonites. "And the sun stood still, and the moon stayed . . . And the sun stayed in the midst of heaven, and hasted not to go down about a whole day. And there was no day like that before it or after . . ." (Joshua 10:13-14). This of course is incompatible w Copernican astronomy.]

КОНЕЦ

APPENDIX ONE:
Proper Nouns In Russian Occurring In Novel.

Августин	Three, III, 5
Адонаи	Two, III, 10
Александр I (Александр Павлович)	One, I, 5
Алеша-пройдоха	Two, II, 15
Алкид	Two, I, 3
Амалик	Three, I, 18
Английская набережная	Two, III, 14
Английский клуб	Two, I, 2
Андрея [орден]	Two, II, 20
Анны[орден]	Two, IV, 1
Апраксин	One, I, 7
Апраксин, С.С.	Two, I, 3
Апшеронский полк	One, III, 15
Аракчеев	One, III, 11
Арбат	Three, III, 26
Арбатская площадь	Two, V, 17
Аристово	Four, II, 15
Армфельд	Three, I, 6
Арнаут	One, III, 7
Архаров	One, I, 12
Астрея	Two, V, 1
Аш	Three, II, 4
Багговут	Four, II, 6
Багратион	One, II, 8
Балашев	Three, I, 3
Барклай	Three, I, 6
"Барыня"	Two, IV, 7
Бахус	One, II, 2
"Бедная Лиза"	Two, V, 5
Беклешов	Two, I, 3
Белая Церковь	Three, II, 17
Бенигсен, or Беннигсен	Two, II, 8
Березина	Three, III, 2
Бертелеми = Barthemy	Four, II, 17
Библейское общество	Ep, I, 13
Бобровск	Four, II, 15
Богемские леса	One, II, 13
Бокль = Buckle	Ep, II, 1
Болотная площадь	Three, II, 18
Болохвитинов	Four, II, 15
Большая Ордынка	Four, II, 14
Борисов	Four, IV, 10
Боровицкие ворота	Three, III, 21
Бородино	Three, II, 7
Браницкий	Three, II, 1
Буксгевден	One, II, 14
Булонская экспедиция	One, I, 16
Бурбоны = Bourbons	One, I, 5
"Буря"	Two, IV, 9
Валлахия	Three, I, 6
Валуев	Two, I, 2
Варварка	Three, III, 23
Варфоломеевская ночь =St.	

APPENDIX TWO:
Location of Definitions of Russian Idioms and Some Other Words

не могу знать	One, III, 13
не раз	One, III, 3
не так	One, I, 6
не то	Two, IV, 7
не то, . . . не то	One, II, 12
не то, что	One, I, 22
ни синь пороха	Three, II, 14
никуда не годиться	One, I, 8
ну, вас	One, II, 21
нумер	One, II, 20
облокачивать	One, I, 3
обмокнуть	Three, I, 2
оброк	Two, III, 1
обросший	One, III, 5
обстричь	Two, II, 17
обсуживать	Two, III, 18
один-на-один	One, III, 4
окромя	One, II, 4
опущенность	Three, II, 8
отбивать	Two, II, 16
отирать	One, III, 6
отстрониться	One, III, 7
отштукатурить	Two, II, 11
перебивать	One, II, 2
переводить/ перевести дух [дыхание]	One, I, 20
перегоняться	Three, II, 13
перехватывать(ся)	Two,I, 1
переход	One, II, 7
перецеловать	Two, V, 6
пиеса	One, I, 1
по делом	Four, IV, 6
по мне	Two, II, 18
по пусту	Three, III, 21
побивать	Four, II, 19
повыехать	Three, III, 12
повыползти	Three, III, 15
повыходить	Three, III, 30
под рукой	One, II, 3
подбадривать(ся)	One, II, 7
подвертка	One, II, 2
подернуть	One, III, 3
подите	One, I, 12
поднимать на смех	Four, II, 5
подрагивать	One, I, 20
подсоблять	Three, II, 9
подстава	Two, I, 8
пока не	Two, V, 10
покряхтывать	Three, I, 23
полно	Two, III, 22
полноте	One, II, 12
порядок	One, II, 8
польский	Two, I, 3
пособлять	Two, II, 9
потрогивать	Three, I, 7
превосходительство	One, II, 1
предвечный	Two, II, 4
при случае	Four, IV, 17
прибить	Two, II, 1
приглядываться	One, III, 14
приготавливать	One, III, 6
приложить уши	Two, IV, 6
принюхиваться	Three, II, 29
присоветовать	Three, I, 11
пристроиваться	Three, I, 22
пробиваться	One, III, 7
пробурлить	One, I, 2
провод	One, II, 9
производить	One, III, 6
противу	Three, II, 1
пускать в ход	One, I, 5
пущай	Three, III, 23
разбирать	Two, II, 1
разбираться	One, II, 2
разводить руками	One, I, 2
расположение	One, III, 5
распускать	One, I, 20

APPENDIX THREE:
Proper Nouns in Latin Alphabet Occurring in Novel

NOTE: In so far as possible, names of historical figures are given in their historical spelling when that contrasts with LNT's spelling, e.g. Barthemy rather than Bartelemi.

Name	Reference
Alicides	Two, I, 3
Amstetten	One, II, 9
Arcola	One, I, 5
Attila	Ep, II, 9
Auersperg	One, II, 10
Auerstedt or Auerstadt see Jena	Two, II, 6
Augezd	One, III, 18
Austerlitz	One, III, 10
Baden see Württem-berg	Three, I, 7
Barclay	Three, II, 1
Bartenstein	Two, II, 15
Barthemy	Four, II, 17
Bassano	Three, I, 3
Beauharnais see Viceroy	Three, II, 27
Beaumarchais	Ep, II, 4
Beausset or Bossuet	Three, II, 26
Belliard	One, II, 12
Bellowitz	One, III, 12
Bernadotte	Three, I, 6
Berthier	Three, I, 2
Bessières	Three, I, 7
Bismarck	Ep, II, 5
Bossuet see Beausset	Three, II, 26
Bourbons	One, I, 5
Branicki	Three, II, 1
Braunau	One, II, 1
Broussier	Four, II, 15
Brumaire (18)	One, I, 5
Brünn	One, II, 9
Bucharest	Three, II, 6
Buckle	Ep, II, 1
Buxhöwden	One, II, 14
Caesar	One, I, 6
Campo Formio	One, II, 10
Castries	Three, I, 5
Caulaincourt	Two, III, 9
Charles I	Ep, II, 4
Charles IX	Three, II, 28
Charles X	Ep, II, 4
Charles XII see Poltava	Three, I, 7
Charon	Three, II, 17
Chateaubriand	Ep, I, 1
Cherubini	Two, III, 13
"[Les] Chevaliers du Cygne"	Three, II, 16
Claparède	Three, II, 34
Clausewitz	Three, II, 25
Code Napoléon [and] Jus-tiniani	Two, III, 6
Compans	Three, II, 27
Confederation of the Rhine	Ep, II, 4
"Contrat social"	One, I, 5

APPENDIX FOUR:
THE TABLE OF RANKS

The "Table of Ranks" was set up in 1722 under Peter I and lasted, with some changes, until 1917. The civil service grades, their military equivalents, and some equivalent court ranks are given here. For a more detailed statement of all this, see the article "Табель о рангах" in the pre-revolutionary *Энциклопедический словарь,* СПБ, Брокгауз и Ефрон, 1890-1904 гг., том 63, стр. 439-444.

1. Канцлер. Генерал-Фельдмаршал.

2. Действительный тайный советник. Генерал-от-кавалерии, или Генерал-от-инфантерии, или Генерал-от-артиллерии. Обер-камергер. Обер-гофмаршал. Обер-церемониймейстер, чин второго класса.

3. Тайный советник. Генерал-лейтенант. Гофмаршал. Обер-церемониймейстер.

4. Действительный статский советник. Генерал-майор.

5. Статский советник. ———. Церемониймейстер.

6. Коллежский советник или Военный советник. Полковник.

7. Надворный советник. Подполковник.

8. Коллежский ассесор. Майор, или Ротмистр.

9. Титулярный советник. Штабс-капитан, или Штабс-ротмистр.

10. Коллежский секретарь. Поручик.

11. Корабельный секретарь. ———.

12. Губернский секретарь. Подпоручик, или Корнет.

13. Провинциальный секретарь, или Сенатский регистратор, или Кабинетский регистратор, или Синодский регистратор. Прапорщик.

14. Коллежский регистратор.

APPENDIX FIVE: SHORT BIBLIOGRAPHY

Any short bibliography of Tolstoy must be highly selective; so much has been written about him, especially, of course, in Russian. Hence, whole categories of Tolstoyana are not represented here at all, e.g. the patriot; the theoretician of art, morality, and religion; the schoolmaster; the forester; the soldier, etc. Similarly neglected here are his interests in music, the Orient, other writers (such as Rousseau and Stendhal), and his reputation in various countries. The reader interested in these subjects is referred to the bibliographies in Section I below.

There are four Sections below. The first mentions a few bibliographies. The second deals with biographical and memoir materials. The third concerns criticism of Tolstoy's art in general, and the fourth focuses specifically on *War and Peace.* None of these sections is exhaustive either, but they should help to give the reader some idea of what has been done in these areas. Of course, there is considerable overlapping between them. Eikhenbaum's criticism, for example, is set very loosely in a biographical framework.

Each Section has been divided into at least two parts. The first of these gives individual works in Russian, followed by English translations thereof (if any), while the second lists books and articles in English (with a very slight smattering, in some cases, of works done in French or German).

I. Bibliographies

A. Russian

1. *Библиография литературы о Л.Н. Толстом, 1917-1958.* Сост. Н.Г. Шеляпина и др. Редакционная коллегия: Б.С. Бондарский, Н.Н. Гусев, К.Л. Ломунов. М: Государственный музей Л.Н. Толстого, 1960, 791 стр.

2. Спиридонов, Василий Спиридонович. *Л.Н. Толстой: био-библиография, т. I*, М: Academia, 1933.

B. English

1. New York Public Library. The Research Libraries. *Dictionary Catalog of the Slavonic Collection.* 2nd ed. Boston: G.K. Hall, 1974. [Vol. 39, pp. 406-499 deals with Tolstoy.]

2. *PMLA: Publications of the Modern Language Association of America, Bibliography.* This is published annually by the Modern Language Association and is indispensable. For Tolstoy criticism, one must look (in recent years) in the International Bibliography volumes under the headings, "East European Literatures. East Slavic Literature. Russian. Nineteenth Century Authors. Tolstoi, L." Before the 1970 Bibliography (for 1969), English and foreign-language literatures were all in the same volume each year.

II. Biographical and Memoir Material

A. Russian

1. Бирюков, Павел Иванович. *Биография Льва Николаевича Толстого.* М: Посредник, 1908-1911, 2 тт. Берлин, Ладыжников, 1921 и М: Государственное издательство, 1922-1923. English tr.: P.I. Biryukov. *Leo Tolstoy: His Life and Work.* N.Y.: Scribner's, 1906. N.Y.: Scribner's, 1911.

2. Булгаков, Валентин Федорович. *Лев Толстой в последний год его жизни. Дневник секретаря Л.Н. Толстого В.Ф. Булгакова.* М: Задруга, 1920, 367 стр. М: Гослитиздат, 1957, 533 стр. First published in 1911 as *У Толстого в последний год его жизни.*

3. Горький, Алексей Максимович [pseud. of А.М. Пешков.] *Воспоминания о Льве Николаевиче Толстом.* 2-ое доп. изд. Берлин: Гржебин, 1922, 80 стр. [Available in other editions, including in his collected works.] English tr.: Maxim Gorky, *Reminiscences of Leo Nikolaevich Tolstoy.* Tr. S.S. Koteliansky and Leonard Woolf. Richmond, England: L. & V. Woolf, 1920, 70 pp. N.Y.: Huebsch, 1920, 86 pp. Part of *Reminiscences.* New York: Dover, 1946, and London: Hogarth, 1968.]

4. Кузьминская, Татьяна Андреевна [Берс]. *Моя жизнь в Ясной Поляне. Воспоминания 1846-1862.* М: Сабашниковы, 1925-1926. English tr.: Tatyana Kuzminskaya, *Tolstoy as I Knew Him: My Life at Home and at Yasnaya Polyana.* Tr. Nora Sigerist and others. Intro. by Ernest J. Simmons. N.Y.: Macmillan, 1948, 489 pp.

5. *Л.Н. Толстой в воспоминаниях современников.* Ред. Н.Н. Гусев. М: Гослитиздат, 1955, 2 тт. [Various editions.]

6. *Лев Николаевич Толстой. Его жизнь и сочинения. Сборник историко-литературных статей.* Сост. Владимир Иванович Покровский. Изд. 2-ое, дополненное. М: Склад в книжном магазине В. Спиридонова и А. Михайлова, 1908, 179 стр.

7. *Лев Николаевич Толстой; материалы к биографии с 1828 по 1855 год.* Ред Н.Н. Гусев. М: АН-СССР, 1954.

8. *Лев Николаевич Толстой; материалы к биографии с 1855 по 1869 год.* Ред. Н.Н. Гусев. М: АН-СССР, 1957, 913 стр.

9. *Лев Николаевич Толстой; материалы к биографии с 1870 по 1881 год.* Ред. Н.Н. Гусев. М: АН-СССР, 1963, 691 стр.

10. *Лев Николаевич Толстой; материалы к биографии с 1881 по 1885 год. Ред. Н.Н. Гусев.* [Отв. ред Л. Д. Опульская и А.И. Шифман.] М: Наука, 1970, 550 стр.

11. *Летопись жизни и творчества Л.Н. Толстого.* Ред Н.Н. Гусев. М: 1936, 874 стр. М: ГИХЛ, 1958-1960, 2 тт. Also later editions.

12. Сухотина-Толстая, Татьяна Львовна. *Друзья и гости Ясной Поляны.* М: Колос, 1926, 196 стр. Her diaries, a different work, are in English tr.: *The Tolstoy Home: Diaries of Tatiana Sukhotin-Tolstoy.* Tr. Alec Brown. London: Harvill, 1950, 352 pp.

13. Толстая, Александра Львовна. *Отец: жизнь Льва Толстого.* Нью-Йорк: Издательство им. Чехова, 1953. English tr.: Alexandra Tolstoy. *Tolstoy: A Life of My Father.* Tr. Elizabeth Reynolds Hapgood. N.Y.: Harper, 1953, 543 pp.

14. Толстая, Софья Андреевна [Берс]. *Дневники, 1860-1909.* Ред. С.Л. Толстой. Л: Сабашниковы, 1928. English tr.: *The Diary of Tolstoy's Wife, 1860-1891.* Tr. Alexander Werth. London: Gollancz, 1928, 272 pp., and *The Countess Tolstoy's Later Diary, 1891-1897.* Tr. Alexander Werth. London: Gollancz, 1929, 267 pp.

15. Толстой, Илья Львович. *Мои воспоминания.* М: Худ. лит., 1969, 455 стр. English tr.: Ilya Tolstoy. *Tolstoy, My Father. Reminiscences.* Tr. Ann Dunnigan. Chicago: Cowles, 1971, 322 pp.

16. Толстой, Сергей Львович. *Очерки былого.* М: Международная книга, 1947. 2-ое изд. М: Гослитиздат, 1956, 399 стр. English tr.: S.L. Tolstoy, *Tolstoy Remembered By His Son.* Tr. Moura Budberg. N.Y.: Atheneum, 1969, 234 pp.

17. Шкловский, Виктор. *Лев Толстой.* М: Молодая гвардия, 1963, 863 стр. 2-ое испр. изд., М: Молодая гвардия, 1967, 654 стр.

B. English, etc.

1. Lafitte, Sophie. *León Tolstoï et ses contemporains.* Paris: Seghers, 1960, 330 pp.

2. Maude, Aylmer. *Life of Tolstoy.* London: Oxford U. Press, 1929-1939, 2 vols. In L.N. Tolstoy, *The Works of Leo Tolstoy,* The Centenary Edition, Vols. 1 and 2. (This replaces an earlier version. N.Y.: Dodd, Mead, 1911.)

3. Simmons, Ernest J. *Leo Tolstoy.* Boston: Little, Brown, 1948, 790 pp.

4. Troyat, Henri. *Tolstoï.* Paris: Fayard, 1965, 889 pp. English tr

Tolstoy. Tr. Nancy Amphoux. Garden City, N.Y.: Doubleday, 1967, 762 pp.

III. Critical and General Material

A. Russian.

1. Бурсов, Борис. *Лев Толстой: идейные искания и творческий метод, 1847-1862.* М: ГИХЛ, 1960, 405 стр.

2. Виноградов, Виктор. "О языке Толстого (50-60-ые годы)." *Литературное наследство,* № 35-36 (М 1939), стр. 117-221.

3. Гудзий, Николай Каллиникович. *Как работал Л. Толстой.* М: Советский писатель, 1936, 246 стр.

4. Ермилов, Владимир Владимирович. *Толстой—романист. "Война и мир," "Анна Каренина," "Воскресение."* М: Худ. лит., 1965, 591 стр.

5. Купреянова, Елизавета Николаевна. *Эстетика Л.Н. Толстого.* Л: Наука, 1968, 322 стр.

6. Ландау, Марк Александрович. [pseud: Алданов.] *Загадка Толстого.* Берлин: Ладыжников, 1923, 127 стр. Republished, Providence, R.I.: Brown U. Press, 1969, Brown U. Slavic Reprint, VII.

7. Ленин, Владимир Ильич. [pseud. of Ульянов.] *О Л.Н. Толстом.* Сост. С.М. Брейтберг. М: Худ. лит., 1969, 188 стр.

8. Леонтьев, Константин Николаевич. "Анализ, стиль и веяние. О романах гр. Л.Н. Толстого. Критический этюд." *Собрание сочинений К. Леонтьева,* том 8, М: Саблин, 1912. Republished, Providence, R.I.: Brown U. Press, 1965. Brown U. Slavic Reprint, III. Bound with В. Розанов "Неузнанный феномен." English tr.: "The Novels of Count L.N. Tolstoy: Analysis, Style, and Atmosphere." *Essays in Russian Literature.* Selected, ed., tr. and with an intro. by Spencer E. Roberts. Athens, Ohio: Ohio U. Press, 1968, pp. 225-357.

9. ———, *О романах гр. Л.Н. Толстого.* М: 1911.

10. Мережковский, Дмитрий Сергеевич. *Л.Н. Толстой и Достоевский.* СПБ: Мир искусства, 1901-1902. 2-ое изд. СПБ: Пирожков, 1905. English tr: Dmitri Merejkowski, *Tolstoy as Man and Artist; With an Essay on Dostoïevski.* N.Y.: Putnam's Sons, 1902, 310 pp.

11. Михайловский, Николай Константинович, "Десница и шуйца Льва Толстого." *Литературно-критические статьи.* М: ГИХЛ, 1957, стр. 59-181. [First published in *Отечественные записки,* 1875, май, июнь, июль, as "Записки профана."]

12. Мышковская, Лия Моисеевна. *Лев Толстой: работа и стиль.* М: Советский писатель, 1939, 298 стр.

13. Овсянико-Куликовский, Дмитрий Николаевич. *Л.Н. Толстой как художник.* Изд. 2-ое, испр. и допол. СПБ: Орион, 1905, 274 стр.

14. Скабичевский, Александр Михайлович. "Граф Л.Н. Толстой, как художник и мыслитель," *Отечественные записки, том 4* (II, стр. 268 ff.), и том 5 (II, стр. 1 ff.). СПБ: 1872. (Reprinted repeatedly.)

15. Страхов, Николай Николаевич. *Критические статьи об И.С. Тургеневе и Л.Н. Толстом (1862-1885)*. СПБ: Пантелеевы, 1885, 484 стр. 4-ое изд., Киев: 1901. Republished, The Hague, Holland: Mouton, 1968, Slavistic Printings and Reprintings, 147.

16. *Толстой, памятники творчества и жизни.* Ред. В.И. Срезневский и А.Л. Бем. Петроград: Огни, 1917-1923, 4 тт. Photostat ed., Ann Arbor, Mich.: Univ. Microfilms, 1967.

17. Храпченко, Михаил Борисович. *Лев Толстой как художник.* М: Советский писатель, 1963, 659 стр. 2-ое изд. М: Советский писатель, 1965, 505 стр.

18. Эйхенбаум, Борис Михайлович. *Молодой Толстой.* СПБ: Гржебин, 1922. Photostat ed.: Ann Arbor, Mich.: Univ. Microfilms, 1967. Republished, München: Wilhelm Fink Verlag, 1968 (Slavische Propyläen, Band 53). English tr.: Eikhenbaum *The Young Tolstoi.* Ed., Gary Kern. Ann Arbor, Mich.: Ardis, 1972, 152 pp.

19. ———, *Лев Толстой, книга первая, 50-ые годы.* Л: Прибой, 1928. Photostat ed.: Ann Arbor, Mich.: Univ. Microfilms, 1964. Republished: München: Wilhelm Fink Verlag, 1968, as part of *Лев Толстой* (Slavische Propyläen, Band 54.).

20. ———, *Лев Толстой, книга вторая, 60-ые годы.* Л-М: Гослитиздат, 1931. Photostat ed.: Ann Arbor, Mich.: Univ. Microfilms, 1964. Republished: München: Wilhelm Fink Verlag, 1968, as part of *Лев Толстой* (Slavische Propyläen, Band 54.).

21. ———, *Лев Толстой, 70-ые годы.* М: Советский писатель, 1960, 294 стр.

B. English, etc.

1. Arnold, Matthew. "Count Leo Tolstoy." *Essays in Criticism: Second Series.* London and N.Y.: Macmillan, 1888. (Reprinted repeatedly.)

2. Bayley, John. *Tolstoy and the Novel.* London: Chatto & Windus, 1966. N.Y.: Viking, 1967.

3. Benson, Ruth Crego. *Women in Tolstoy.* Urbana, IL: University of Illinois Press, 1974, 141 pp.

4. Christian, Reginald Frank. *Tolstoy: A Critical Introduction.* Cambridge, England: Cambridge U. Press, 1969.

5. Feuer, Kathryn Beliveau. "Recent Works on Leo Tolstoy." *Russian Review,* 28(1969), pp. 217-224. (Review article.)

6. Hamburger, Käte. Leo Tolstoi: *Gestalt und Problem.* Bern: Francke, 1950, 189 pp. 2nd revised ed., Göttingen: Vandenhoek & Ruprecht, 1963.

7. Hayman, Ronald. *Tolstoy.* N.Y. Humanities, 1970, 116 pp.

8. Jones, Malcolm, ed. *New Essays on Tolstoy.* Cambridge, England: Cambridge University Press, 1978, 251 pp.

9. Lavrin, Janko. *Tolstoy: An Approach.* 2nd ed. London: Methuen, 1948, 167 pp.

10. Lenin, V.I. *Articles on Tolstoy.* M: Foreign Languages Publishing House, 1951, 54 pp.

11. *Leo Tolstoy: A Critical Anthology.* Ed. Henry Gifford. Hammondsworth, England: Penguin, 1971, 415 pp.

12. Lettenbauer, Wilhelm. "Zu L, Tolstojs Erzählkunst und Erzähltechnik." *Die Welt der Slaven,* Wiesbaden, 9(1964), pp. 1-13.

13. Simmons, Ernest J. *Introduction to Tolstoy's Writings.* Chicago: U. of Chicago Press, 1968.

14. Steiner, George. *Tolstoy or Dostoevsky: An Essay in the Old Criticism.* N.Y.: Knopf, 1959, 354 pp. London: Faber and Faber, 1960.

15. *Tolstoy: A Collection of Critical Essays.* Ed. with intro. by Ralph E. Matlaw. Englewood Cliffs, N.J.: Prentice Hall, 1967.

IV. Criticism of *War and Peace.*

A. Russian

1. Анненков, Павел Васильевич. "Исторические и эстетические вопросы в романе гр. Л.Н. Толстого *Война и мир.*" *Вестник Европы,* СПБ, 1868, т. I, стр. 774-795.

2. Бирман, Ю. "О характере времени в *Войне и мире.*" *Русская литература,* № 3 (1966), стр. 125-131.

3. Борисова, И. "Народные сцены в *Войне и мире.*" *Вопросы литературы, № 3 (1960), стр.* 170-191.

4. Бочаров, С. "Мир в *Войне и мире.*" *Вопросы литературы,* 14, viii (1970), pp. 76-90.

5. ———, *Роман Л.Н.Толстого "Война и мир."* М: ГИХЛ, 1963, 140 стр.

6. Волков, Г. "*Война и мир.* Неизданные тексты." *Литературное наследство,* 35-36. Ред. В.В. Жданов. М: Издательство Академии Наук СССР, 1939, стр. 285-380.

7. Гудзий, Николай Каллиникович. "Еще о каноническом тексте *Войны и мира.*" *Вопросы литературы,* VIII, ii (1964), стр. 190-200.

8. Гусев, Николай Николаевич. "О каноническом тексте *Войны и мира.*" *Вопросы литературы,* VIII, ii (1964), стр. 179-190.

9. Ермилов. В. *Толстой-художник и роман "Война и мир."* М: Гослитиздат, 1961.

10. Зайденшнур, Эвелина Ефимовна.*"Война и мир" Л.Н. Толстого: создание великой книги.* М: Книга, 1966, 401 стр.

11. Каммев, Алексей. "Русский перевод французских текстов Л.Н. Толстого: К столетию первого издания *Войны и мира.*" *Slavia,* 36 (1967) , стр. 629-637.

12. Кандиев, Богдан Иванович. *Роман-эпопея Л.Н. Толстого"Война и мир":комментарий,* М: Просвещение, 1967, 390 стр.

13. Краснов, Георгий Васильевич. *Герой и народ: о романе Льва Толстого "Война и мир."* М: Советский писатель, 1964, 269 стр.

14. ———, "Наташа Ростова: К проблеме героя . . . *Войны и мира." Филологические науки,* V, I (1962), 118-128.

15. Леушева,С.И. *Роман Л.Н Толстого "Война и мир."* М: Учпедгиз, 1957.

16. Наумова, Н. "Проблема характера в *Войне и мире." Русская литература,* № 3 (1960) , стр. 100-116.

17. Потапов, И.А. *Роман Л.Н.Толстого "Война и мир": Современное и историческое в романе, проблемы композиции, роль пейзажа.* М: Просвещение, 1970.

18. Ржевский, Леонид. "Об одном образе в романе *Война и мир." Новый журнал,* Нью-Йорк, № 82 (1966) , стр. 113-119.

19. *Роман Л.Н. Толстого"Война и мир," вопросы поэтики: Семинарий.* Горький: Издание Горьковского гос. университета, 1969.

20. *Русская критическая литература о произведениях Л.Н. Толстого. Хронологический сборник критико-библиографических статей.* Сост: В.А. Зелинский, М: Баландин, 2-ое изд. Часть 3-ья, 1901, 214 стр. (1866-1868) ; Часть 4-ая, 1902, 255 стр. (1868) ; Часть 5-ая, 1903, 247 стр. (1869-1870) ; Часть 6-ая, 1900, 198 стр. (1870-1872) . The years mentioned from 1866 to 1872 indicate when the criticism of *War and Peace* collected here was first published.

21. Сабуров, А.А.*"Война и мир"Л.Н. Толстого, проблематика и поэтика.* М: Издательство Московского университета, 1959, 599 стр.

22. *Сборник"Война и мир."* Ред В.П. Обнинский и Т.И. Полнер. М: Задруга, 1912.

23. Селинов, В. "Архитектоническая основа романа *Война и мир ." Slavia,* Praha, Czechoslovakia, 8(1929-1930), стр. 741-760.

24. Фейн, Герман Наумович. *Роман Л.Н. Толстого "Война и мир"; целостный анализ.* М: Просвещение, 1966, 273 стр.

25. Чирков, Н. "*Война и мир* Л.Н. Толстого как художественное целое." *Русская литература,* № I (1966), стр. 43-66.

26. Чичерин, А.В. *О языке и стиле романа-эпопеи"Война и мир."* Львов: Издательство Львовского университета, 1956.

27. Шкловский, Виктор. *Матерьял и стиль в романе Льва Толстого*

"Война и мир." М: Издательство "Федерация", 1928. Photostat ed.: Ann Arbor, Mich.: Univ. Microfilms, 1967.

28. Штильман, Лев Наумович. "Наблюдения над некоторыми особенностями композиции и стиля в романе Толстого *Война и мир."* *American Contributions to the Fifth International Congress of Slavists, Sofia, September, 1963,* Vol. 2, The Hague, The Netherlands: Mouton, 1963, pp. 327-371. (By Leon Stilman.)

B. English, etc.

1. Berlin, Isaiah. *The Hedgehog and the Fox: An Essay on Tolstoy's View of History.* N.Y.: Simon & Schuster, 1953. [Republished in various editions.]

2. Bier, Jesse. "A Century of *War and Peace*—Gone, Gone with the Wind." *Genre,* 4(1971), pp. 107-141.

3. Chapple, Richard L. "The Role and Function of Nature in L.N. Tolstoy's *War and Peace." New Zealand Slavonic Journal,* 11(Winter, 1973), pp. 86-101.

4. Christian, Reginald Frank. *Tolstoy's "War and Peace."* Oxford: Clarendon Press, 1962, 184 pp.

5. Cook, Albert. "The Unity of *War and Peace." Western Review,* 22(1958), pp. 243-255. Reprinted in *The Meaning of Fiction.* Detroit: Wayne State U. Press, 1960. Reprinted again as "The Moral Vision of Tolstoy," *Tolstoy: A Selection of Critical Essays.* Ed. Ralph E. Matlaw, Englewood Cliffs, N.J.: Prentice Hall, 1967, pp. 111-127.

6. Curtis, James M. "The Function of Imagery in *War and Peace." Slavic Review,* 29(1970), pp. 460-480.

7. Debreczeny, Paul. "Freedom and Necessity: A Reconsideration of *War and Peace." Papers on Language and Literature,* 7(1971), pp. 185-198.

8. Feuer, Kathryn Beliveau. "The Genesis of *War and Peace."* Diss. Columbia U., 1965.

9. ———, "Alexis de Tocqueville and the Genesis of *War and Peace." California Slavic Studies,* 4(1967), pp. 92-118.

10. ———, "The Book that Became *War and Peace." The Reporter,* 20(May 14, 1959), pp. 33-36.

11. Friedberg, Maurice. "The Comic Element in *War and Peace." Indiana Slavic Studies,* IV(1967), pp. 100-119.

12. Greenwood, E.B. "Tolstoy's Poetic Realism in *War and Peace." Critical Quarterly,* 11(1969), pp. 219-233.

13. Hagan, John. "A Pattern of Character Development in Tolstoy's *War and Peace:* P'er Bezukhov." *Texas Studies in Literature and Language,* 11(1969), pp. 985-1011.

14. ———, "On the Craftsmanship of *War and Peace." Essays in Criticism,*

Oxford, 13(1963), pp. 17-49.

15. ———, "Patterns of Character Development in Tolstoy's *War and Peace:* Nicholas, Natasha, and Mary." *PMLA,* 84(1969), pp. 235-244.

16. Harkins, William E. "A Note on the Use of Narrative and Dialogue in *War and Peace." Slavic Review*, 29(1970), pp. 86-92.

17. Lanoux, Armand. "Pourquoi Tolstoï écrivit *Guerre et Paix."* 72(octobre, 1965), pp. 54-67.

18. Lettenbauer, Wilhelm. "Zur Dreigliedrichkeit des Ausdrucks in Tolstojs *Vojna i mir." Slawisten-Studien zum V. Internationalen Slawisten-kongress in Sofia, 1963.* Ed. Maximilian Braun, Erwin Koschmieder, and Irmgard Mahnken. (Opera Slavica 4). Gõttingen: Vandenhoek & Ruprecht, 1963, pp. 427-435.

19. Lewis, Robert P. "Deception and Revelation: A Study of Three Systems of Characterization in Tolstoy's *War and Peace."* Diss. Columbia U., 1973.

20. Lyngstad, Alexandra H. "Tolstoj's Use of Parentheses in *War and Peace." Slavic and East European Journal,* 16(1972), pp. 403-413.

21. Nedeljković, D. "Principe et unité de *Guerre et Paix." Neophilologus,* Groningen, The Netherlands, 62(1968), pp. 235-248.

22. States, Bert O. "The Hero and the World: Our Sense of Space in *War and Peace." Modern Fiction Studies,* Vol. 11, No. 2(Summer, 1965), pp. 153-165.

23. Thale, Jerome. "*War and Peace.* The Art of Incoherence." *Essays in Criticism,* 16(1966), pp. 398-415.

24. Tolstoy, Leo. *War and Peace.* Tr. Louise and Aylmer Maude. Ed. George Gibian. New York: Norton, 1966. The text is followed by "Background and Sources," pp. 1355-1377, and then by "Essays in Criticism," pp. 1377-1482.

25. Wasiolek, Edward. "War and Peace." *Tolstoy's Major Fiction.* Chicago: University of Chicago Press, 1978, pp. 65-129.

26. Wedel, Erwin. *Die Entstehungsgeschichte von L.N. Tolstojs "Krieg und Frieden."* Wiesbaden: Otto Harrassowitz, 1961.

C. Those interested in published drafts of *War and Peace* are referred to the *Полное Собрание Сочинений Л.Н. Толстого* (Юбилейное издание), т. 13, М: ГИХЛ, 1949, 880 стр., т. 14, М: ГИХЛ, 1953, 446 стр., т. 15, М: ГИХЛ, 1955, 335 стр. и т. 16, М: ГИХЛ, 1955, 254 стр. Vols. 15 and 16 are bound together. Vol. 13 has plans, notes, introductions, variants of the beginnings to the work, and variants to Volumes One and Two. Vol. 14 has rough editings, typed manuscripts and proofs to Vol. Three. Vol. 15 has variants to Volume Four, Parts I through IV, and to both parts of the Epilogue. Vol. XVI contains "Несколько слов по поводу *Войны и мира,"* and various valuable commentary material by Soviet scholars.

APPENDIX SIX:
REFERENCE WORKS REPEATEDLY CONSULTED.

I. Notes In Annotated Editions. All by L.N. Tolstoi (Tolstoy).

A. Russian

1. *Полное собрание сочинений.* М и Л: Гослитиздат том XII, первый тираж, 1933.
том XII, второй тираж, 1937.

2. *Собрание сочинений в 14-и тт.* М: ГИХЛ, том 7, 1951, стр. 365-379.

3. *Собрание сочинений в 12-и тт.* М: ГИХЛ, том 7, 1963, стр. 462-493.

4. *Война и мир.* М: Гос. учебно пед. издательство. Министерство просвещения РСФСР, 1957, стр. 777-807.

5. *Война и мир.* М: Детская литература. Школьная Библиотека. 1964, 2 тт. том 1, стр. 663-689, и том II, стр. 679-700. 1966.

6. *Война и мир.* М: Художественная литература, 1968, 2 тт. Notes in each volume by L. Opul'skaia, basically following her notes for 12-vol. ed. above, but with a few changes.

B. English

1. *War and Peace.* tr. Louise and Aylmer Maude. Ed. George Gibian. N.Y.: Norton, 1966. [The Maude notes are also available in other eds., and are most helpful. Gibian has "silently corrected" a few of them in this ed.]

II. Dictionaries and Encyclopedias.

A. Russian-English

1. Александров, А. *Полный русско-английский словарь.* Изд. 3-е, испр. и допол. СПБ: Главный склад издания в Книжном и Географическом Магазине изданий Главного Штаба, 1904.

2. *Русско-Английский Словарь.* под общим руководством А.И. Смирницкого. Изд. 7-ое. М: Советская Энциклопедия, 1965. Other editions were also consulted.

3. Segal, Louis. *New Complete Russian-English Dictionary.* 2nd ed., revised and enlarged. London: Lund, Humphries & Co. Ltd, 1943. More recent editions were also consulted.

4. Wheeler, Marcus. *The Oxford Russian-English Dictionary.* Gen. Ed. B.O. Unbegaun. Oxford, England: Clarendon Press, 1972.

B. Russian

1. Академия наук СССР. Институт русского языка. *Словарь современного русского литературного языка.* М и Л: АН-СССР, 1950-1965. 17 тт.
2. Академия наук СССР. Институт Языкознания. *Словарь русского языка.* М: Гос. издательство иностранных и национальных словарей, 1957-1961. 4 тт.
3. Ашукин, Николай Сергеевич и Ашукина, Мария Григорьевна. *Крылатые слова.* М: Художественная литература, 1966.
4. *Большая Советская Энциклопедия.* 1-ое изд. Главный ред. О. Ю. Шмидт. М: Советская энциклопедия, 1926-1931. 65 тт.
5. *Большая Советская Энциклопедия.* 2-ое изд. Главный редактор С.И. Вавилов [тт. 1-7] и Б.А. Введенский [тт. 8-51]. М: Большая советская энциклопедия, 1949-1958. 51 т.
6. Даль, Владимир Иванович. *Толковый словарь живого великорусского языка.* М: Гос. издательство иностранных и национальных словарей, 1955. Reprinted fr 2nd edition, СПБ и М: М.О. Вольф, 1880-1882.
7. *Краткая Литературная Энциклопедия.* Главный ред. А.А. Сурков. М: Советская энциклопедия, 1961-1975.
8. Михельсон, М.И. *Ходячие и меткие слова.* 2-ое изд. СПБ: Императорская Академия Наук, 1896.
9. *Театральная Энциклопедия.* Главный ред. С.С. Мокульский [т. 1] и П.А. Марков [тт. 2-5]. М: Советская энциклопедия, 1961-1967. 5 тт.
10. *Толковый словарь русского языка.* Ред. Д.Н. Ушаков. М: Гос. институт "Советская Энциклопедия", 1935-1940. 4 тт. Republished Ann Arbor, Mich.: Edwards Bros., ca. 1948, American Council of Learned Societies. Reprints, Russian Series, Nos. 1-4.
11. *Фразеологический словарь русского языка.* Ред. А.И. Молотков. М: Советская энциклопедия, 1967.
12. *Энциклопедический словарь.* Ред. И. Андреевский [Letters А и Б], К.К. Арсеньев и Ф.Ф. Петрушевский [Letter В on], Supplement ed. Арсеньев и В.Т. Шевяков. СПБ: Ф. Брогкауз (Лейпциг) и И.А. Ефрон

(СПБ) , 1890-1907. 82 vols, plus 4 supplementary vols.

C. English, etc.

1. *The Columbia-Viking Desk Encyclopedia.* 2nd ed. Ed. William Bridgewater, *et alii.* N.Y.: Dell, 1966. Paperback.
2. *Encyclopedia Britannica.* 11th ed. Cambridge, England, and N.Y.: Cambridge U. Press, 1910-1911. 29 vols.
3. *La Grande Encyclopédie.* Paris: Société anonyme de la Grande Encyclopédie [1886-1892] , 31 vols.
4. *Grove's Dictionary of Music and Musicians.* 5th ed. Ed. Eric Blom. N.Y.: St. Martin's Press, 1959-1961. 10 vols.
5. *McGraw-Hill Encyclopedia of Russia and the Soviet Union.* Ed. Michael T. Florinsky, *et alii.* N.Y.: McGraw-Hill, 1961.
6. *Meyers Konversations-Lexikon.* 4th revised ed. Leipzig: Verlag des bibliographischen Instituts, 1885-1890. 16 vols.
7. *Random-House Dictionary of the English Language.* Ed. Jess Stein. N.Y.: Random House, 1966.
8. Six, Georges. *Dictionnaire biographique des généraux et amiraux français de la Révolution et de l'Empire (1792-1814).* Paris: G. Saffroy, 1934, 2 vols.
9. Utechin, S.V. *A Concise Encyclopedia of Russia.* N.Y.: Penguin, 1961.
10. *Webster's New International Dictionary of the English Language.* 2nd ed. Unabridged. Springfield, Massachusetts: 1960. This ed. contains more words than the more recent 3rd ed.

III. Other Works Consulted

A. Russian

1. Академия Наук СССР. *История Москвы в шести томах.* М: АН-СССР. том II, 1953, ред. С.В. Вахрушин; том III, 1954, ред. Н.М. Дружинин и М.К. Рожкова.
2. Академия Наук СССР. Институт Русского Языка. *Грамматика русского языка.* ред. В.В. Виноградов и другие. В двух томах (трех книгах) . М: 1960.
3. Е. Молоховец. *Подарок молодым хозяйкам.* Нью-Йорк. Мартьянов. [1958] (Reprint of 19th-cent. St. P cookbook.)
4. Сытин, П.В. *Из истории московских улиц (очерки).* Изд. 2-ое, пересмотренное и допол. М: Московский рабочий, 1952.

5. *Экскурсии по Москве,* М: Московский рабочий, 1959.

B. English, etc.

1. Baedeker, Karl. *Russia with Teheran, Port Arthur, and Peking.* Leipzig: Karl Baedeker, 1914. This contains two excellent maps of Moscow in English.
2. Florinsky, Michael T. *Russia: A History and an Interpretation.* New York: Macmillan, 1955. 2 vols.
3. Palmer, Alan Warwick. *Alexander I: Tsar of War and Peace.* London: Weidenfeld & Nicolson, 1974.
4. ———. *Napoleon in Russia.* N.Y.: Simon & Schuster, ca. 1967.
5. Pushkin, Alexander. *Eugene Onegin: A Novel in Verse.* Tr. w commentary by Vladimir Nabokov. N.Y.: Pantheon 1965, Vols. 2 and 3. I used 1965 ed. (2nd rev. ed., Princeton, N.J.: 1975.)
6. Shaw, Joseph Thomas. *The Transliteration of Modern Russian for English-Language Publications.* Madison, Wis.: U. of Wisconsin Press, 1967.
7. Strong, James. *The Exhaustive Concordance of the Bible.* N.Y.: Hunt & Eaton, and Cincinnati: Cranston & Curts, 1894.
8. Tarlé, Eugene. *Napoleon's Invasion of Russia: 1812.* Tr. G.M. N.Y.: Oxford, 1942.
9. Thiers, Adolphe. *Histoire de l'Empire,* Vol. III. Paris: L'Heureux, 1867.
10. Werlich, Robert. *Russian Orders, Decorations, and Medals, Including Those of Imperial Russia, The Provisional Government, and the Soviet Union.* Washington, D.C.: Quaker Press, 1968.

APPENDIX SEVEN: UNSOLVED QUESTIONS

The following questions remain unsolved despite my best efforts and those of scholars ranging from Berkeley to Moscow. Should any reader know the answers, I hope he (or she) will write me c/o the Russian Department, Washington University, St. Louis, MO 63130, U.S.A.

1. p. 62. Volume Two, Part I, Chapter 15, Entry 7. *Oh, mio crudele affetto.* At first, it seemed that this would be easy to track down, but this supposition proved untrue. My letter in the *Times Literary Supplement* of London for September 8, 1978, elicited no response about this problem from anyone. Mr. Rembert Herbert of the Music Division of the Library of Congress in Washington explained to me (in a letter dated January 12, 1978) that arias are generally indexed by their first lines, and *Oh, mio crudele affetto* does not appear, from Tolstoy's text, to be the first line. He added, "It would take days to go through our volumes of Cimarosa alone." Having no budget, I could not follow this lead further.

Leonard J. Lehrman (the American composer whose interest in Russia is shown, among other things, by his opera "Sima," who has a doctorate in music from Cornell University, and who is also my nephew) spent hours in the New York Public Library at my request hunting through Cherubini for this phrase, but with no results. Nor could his contacts at the Metropolitan Opera Company, where he was then employed as an assistant conductor of the offstage chorus, help. (Tolstoy terms Cherubini Natasha's favorite composer.) The idea of Cherubini also occurred to Evelina Zaidenshnur of the Tolstoy Museum in Moscow, but her friends in music there discouraged the idea on the very logical grounds that the libretti to Cherubini's operas were in French, rather than Italian. Such a distinguished American musician of Russian background as Boris Goldovsky (of the Goldovsky Opera Institute near Boston) could not identify the piece either.

My colleague in the Music Department of Washington University in St. Louis, Professor Mark Lindley, has been full of good ideas as to how to keep after this problem. At his suggestion, I wrote to Professor Boris Schwarz of Queens College in New York. Schwarz answered that he did not know, but Professor Philip Gossett of the University of Chicago might. So might Nicholas Slonimsky, another distinguished American musician of Russian background. Very courteous letters from both Gossett and Slonimsky indicated that they could not answer this question either.

Again at this point Evelina Zaidenshnur demonstrated yet another kindness to me. She had the first, unpublished draft of the relevant passage typed out in Russian and sent it to me on October 4, 1978. This passage mentions another line in Italian, *"La madre del' suo cor,"* hints that there is a high *si* (B natural) in the piece, and states that Countess Perovskaia had just (around 1808) brought the melody back from Italy. Tolstoy characterizes the melody in the first draft as a barcarolle which became enormously popular for a brief period and was then just as completely forgotten.

My next stop was to hunt up and check all references to Perovskiis in the ninety-volume Jubilee Edition of Tolstoy. Unfortunately, this produced no results. Then, on a business trip to New York in December of 1978, I sneaked away to the New York Public Library to see what they had by or about anyone named Perovskii. My excitement was great because, as I remembered from Shklovskii's *Матерьял и стиль,* one of Tolstoy's sources for the novel was Perovskii's *Записки.* The disappointment was equally great when the *Записки* in question turned out to deal with the negotiations between the advancing French and the retreating Russians about the giving up of Moscow in 1812. Nothing relevant was to be found in any of the other Perovskii references in the New York Public Library, including the works of Алексей Алексеевич Перовский (1787-1836), who wrote under the name of Антоний Погорельский.

In the same letter mentioned before, Zaidenshnur wrote that the Director of the Museum of Musical Culture in Moscow had told her that the person to write about *Oh, mio crudele affetto* would be Dr. Emilia Zanetti, who is associated with one of the musical museums in Rome (of which there are over thirty), the exact name of which the person giving the information could not think of.

Through the aid of the marvellous reference librarians at both the Music Library and Olin Library of Washington University, I was able to locate Dr. Zanetti as the Librarian of the Biblioteca Musicale Santa Cecilia in Rome; I wrote her on October 30, 1978. (My colleague Anna di Palma Amelung was kind enough to translate both my letter and my English version of Tolstoy's first draft into Italian for me; she has also translated other letters to and from Italy for me, and I am very grateful to her also.) On December 2, 1978, Dr. Zanetti wrote me in Italian that she does not know the answer to this question, but suggested I write to others, such as Mr. James Fuld (the well-known bibliographer) in New York, and also to the British Museum. She added that she had referred the matter to a well-known professor in Rome who would try to look into the question. She mentioned also that neither the "Gogol" Russian Library in Rome nor Tolstoy's granddaughter there was able to help. I would like to thank Dr. Zanetti too for the troubles she has taken on my behalf.

Meantime, I asked Dr. Leonard J. Lehrman if there was some Americ publication to which I might write a letter about this. He suggested my submitting the question to Professor Nicholas Temperley, the Editor of the *Journal of the American Musicological Society,* at the University of Illinois. Mr. Wayne D. Shirley of the Music Division of the Library of Congress, in his letter of October 27, 1978 to me, seconded my nephew's motion. Therefore, on October 30, 1978, I wrote to Professor Temperley who very kindly consented to publish my letter in the Spring, 1979 edition of *JAMS.* (Scholarly delays in perhaps every field are simply unavoidable.)

Letters to Mr. Fuld and to the British Museum produced courteous, but negative responses. O.W. Neighbour, the Music Librarian of the British Museum, added in his letter to me of February 5, 1979 that this question had arisen before. Mr. Fuld suggested that I might write to Mr. Harold Barlow, the well-known music specialist in New York. Mr. Barlow answered by telephone and we had a pleasant talk; unfortunately, however, the question remained unanswered.

Again I turned for help to my colleague, Mark Lindley. He suggested my writing Dr. Pierluigi Petrobelli in England. Dr. Petrobelli kindly answered me on February 11, 1979 to suggest that, after speaking with his colleague Dr. Reinhard Strohm, the two men concluded that perhaps Tolstoy had made the whole thing up himself. This, of course, is always possible—but it is not the way Tolstoy generally worked.

Dr. Lindley had also suggested that I write Dr. Carlo Bianconi in Bologna about this question, which I did on January 29, 1979. In an undated letter which I received by air mail in early March, 1979, Dr. Bianconi wrote that Mr. Carlo Vitali of Bologna had recently taken inventory of the musical holdings in the archives of the Oratorio dei Filippini in Vicenza, Italy, and run across something which might be relevant; unfortunately, even though Dr. Lindley happened to know Mr. Vitali's address, the courteous Mr. Vitali could not help me further.

The musicians Tolstoy mentions in *War and Peace*—such as Cherubini, Dussek, John Field and Steibelt (whose music is mentioned, if not his name)—all spent time in Russia. By contrast, Mozart, Beethoven, Bach and othes who did not spend time in Russia are not mentioned in *War and Peace.* I therefore suspect the piece may be by an Italian who spent some time in Russia. In any case, the trail is cold. (This presumes, of course, that Tolstoy did not make up the Italian phrase or phrases). If any reader can help, I hope he will write me.

2. p. 97. Volume Three, Part I, Chapter 1, Entry 6. memorandum за No. 178. Attempts to trace this further have been to no avail. I have looked in such works as:

1. Armand, marquis de Caulaincourt, *With Napoleon in Russia,* ed. by y Georges Libaire, N.Y. ca. 1935;

2. *Mémoires du Prince Adam Czartoryski et correspondance avec L'Empereur Alexandre I-er,* Paris, Plon, 1887, 2 volumes

3. Armand Lefèbvre, *Histoires des cabinets de l'Europe pendant le Consulat et l'Empire, 1800-1815,* II-e édition, Vol. 5, Paris 1869;

4. Alan Palmer, *Alexander I,* New York, 1974;

5. Albert Sorel, *L'Europe et la Révolution Française,* 10-e édition, Vol. VII, Paris, 1914;

6. Serge Tatistcheff, *Alexandre I-er et Napoléon, d'après leur correspondance inédite, 1801-1812,* Paris, Perrin, 1891.

7. Albert Vandal, *Napoléon et Alexandre I,* Paris, Plon, ca. 1894. (Reprinted in Nendeln, Lichtenstein, 1976.) 3 volumes. This work contains the Champagny-Caulaincourt correspondence listed separately in the National Union Catalogue of pre-1956 imprints as being held by the University of California at Berkeley and entitled *Projet de mariage de Napoléon I-er avec la Grande Duchesse Anne de Russie;* this correspondence gives as obstacles to a match between Napoleon and Anna Pavlovna, such facts as the girl's age and religion, but says nothing about the memorandum in question.

8. Генерал-майор М. Богданович, *История отечественной войны 1812-го года по достоверным источникам составлена по высочайшему повелению,* СПБ, 1859, 3 тома. Soviet scholars are quite right to cite Bogdanovich as one of Tolstoy's sources; however, Volume I, Chapter 2 says nothing about any French memorandum stating that an alliance with Russia would not be to Napoleon's interest because Russia was so influential in northern and eastern Europe.

Although the problem of this memorandum was mentioned in the letter from me which the *Time Literary Supplement* of London published on September 8, 1978, the only response my request elicited was to articles by Oscar Harnack and to the book mentioned above by Albert Vandal. Neither citation was productive. (It is, of course, possible that Tolstoy invented the memorandum himself.) This matter must be considered still open. If some reader does know the answer, I hope he will write me.

I would like to conclude this work as I opened it: with a statement of deep gratitude to those scholars, both American and Soviet, without whose aid this volume (which at times made me feel that I was "pursuing the horizon") could never have been completed. To finish this book took me six years.

ADDITIONS

1. p. 17. Volume One, Part I, Chapter 10, Entry 1. I thank Patricia Carden for correcting this entry.
2. p. 18. Volume One, Part I, Chapter 10, Entry 8. According to tradition, the house LNT had in mind when he described the Rostovs' residence is the present building of the Board of the Union of Soviet Writers at 52 Vorovsky Street.
3. p. 28. Volume One, Part I, Chapter 28, Entry 6. Nothing like the quotation attributed to Sterne can be found in *Tristram Shandy* either, and I have not seen any evidence that LNT knew of Sterne's writings beyond the two books mentioned.
4. p. 110. Volume Three, Part I, Chapter 19, Entry 3. LNT's source (М. Богданович, *История отечественной войны,* СПБ, 1859, I , 435) does indeed give the first word as "Le" (rather than "L' ") in *Le Empereur Napoléon.*
5. p. 183. Epilogue, Part II, Chapter 1, Entry 5. Talleyrand's chair was also identified by Hugh McLean of the University of California at Berkeley, who even sent me a photostat of the printed source. I thank him too.
6. p. 185. Epilogue, Part II, Chapter 4, Entry 15. Keenan was answered in Р. Г. Скрыпников, *Переписка Грозного и Курбского: парадоксы Эдварда Кинана,* Л, Наука, 1973.
7. p. 159. Volume Four, Part II, Chapter 15, after Entry 5:
   Аристово — Aristovo [Village in Borov District, NE Kaluga Province, near Tarutino]